Orson Welles Remembered

Orson Welles Remembered

Interviews with His Actors, Editors, Cinematographers and Magicians

Peter Prescott Tonguette

McFarland & Company, Inc., Publishers
Jefferson, North Carolina, and London

Frontispiece: Orson Welles in a test shot for a film of *King Lear*, 1985 (photograph courtesy of Gary Graver).

LIBRARY OF CONGRESS CATALOGUING-IN-PUBLICATION DATA

Tonguette, Peter Prescott, 1983–
Orson Welles remembered : interviews with his actors, editors, cinematographers and magicians / Peter Prescott Tonguette.
p.   cm.
Includes bibliographical references and index.

ISBN-13: 978-0-7864-2760-4
(softcover : 50# alkaline paper) ∞

1. Welles, Orson, 1915–1985 — Anecdotes.   2. Motion picture producers and directors — United States — Anecdotes.   3. Motion pictures — Interviews.   I. Title.
PN1998.3.W45T66   2007
791.4302'33092 — dc22   2006037131

British Library cataloguing data are available

On the cover: Orson Welles ©2006 Photofest. Background images ©2006 Brand X Pictures

Manufactured in the United States of America

McFarland & Company, Inc., Publishers
Box 611, Jefferson, North Carolina 28640
www.mcfarlandpub.com

For my mother and father

Acknowledgments

For their assistance and suggestions, I wish to thank Raymond Bally, David Baron, Dann Cahn, Fred Camper, Michelle Carey, Tomm Carroll, Stefan Droessler, Bilge Ebiri, Filipe Furtado, Ruy Gardnier, Joe Kaufman, Robert F. Keser, Oja Kodar, Bill Krohn, Vincent LoBrutto, Joseph McBride, Meghan McElheny, Patrick McGilligan, Jonathan Rosenbaum, Marion Rosenberg, Dee Dee Sadler, Roberto Silvi, Bill Smith, Del R. Tonguette, Diane Tonguette, Patrick Tonguette, Tom Watson, Jake Wilson, and Jeff Wilson.

The interview with Curtis Harrington first appeared, in somewhat different form, in *Bright Lights Film Journal*. The interviews with Keith Baxter, Mike Caveney, Norman Lloyd, and Jim Steinmeyer as well as some of my own prose from those chapters, first appeared, again in somewhat different forms, in *The Film Journal*. A majority of my interview with Abb Dickson, and select portions of my interview with Gary Graver, as well as some of my own prose from those chapters, first appeared as part of my article, "The Company of Magicians: Orson Welles, Abb Dickson, Scarlet Plush, and Purple Hokum," published in *Senses of Cinema*. I've also taken material from my article, "From the Beginning: Notes on Orson Welles' Most Personal Late Film," first published in *Senses of Cinema*; this piece was later re-printed (and slightly revised) in the book of Welles-related essays, *The Unknown Orson Welles*, published by Belleville/Filmmuseum Munchen, and it also appeared in Portuguese translation in Contracampo. My profound thanks to all of the editors of the aforementioned publications.

Contents

Preface

Orson Welles Remembered is an oral history. It consists of interviews I conducted between 2003 and 2005 with individuals who worked with Orson Welles. They include actors, editors, cinematographers, camera assistants, and magicians; the interviews number thirty-three in all.

I was inspired to begin this project largely thanks to two people: Jonathan Rosenbaum and Jim Steinmeyer. By way of thanks, allow me to briefly recount their involvement.

It was the spring of 2003 when I first read Welles's brilliant un-produced screenplay, *The Cradle Will Rock,* published posthumously by Santa Teresa Press in 1994. The book included an afterword by Rosenbaum, the film critic for the *Chicago Reader* (and who also edited *This Is Orson Welles*, Peter Bogdanovich's interview book with the director). Several pages into the essay, Rosenbaum made mention of Steinmeyer, whom he described as "a magician [Welles] met in the early '80s, saw on average of once a week, and discussed *The Cradle Will Rock* with at length."[1]

I was moved by Rosenbaum's reference to this friendship (which I had never read about before) to see if I could locate Steinmeyer and speak with him. I found him, contacted him, and proposed an interview to be published in a magazine I was writing for at the time. Most graciously, he agreed to talk to me on the record about Welles. The resulting interview appears in chapter 9 of this book.

Steinmeyer's memories of Welles lived up to the expectations I had on the basis of Rosenbaum's brief but tantalizing allusions to them. Just as importantly, speaking with Jim instilled in me a desire to speak to other people like him: people who had fascinating things to say about Welles, but who hadn't necessarily been interviewed at any great length before. A number of the people on the final list of interviewees in *Orson Welles Remembered* fit that profile.

George Plimpton, author of several "oral biographies," once said in an interview, "If you're doing a biography on contemporary figures, because of the magic of the tape recorder, most biographies are put together by writers going out and interviewing people who knew the subject. They have the advantage afterwards of picking out the one or two sentences from the interview they want. But I'm fascinated by the entire transcript, by the depth of material that's available in it."[2] I happen to share Plimpton's fascination with "the entire transcript," and "the depth of material" contained therein, which is why I chose to present the interviews I conducted in a Q&A format rather than write another biography of Welles. That isn't to imply that what appears here are unedited transcripts; to the contrary, the vast majority of my work consisted of many months of editing the interviews.

Writing about his oral biography of Truman Capote, Plimpton also said that "the editors of oral biography do not have the luxury of being guides and interpreters of the subject's life: they are more or less at the mercy of others' verbiage."[3] I think that, too, is true, and it is one of the reasons I'm so proud of this book. It is called *Orson Welles Remembered* and indeed the very *essence* of the book is the memories of those who knew Welles. I have added my own commentary at various points throughout the Q&As, but only when I felt it essential to add context to what the interviewee was talking about. (For example, some readers will very likely be unfamiliar with Welles's later films from the '70s and '80s, which are covered in great detail in chapters 7 thru 11.)

The interviews appear chronologically according to their subject matter. Thus, the book opens with Norman Lloyd recalling the Mercury Theatre, while Jim Steinmeyer remembers, near the close of the book, the very evening before Welles died in October 1985.

This chronological order of the book resulted in a wonderful coincidence. One of the earliest chapters is devoted to the recollections of one film editor (Robert Wise, editor of *Citizen Kane*), and one of the last chapters in the book contains the recollections of another. The latter man is Jonathon Braun, an editor who, forty years after *Kane* was released, worked alongside Welles in his Hollywood home, editing several of the director's unfinished and unreleased works. This chance symmetry was particularly meaningful because it reminded me of Welles's views of the editing process. "[F]or my style, for my vision of film," he once told an interviewer, "editing is not an aspect, *it is the aspect*."[4]

Braun concluded his comments to me by referencing one of the final lines Marlene Dietrich's character, Tanya, speaks in *Touch of Evil*. In the film, talking about Welles's character, Hank Quinlan, Tanya says, "He was some kind of man." If these interviews confirm anything, it is, indeed, that sentiment. As magician Mike Caveney told me, "This was the guy who had achieved everything that everyone in this business hoped to achieve. Whether they wanted to be a movie director — this was a guy that made the greatest movie in history. Whether they wanted to be in radio — hey, this is a guy that made the greatest radio show in history." When I think of my personal heroes, I think of Churchill, Roosevelt, and William Sloane Coffin, but also of

Welles — and largely for the reasons Caveney alluded to. Perhaps Marie-Sophie Dubus (speaking to me of how intimidating it was to meet Welles for the first time) put it most succinctly of all: "Orson Welles is Orson Welles and there's only one on the Earth."

Peter P. Tonguette
New Albany, Ohio
January 2007

1

The Mercury Theatre

Norman Lloyd

Norman Lloyd: I'd been on the Federal Theatre in *The Living Newspaper* and I played prominent roles in the first three *Living Newspapers*. So when Orson and John Houseman left the Federal Theatre to form the Mercury, they asked me to go with them because of my work on *The Living Newspaper*.

Peter Prescott Tonguette: I see. And this would be 1937?
 NL: That's correct.

PPT: What productions did you act in at the Mercury Theatre?
 NL: *Julius Caesar* and *Shoemaker's Holiday.*

The Mercury's first production — and the first Lloyd acted in as a member of the Mercury — was Caesar. *Lloyd played Cinna the Poet. In his marvelous autobiography,* Stages of Life in Theatre, Film, and Television, *Lloyd wrote of the staging of the scene in which Cinna is mobbed. Lloyd writes, "I think it is fair to say — and I have heard Orson say it publicly — that in this version, Cinna's scene became 'the' scene of the play: the fulcrum around which the rest of the play swung."*[1]

PPT: What was Welles like as a director?
 NL: Orson was, in my view, the most talented director that our theatre ever had. He was the first American director to bring a totality to a production. That had been done in Europe, I believe, by Reinhardt and Otto Brahm and those people. In America, the men who directed were very professional, very good, but it was more or less staging of fairly simple physical productions. And they were very good, these men. George Kaufman was superb. And George M. Cohan: superb. They knew how to do that kind of play very well.

But when Orson came along, he brought together all the elements of theatrical staging. That is to say the actors and of course the script, which he would affect considerably because he would re-cut it and change the continuity and so forth, sometimes for the better — of course, he was dealing with classics in my experience with him, so you could do that. There was no author around to scream bloody murder. But he would then involve lighting, staging, set design, music, sound, all blended together with the actors and have a totality of production that absolutely overwhelmed the audience.

Even when it got to a comedy like *Shoemaker's Holiday*, you had a kind of theatricality which was unique to Orson and, in my view, made him the most talented of all our directors.

PPT: Was he easy to act for?
NL: Yes, very.

Welles loved to tell stories at rehearsal. Rehearsals never started right on time. They started with stories. But that was part of the whole process. It was part of sort of warming up, if you will, part of thawing out. You know, instead of just coming in and, "All right, Act 1, Scene 1," he would sit down and tell stories. There'd be a lot of laughs and people would get to moving around and then doing the rehearsal.

PPT: Do you remember Welles's chauffeur from this time?
NL: Shorty?

PPT: Yes, Shorty! Do you have any memories or stories about him?
NL: I don't have any except that I remember that he wasn't a dwarf, but he wasn't much taller than one. He was very short. And very, very strong. He could sort of push you over with his finger.

I was to hear about George "Shorty" Chirello from several other interviewees; Welles himself mentioned him during the last interview he was ever to give, on The Merv Griffin Show, *the evening before he died in October 1985.*

PPT: Did you participate in any of the Mercury Theatre On the Air productions?
NL: None. Now, at that particular time, he had two separate companies. He had the theatre company and he had the radio company. Now, one or two of the actors lapped over and were in both — Jo Cotten and sometimes George Coulouris. But for the most part, they were kept separate. Ray Collins, Paul Stewart, Everett Sloane, and Agnes Moorehead were all in the radio company.

When he made his first journey out to Hollywood to do *Heart of Darkness*, he blended both companies. He joined the two companies together. And both companies arrived as one company in California.

PPT: And that included you, of course.
NL: Yes.

PPT: So you were going to act in *Heart of Darkness?*
NL: Yes.

PPT: What role were you going to play?

NL: You know, I can't remember. It was one of the guys going up the river. The only character's name I remember is Marlow, which Orson was going to do. Orson was going to be the camera. You were just going to hear his voice.

Welles was to film Heart of Darkness *subjectively so that "the audience would see what the camera/character sees,"*[2] *as biographer Frank Brady wrote.*

NL: And it was a very good script, but somehow the studio, RKO, suddenly said, after we were there six weeks, "We're not going to make it."

PPT: Did you have any rehearsals during those six weeks?

NL: We had one reading of the script. And that was it. We hung around while they discussed whether to make it or not and finally the answer came, "No."

PPT: But you stayed in Hollywood because just a few years later you were in Alfred Hitchcock's film, *Saboteur* (1941)?

NL: Well, I didn't stay in Hollywood. That's part of the story. That is to say, Orson asked us at the end of the six weeks when they ruled that they were not going to make the picture. He asked us to stay while he worked out another deal. He had another idea. There was a book called *The Smiler with a Knife* and that was written by Nicholas Blake, I believe. Nicholas Blake was the pen name of C. Day Lewis, the poet, who is the father of Daniel Day Lewis, the actor. But the studio wouldn't make that.

Orson asked us to stay around. Well, I elected not to because we weren't going to get paid. Some of the other actors were better off financially than I was at the time, particularly the radio actors. The radio actors had done very well economically. But those of us who were strictly from the theatre, we were not very rich, let's put it that way. So my wife and I went back to New York. And when I came back in 1942, that was at the behest of Alfred Hitchcock. Orson had nothing to do with that.

PPT: Did you and Orson ever discuss collaborating on film projects again?

NL: No. I did go backstage to see him after *Danton's Death*. He said to me, "When are you coming back?" He spoke to me very briefly, just sort of casually, that in doing what eventually became *The Five Kings*, he had in mind that I might do Jack Cade, which is a wonderful part in *Henry VI*.

Initially, *Chimes at Midnight* (1965) was a production in the theatre called *The Five Kings*. That closed out of town. The Theatre Guild was producing it and it closed. It never came into New York. Orson was in it and Burgess Meredith and quite a few familiar names.

PPT: And Meredith played Prince Hal in the play?

NL: Yes. But that eventually became *Chimes at Midnight*, which is one of his better pictures.

PPT: I think it's his best, actually.

NL: It's a wonderful picture. There's no question about Orson's gifts. He was the best. I mean, he was the most talented that we've had. The tragedy, as far as Hollywood is concerned, is that they thought he was too rich for their blood. It's unfortunate.

It's based on economics. You know, we did the Mercury on $6,000, I believe. True, it was the depths of the depression, 1937, so $6,000 represented a lot of money. But still it wasn't a lot of money, even as far as productions on Broadway went. When you get into pictures, the phrase I gave you — "Too rich for my blood" — came from the head of a studio who said that to me. I was going in to see Ben Kahane, who headed RKO, and we were talking about the possibility of my producing there. And he said, "I see you worked with Orson Welles — well, that's too rich for my blood." And I knew I was a goner right there.

They had this fear that he would in financial ways get them into a bind, which is a laugh when you consider what's happening today. But he did have trouble in the theatre when he did *Around the World in 80 Days*. He got himself into a bind for a tremendous amount of money — I think about $300,000; I could be proved wrong. And as a result, because he was set up wrong — he wasn't set up as a company, he was set up as an individual — he had to really go to Europe for about eleven years because of tax problems.

PPT: Were you in touch with Welles after this period?

NL: I saw him twice subsequent to that. Once was the night the AFI [American Film Institute] honored him. We were invited — not by Orson, but by MCA, my agency at that time. They had a table and they knew I had worked with Orson, so they invited me. And we had a little chat, very nice, and that was it.

Then the next time I saw him was at a panel at the Director's Guild near the end of his life where they devoted an entire week to Orson Welles. These panels were in the evening. On the second evening, there was a panel devoted to what Orson brought from the theatre into film. And on that panel Kenneth Tynan, Roger Hill, who was his teacher at The Hill School, and Orson appeared, and there were a couple of other people. I've forgotten who chaired the panel, but maybe Bob Wise, who had been the cutter for *Citizen Kane* (1941), appeared. Orson came and it was a surprise because everyone thought that he wouldn't show up, although he had been invited. But he did show up. And then after it, I went over to greet him and he embraced me in an enormous bear hug and whispered in my ear, "You son of a bitch." *[Laughs.]* And that was the last time I saw him.

PPT: That's not a bad good-bye.

NL: Not a bad good-bye. You see, Orson was a jolly fellow when he had humor. He was a temperamental fellow. He was difficult to discipline. I always regretted that my relationship with him always had a kind of tension in it. Now part of that is due to the fact that we were very young at the time. We were 22, then became 23 during that period. There was this enormous success and there were jealousies involved, maybe not on his part, but I think on my part I was cocky — not jealous so much as I had a chip on my shoulder. I always regretted that I didn't have a warmer relationship with him. But I have been told by many people, many people — and John Houseman was very close to us, we were a family with John — that it was impossible to have a warm relationship with Orson. And that's unfortunate. His best friend, I guess, was Jo Cotten. Jo was a wonderful man, really a rare and beautiful person, and if anyone couldn't get on with Jo, then they couldn't get on with anybody. But he did get on with Jo; they were dear friends.

PPT: The subject of that Director's Guild panel you mentioned raises an interesting question, and one which I'll ask you. What do you feel Welles brought to his film work from the theatre?

NL: Well, mainly in staging. Maybe others did it before him, maybe it came through the influence of the great cameraman who worked with him on *Citizen Kane*, Gregg Toland, but deep focus, the staging of people in depth. Curiously, much of the staging could have been in the theatre — although Orson had great sense of camera, I mean, remarkable. He staged it in such a way that it was cinematic.

I think that that was the main thing he brought and he brought, a certain theatricality. You know, if you say, "What was Chaplin about?" You'd say, "Well, he really brought the immigrant into the world." Jean Renoir brought France, if you want to know what France was, and a certain humanitarianism. Orson's story was theatricality. It was about a great theatricality. And he brought that from theatre. It was bigger and broader than a lot of picture work.

PPT: Do you have any favorite memories of Welles?

NL: Well, my memory of Orson — at this instance, which is sixty-seven years later — is of a very vital, enormous gift to the theatre. The rehearsals and so forth. The richness of his personality. The energy, the vitality, the bigness, full of ideas, and laughing all the time. I remember him laughing all the time, except when he and Houseman were screaming at each other. They screamed a lot! They screamed so much that you didn't hear it. You know what I mean? You can hear people screaming and it just goes over your head. We would just sit, reading the newspapers. *[Laughs]*

But, as you indicated a moment ago, I've been privileged to work with some great guys. Each quite different from the other, by the way. For example, Orson and Chaplin, who knew each other, thought that Jean Renoir was the great man. And that's very possible. But I remember that Orson was what theatre was about. The vitality, the theatricality, the ideas, even the terrible accidents, such as Orson stabbing Joe Holland when we did *Caesar*. These things happened with Orson.[3] He was that kind of person. So I remember him as a tremendous, big theatrical force. When you were working with him, you were working in the theatre at its best, the theatre that you loved, the theatre that you went into.

By the time our conversation was nearly over, Lloyd and I were simply chatting about Welles's many films, including the unreleased The Other Side of the Wind, *the making of which is detailed in chapter 7.*

NL: I don't know anything about the picture. I've seen a little footage of it. I saw some scenes with John Huston. But I'm sure it's brilliant. He made brilliant films. Even the ones that weren't very good! I mean, *Mr. Arkadin* and *The Trial*, I found them boring, but they're wonderful to watch! *[Laughs.]* Because anything he touched always had some unique quality to it.

PPT: Have you ever seen *The Immortal Story* (1968)?
NL: No. Isn't that the one with Jeanne Moreau?

PPT: Yes, and it's based on the short story by Isak Dinesen.
NL: Yes. But that has always been put down.

PPT: Well, I love it.
NL: Ah, good.

PPT: I think it's one of his best films.
NL: Did he ever get it released?

PPT: It was released briefly in the United States, but I believe that it was more successful in Europe.
NL: Well, that's unfortunate. He died, and he's buried in Spain. I mean, he's like a permanent exile. After all, he's a Midwestern boy! *[Laughs.]*

Welles was born in Kenosha, Wisconsin; Frank Brady writes in his biography, Citizen Welles, *that his ashes are buried in Ronda, Spain, on bullfighter Antonio Ordonez's farm.*[4]

May 6, 2004 and October 20, 2005

2

Citizen Kane

Robert Wise

Wise was the editor of two Welles films: Citizen Kane *and* The Magnificent Ambersons *(1942).*

Robert Wise: I was at RKO and they had signed Orson. And I was just finishing editing, as I recall, a picture being directed by Garson Kanin called *My Favorite Wife* [1940]. As I recall — I have to think way back here, you see — Orson was very young himself then. He was only about 25. They had assigned a rather old-time hack editor to do *Citizen Kane* and Orson wasn't happy with that. He wanted somebody younger and near his own age. We were roughly the same age, Orson and I.

So I was sent over to meet him and we chatted for a few minutes about working operandi. When I got back to my cutting room, I got a call from my boss saying I had got the job. And I was absolutely thrilled because I was so impressed by Orson. Here he was at this very tender age — I think 25 or 26, we were roughly the same age — going to do his first motion picture. I felt it was quite an honor to be given the assignment to edit the film for him.

And I think one of the things that made it all work so well for Orson too was the fact that he brought his Mercury Theatre actors out from New York. So audiences were seeing not only a fine film, but fine actors whom they weren't familiar with and didn't know. And I think that was a very important plus for him, for Orson and for the film.

Peter Prescott Tonguette: Did you re-do all of the scenes that that older editor had been working on?

RW: No, some of them were all right. But I changed those that I felt could be improved, that's all.

PPT: Was he still shooting while you started cutting?

RW: Oh, sure. I always do. Today's work that you shoot you see tomorrow in rushes. And when you get a whole sequence complete, maybe after several days of work, that's all done, then you go to the cutting room and start putting it together.

I went off and edited on my own. You see, it's the usual routine. You see your rushes every day from the day's work before and, if he printed up two or three takes, he might say, "Use take two," or he might say, "Use the first half of take two and the last half of take three," things like that. You make your notes and go back to the cutting room and put it together according to what those instructions were. When I got a sequence entirely edited, completely edited, I'd show it to him, the cut version, and he, of course, might want some changes. I broke in with an old-time editor who said, "Bob, the only thing that the director wants you to do is to make the sequence play. You might cut it together a little differently than he had envisioned, but if you make that play, that's all he wants from you." And he was right.

PPT: Did you have a chance to visit the set?

RW: Yeah, I used to go to the set a couple times a day, maybe once in the morning, if they were shooting on the lot. Sometimes they were out on location and I wouldn't do it, but if they were on the lot shooting I'd wander up to Stage 10 for a while in the morning. As a matter of fact, that's one of the things that helped me when I started directing, myself, with *The Curse of the Cat People* (1944). That was my first picture. I was editing the film and the director, whose first feature this was, got way behind and they couldn't seem to make him understand that he had to shoot more pages every day. He used up all of his time and he only shot half of the script. And that's when they kind of called me and said, "You've been wanting a chance to direct. Gunther — his name was Gunther von Fritsche — can't seem to understand he has to shoot more every day, so why don't you take over on Monday morning?" And I did. I took over Monday morning. They gave me 10 days to finish it and I did it in 10 days. They signed me to a contract and that started my directing career.

As Wise indicated earlier, Welles was not a domineering presence in the cutting room.

RW: Of course, all the time he was shooting, he was there. When he finished shooting, he might go off for a week or 10 days and let me finish my cut and then come back and see the cut and then stay with me to make whatever changes he wanted, or we felt together we wanted.

Welles once remarked, "I think it's very harmful to see movies for movie-makers because you either imitate them or worry about not imitating them."[1] Nevertheless, Welles watched and studied John Ford's Stagecoach *(1939), and several other Ford films, numerous times.[2] Wise commented:*

RW: And he had studied. He had gone to see other films and kind of studied them and studied how they were done and how they were shot and how they were photographed and the acting and all that.

PPT: Can you describe a typical working day on the film?

RW: It depends on whether you're in pre-production, production, or post-production. Let's say you're in pre-production. You're getting everything ready and getting the cast all set and the staff all set, making sure the script's fine. And production, of course, is when you actually are shooting, whether you're shooting in the studio or on location or whatever. And then once the shooting is finished, then you go into what we call post-production, where you're back in the studio in the editing room and doing all the editing, getting a final cut of a thing, and then getting the sound fixed and the music score put in. And then very often, in those days, once you did that you'd go out for what we call "sneak previews." Once you'd buttoned it up, you'd go out to some town like Santa Barbara, let's say, and the theatre would advertise "sneak preview tonight" so the audience would know they were going to see something besides the film that had been playing there advertised. You go in for your previews and you get the audience reaction. Most times you had preview cards, where the audiences could write their opinion of the film, what they liked and didn't like. And then you go back to the cutting room if you need to make changes, and sometimes you'd do re-dubs and make changes and that was it.

PPT: But there wasn't a preview process for *Kane*?

RW: No, he never previewed it. *[The Magnificent] Ambersons* we did, but *Kane* we never did. I had to take it to New York. There was a big concern about what the reaction of William Randolph Hearst would be to the picture because Hearst was a big newspaper publisher and they were afraid he might come down on the film badly and it would hurt the film. So I had to fly to New York myself, when we got a completed print — sound, music, and everything in it — and I went over to Radio City Music Hall where they had a small preview, revue theatre and I ran it for a lot of the top executives in the various studios. And they all said, "There's no problem with this." I think I had to get some of the actors in to re-dub and change a few words here and there. I might have had to have a newspaper printed up again with a different date or headline, but nothing major. And then the picture went out.

I asked Wise about a famous scene in the film featuring Kane and his first wife, Emily (Ruth Warrick).

RW: It was in the script, it was shot that way, but the whole rhythm of it — what we call whip pans, the speed of those whip pans and where they come out and all of that — was done over a period of weeks with me and my assistant editor, Mark Robson, who later became a director too. We would get a version of it that we liked and think was pretty good and then we'd put it away for awhile. And then we'd get it out again, look at it and say, "Well, no, maybe this whip pan could be done here or this one should be a little faster," whatever.

Wise viewed rushes every day, so it was always unmistakable to him that Kane *was a special film.*

RW: Oh, I don't know. I think we pretty well thought that was happening when we saw these marvelous rushes coming in all day. First off, we had a tremendous cinematographer in Gregg Toland. And then all these actors that he brought out from the Mercury Theatre in New York were all new to us and all just great. And we were all thrilled and couldn't wait to see the rushes every day. We knew we'd see exciting film and new faces.

PPT: I was curious if there were scenes which Welles shot but altogether cut out of the final film?

RW: I don't think so. I think on *Ambersons* we did some of that, but not on *Kane*. *Kane* we didn't have any sneak previews on. That was it; it went out.

On *Ambersons,* we did have, and we had some problems with the previews. And we had to come back and make some changes. It was very long to start with and I cut it down some. And occasionally what happens too sometimes on a sneak preview, when you get a film out in front of an audience, suddenly you'll get a laugh that's unintended, what we call a bad laugh.

Welles's first film after Kane *was* The Magnificent Ambersons, *his great adaptation of Booth Tarkington's novel, also made for RKO. Wise was again the editor. I asked him if they worked in the same way that they had on* Kane.

RW: Pretty much. Pretty much the same way, yeah.

PPT: What were the biggest challenges of editing *Ambersons*?

RW: Well, the biggest challenge of *Ambersons,* I guess, was how to get a version of the film that would play to the audiences. When we took it out for previews, it played well in some spots and in other spots it just was very bad. It had bad laughs in it. And you never know about that, you don't see those things until you take it out in front of an audience. The minute that happens, you think, "Oh, gosh, I should have known that they'd take that that way." It takes that audience to tell you, you see. Then we go back and cut around it, try to get rid of it, whatever was causing the bad laugh, and with *Ambersons,* part of it was just plain length. It was just too damn long.

Before a final cut of the film could be delivered, Welles flew to Brazil to commence work on his documentary. It's All True.[3] *As a result, Welles was not at hand for the previews of the film Wise mentioned.*

RW: As a matter of fact, as I recall, I flew down to Miami, taking the reels of film down there, and met him down there. There was a little studio down there that had a dubbing player, Flicker Flashbacks or something. And I ran, with him, all the film we had, until I got all of his notes and all of the suggestions he had about the final cut of the film. Then he got on one of those old flying boats and flew down to Brazil, and I came back to L.A.

I was supposed to fly down to Brazil to take the print down to him. But at the last minute, our government put an embargo on civilians flying abroad, so I had to ship the print down to him there. And I don't know whatever happened to the print. That was it. Too bad, because it would have been fine to have that print of *Ambersons* in the original form around.

Wise received instructions from Welles while he was in Brazil.

RW: He would give me some by cable and some by phone. He gave me instructions of what he wanted changed or dropped out.

They were different pictures. *Kane* was kind of just a neat package itself. *Ambersons* was long and there were performances that got laughed. Aggie Moorehead got some laughs with her performance and we had to work around that. It was a different kettle of fish.

Wise eventually had to direct several new scenes for Ambersons *himself. Wise told me, "I tried to shoot it in the style he did so there would be a consistency to it in terms of the photography and the angles." I asked him when it became clear that such scenes were required.*

RW: Oh, I don't know, after the second or third preview. I can't tell you right now because it's been so long ago, but it just became apparent. As I remember, there was a scene between Dolores Costello and Tim Holt, her son, and we needed a new sequence there. Of course, Orson was in South America so I went in and directed that. And there might have been another couple, I can't remember now, too long ago.

I think the fourth preview we had — I believe it was in Long Beach — it played well and it ran well. It didn't get any bad laughs. And that was it. We said, "Okay, let's ship it."

The version of Ambersons *previewed in Long Beach ran 87 minutes, and in the end the film was released to the general public running 88 minutes.*[4] *When I asked Wise if he felt the film was better in one of its original forms (which had run as long as 132 minutes), he said, "Oh, possibly so, I don't know. I can't remember"—understandable given just how long it has been since Wise viewed any deleted material from the film.*

PPT: Welles probably wasn't happy with all of this being done in his absence ...

RW: No, he wasn't.

PPT: But you think that he probably understood ...
RW: Steps had to be taken, yeah.

PPT: Of *Kane* and *Ambersons,* do you have a preference as to which is your favorite?
RW: *Kane*. No doubt. Outstanding film.

After editing with Welles, Wise went on to have an extraordinary career as a film director. The Set-Up (1949), The Day the Earth Stood Still (1951), West Side Story (1961), and The Sound of Music (1965) are among his many great films. As our conversation drew to a close, I had to ask if Wise felt he had been influenced by Welles.

RW: I think probably a little bit, yeah. But how much, I couldn't tell you.
December 17, 2004

Sonny Bupp

Bupp played Kane's son, Charles Foster Kane, Jr., shooting his small role in "about a week." He told me, "Like most professionals I consider Citizen Kane *to be one of the greatest films ever produced."*

Sonny Bupp: It's interesting about how I was selected for the part in *Citizen Kane*.

Several children of my age were brought into the casting director's office for an "interview," that is, who would be chosen for the child's part. This is standard procedure. While we were waiting, Orson Welles came into the office, looked at the assembled children, pointed directly at me, and said "That's the one," then left. We can only assume he thought I looked like him.

Later, when I was on the set I had a chance to speak with Orson. He was very kind and attentive.

The atmosphere on the set was businesslike.

Welles was very demanding but also very precise. Not too many scenes required re-shooting. After all, most of the performers were from his other work.

Welles was an incredible person. He acted, directed for the entire picture, running from his spot in the scene to be shot to the script girl and cameramen. What a guy!

January 29, 2005

3

Macbeth

Dann Cahn

Cahn's professional relationship with Welles began as assistant editor on his film adaptation of Shakespeare's Macbeth, *made for Republic Studios and released in 1948.*

Dann Cahn: I had as a teenager been a fan of *The Shadow* and that amazing *War of the Worlds* on radio. During World War II, I was in the army air force. After the war, by fate, I was at Republic Studios working on Westerns and I fell into this *Macbeth* thing. I got to know Orson very well and this is how it happened. I told you that he had trouble with George Chirello, who was his driver. George was a little dwarf and we called him "Shorty." There was some argument over money that Orson owed Shorty. Anyway, Shorty took the car and left ... and left ... and left. And I wound up chauffeuring Orson around in my car.

We would work late at night, 8, 9 o'clock at night — maybe as late as 10. I was single and young, about 23 or 24. I'd drive him around and got to know him well. We'd talk about all kinds of things. I told Orson that I'd seen his magic act when I was in the service. I'd seen him at the Hollywood Canteen where he cut Marlene Dietrich in half. He told me that someday he wanted to do his act on television. Fatefully, almost 10 years later, I was the supervising editor at Desilu and he came to the studio to do that famous *I Love Lucy* show where he meets Lucy. There's that great scene where she's in this scuba outfit, shopping in a sporting goods store, trying on flippers and wearing a scuba mask to go to Miami to meet Ricky Ricardo and their kid. Orson looks at her and she says to him, "I'm on my way to Miami." And he replies, "Under water all the way?" It got a big laugh. *[Laughter.]*

Well, he didn't saw Lucy in half but he did this gag that was pretty visual where Lucy is lying on top of a broom and then Orson takes the broom away and she's floating in air. It was quite a trick. So there Orson was on TV doing his magic act and, ironically, I'm with him.

Back in the *Macbeth* days, we talked about a lot of things. He kept cautioning me like a mentor, "Danny, don't get married too young." He was 19 years old when he married Virginia Nicholson and they produced his first child, Christopher. Christopher was the first of three daughters produced by Orson, each with a different wife.

Welles's other daughters were Rebecca, by his second wife, Rita Hayworth, and Beatrice, by his third and final wife, Paola Mori.

DC: Christopher was eight or nine years old when we made *Macbeth* and Orson brought her in to play Macduff's child, who was murdered by the assassins. This was quite a performance. Because she was dressed as a little boy and with a name like Christopher, for a long time I thought Christopher was a boy. When I finally was told that Christopher was a little girl, I never did ask why she had that name.

He cautioned me several times about getting married too young. He made a big thing about that. Of course, 10 years later I was married with a couple of children and he got a laugh out of that. I didn't get too much into his personal life, but at the time we were making *Macbeth* he was estranged from Rita Hayworth and made several personal calls to her in Europe from the cutting room.

Cahn said that Welles told him that he loved the editorial process.

DC: Editing the film and dubbing sound was a big thing with him — of course, Orson came from radio and was really into sound. But he adapted readily to film. In *Macbeth,* we used all these original film shots, transitions, no one else had used them. Now they do *thousands* of tricks, it's old hat. He would have been absolutely in his glory if he were alive today. And, boy, that is the truth. He said that when he got to RKO and worked with the camera and the cutting departments and the art department, that it was the best electric train set a kid could ever get. He did say that to me personally and he did say it to other people too.

Cahn discussed the pre-recorded soundtrack of Macbeth.

DC: I came in, I think, four, five days in, right in the first week of shooting. This other fellow, who had the assistant editor's job, couldn't handle it. His wife was having a baby. I wound up sleeping there at night. Orson got a cot for me and put it in the corner of one of the stages where we were shooting. I literally stayed at the studio for several days for 24 hours at a time, Orson was so absorbed in the pre-recording. We pre-recorded the sound with the actors and then they worked to playback on the set. The studio thought the pre-recording was a fiasco and they pulled it all out and re-looped it all later. We did that whole thing to playback, like a musical number.

The actors included Jeanette Nolan as Lady Macbeth, Dan O'Herlihy as Macduff, Peggy Webber as Lady Macduff and Roddy McDowall as Malcolm. George "Shorty" Chirello, Orson's real life driver and Man Friday, played the character of Seyton, who was Macbeth's Man Friday. He was dubbed by another actor. I believe it was Bill Alland, who also played one of the three witches and one of the assassins. He was a triple-header there and became a successful producer at Universal.

Orson made so many takes of those actors that when we pre-recorded the track, we took a deck of cards, 52 in all, and we called each take by a card. I would flip the cards over — the five of hearts, the ten of spades — and each one was a take number. Orson would say, "Let's try the five of spades" or "Let's try the ten of hearts." We literally did that when we pre-recorded the actors.

Later in post-production, the editor and Orson took a dupe of the picture to Italy where he was doing his next film, *Black Magic* (1949). They were in Rome, playing with the dupe. We didn't have faxes or anything like that. So they'd send me these little recorded discs of changes and give me the film edge numbers and I'd make the changes in the production work print. So I sort of became an associate editor at the end of the thing. I had a wonderful experience with the guy who was the editor, Lou Lindsay.

Peter Prescott Tonguette: Did Welles shoot a lot of film or more than was typical?

DC: Less than typical. Because we were working to the playback and he had this *Macbeth* in his head the way he did it on the stage. He was pretty good on schedule for shooting, but after we got in the cutting room there were a million ways of playing it because he had enough coverage. And he was being innovative with all these zoom lens tricks. Some of them he did on stage and some of them we did post-production, as we did 10 years later while shooting *The Fountain of Youth* (1958).

> *Echoing Robert Wise's comment to me that he "went off and edited" on his own while working on* Kane, *Cahn said that Welles was not always in the editing room on* Macbeth.

DC: Welles had respect for editors and was not necessarily in the cutting room during the editing. He would look in the Moviola, give his notes, and then he would go off being a bon vivant, socializing, or planning his next project — or his next three projects! He would deliver the notes. He had respect for us. But he was very explicit in what he wanted done and it was fine to do it.

He'd waltz in at six in the evening and we'd play around for three or four hours.

November 15, 2004

Peggy Webber

Peggy Webber: I first met Orson on the telephone. He called NBC, where I was broadcasting one of my daily soaps. I was just 19. We broadcast first to New York and then to the West Coast. I was called into the control booth in Studio G to answer the call and he asked me to hurry over to CBS as soon as I got off the air.

As an 11 year old, living in San Antonio, Texas, I was home alone one Saturday afternoon and, by accident, heard Orson on the air from New York on a sustaining show. Probably a summer replacement. I fell in love with him for his intelligence, his timing, his way of not talking down to his audience, but taking them into his wonderment and joy of life. I loved the music he chose with Bernard Herrmann, the material, and of course, his voice, and determined then and there, that what he did was what I wanted to do with my life.

I proceeded to write a series of radio scripts and took a little band of actors I had culled from my junior high school class to audition at WOAI. I trained my "actors" and created sound effects and played many voices. We created a sensation at the station and they put us on the air a few times. My career had started when I was two and a half, singing and dancing solo, between motion pictures and in mining camps and oil fields in Laredo, Texas, then in Merced, Mariposa and Fresno, California, where I performed for Governor Rolph and Vice President Nance Garner on two separate occasions as well as for other organizations. Then I continued performing and model-ing and developing a one person show where I imitated famous personalities, and continued with appearances in Seattle, Glendale, California, San Antonio and Tucson, Arizona, where I finally got my own weekly, sponsored show on KVOA for my sophomore, junior and senior years at Tucson high school. I graduated at 16 years of age (the war had started in December 1941, now it was July of '42) and went to Hollywood (my father had died in April, and my mother and I went as far as the money would take us, and that was L.A.).

But before that, when we were living in the Arizona desert near the Cochise Mountains, I was allowed to listen to the car radio once a week because we had no electricity, and my father was trying to develop a gold mine in the mountains. I listened to Orson Welles's Mercury Theatre with the moon shining and the coyotes and other wild creatures circling around me while dreaming of the day when I might be doing what "he" was, or at least meet him.

So when that phone call came, I was out of my mind for many hours. (*Time* magazine had written me up around this time and had followed me for a week as I appeared on 21 shows performing different characters on each show. This and the accompanying complimentary article had put me into orbit in the network radio world.)

I never exactly knew, on that first Welles show, what I was doing or why, but guessed I was replacing someone important on the show. I played a romantic lead opposite him for the scenes I had and, as I recall, I spoke with a Russian accent. I was told that I was to smash a champagne glass against the wall of the studio (it was an audience show at CBS) with the rest of the cast at a given moment! And as I told you earlier, there was tremendous cutting of the script before I got on mike, very shortly before we went on the air. From what Dick Wilson told me, this was customary, as was Orson dropping his script, just as he walked up to the mike.[1] It seemed to be his theatrical way of getting the audience on the edge of their seats. Of course, at the right moment, he would pull a script from his coat pocket and proceed.

I have memories of "new" scripts being written in the middle of the night by very disgruntled girls from script departments having to work past their normal hours. Whether this was something I heard about from others or actually experienced, I find it difficult to remember. But that did seem to be Orson's way of working. He did not adhere to any of the orderly protocol, which other directors and producers had developed in the scheme of network radio, as I knew it. But I expected him to be "the magician," or the greatest showman on Earth, the P.T. Barnum of our age, only a more sensitive artist.

The only Welles-directed film Webber actually appeared in (she looped several others after they were completed, as we shall learn) was Macbeth.

PW: The next memory I have of him is his asking me to meet him at Republic Studios to read for Lady Macduff. I never resorted to such things as sun lamps, but because I was working so much I thought I did not get out enough in the sun to look healthy. My hours were from 6 in the morning at NBC for the soaps, to 2 A.M., after midnight, recording such shows as *The Saint* or *Box 13*, getting home just long enough to crawl into bed and be up at 5:30 to get back to work. And so in order to look "healthy," I decided to buy a sun lamp before I went to Republic to see him. I got under the sun lamp ... and I fell asleep. When I awakened, my face proceeded to swell. And I was horrified that that was the way he was going to see me.

When I got to the studio, they sent me upstairs to the projection booth over the top of the sound stage, where they recorded and looped in those days. Orson was wearing a Mexican peon's outfit: loose fitting white pajama-like bottoms and a loose fitting top with bell type sleeves. He was overjoyed to see me and asked me to read the main Lady Macduff's scene. When I finished, he shouted, "That's it! That's it!" and told me to go right down stairs and record it. He said, "Dick Wilson is down there, Jeanette Nolan and Edgar Barrier." These were my old friends and so I was a bit mollified, but apprehensive as to how I would feel, later, after I had worked on the part. I apologized for my swollen face and he said, "Nonsense. I want her to be very feminine and blonde. Like a child bride, compared to Lady Macbeth." Then he pressed the "talk back" and told Dick Wilson that I was on my way down to record my part.

In a highly novel move, Welles elected to pre-record the film's dialogue before shooting ever began.[2]

PW: I was frightened at acting to my audio reading of lines before I was "set" in the character. Orson saw this and had me say the lines in the second take without the audio. I do not know which was used. Actually, we re-dubbed so much it did not matter.

However, in the two and more years that followed, we had been criticized by the British press as being too Scottish with the accents and so we re-recorded the show with Mid-Atlantic accents, then with softer Scottish accents and then with British accents. I think he had me doing the voices of the gentlewoman in the scene with the doctor, the screams of Jeanette, the children's voices, the witches' voices.

We only had 21 days to film the whole picture. Orson had a bet with [Herbert] Yates (the owner of Republic) that he could make a film, and what's more a Shakespearean film, in three weeks. Olivier had just made *Hamlet* and Orson was throwing his hat in the ring, proving that he was not a spend-thrift, and could be as disciplined as anyone ever had been.

Nevertheless, the dubbing process alluded to above took two-and-a-half years.

PW: The reason it took so long was in those days we recorded on glass disks and they had to be shipped to Orson in Europe, who would then record his directorial comments to each of us and we would listen and then do what he told us. Then that would be shipped back to him and if he still wanted changes those were shipped back to us. Sending mail to Europe in 1948 took weeks.

Peter Prescott Tonguette: Would Welles do a lot of takes?

PW: No. He did not do a lot of takes. Only on the special effects, like the melting of the witches or the dampness of the hillocks in the Macbeth compound. We were watered down a lot. The horses did what came naturally and the long dresses trailed in the two or three inches of water where all things commingled.

PPT: How was he to work with as a director?

PW: I believed he was the best director in the world. But I was quite chagrinned that he was shooting on the next set simultaneously. After he would rehearse us once or twice, he sometimes would leave us to Dick or to the cameraman. I believe I would have been shot much better had he been there to oversee my close-ups. I am still very embarrassed about myself in that picture. I did work a few years later which is one hundred percent better, but, then, I learned a little about film technique after *Macbeth*.

He was able to shoot on two sets at once because he was not concerned with sound. He sat thru one complete shot of my scene with my child (Chris Welles, his own eldest child, played my little boy, although she was a she). Then he would set up another shot that was not so crucial and leave it to his second crew and walk over to the next set and rehearse that scene. Then he might return and do another scene with me and Alan Napier and then go back and shoot the one he had rehearsed on the adjoining set. He was totally in control and knew when to expend his energies.

He lost about forty or fifty pounds during the shoot. He was on pills and so he did not sleep, which aided him in his last scenes. (He absolutely never drove a car, refused to drive, and when he was on the dubbing sound stage, he was on the phone to people all over the world no matter what time it was "their" time. He talked to Sir Carol Reed, Hitchcock, and other notables all the time that he was on the sound stage when we were dubbing.)

Welles later engaged Webber to re-dub a part in Black Magic.

PW: Orson asked for me to redo all of Valentina Cortese's role in *Black Magic*, which was her debut. As I recall, the scenes were with him, which I did, and he directed me long distance, as he did on *Macbeth*, when we looped. But he seemed to like what I did, because there was not a lot of correction. I thought he directed the film. That is what Dick Wilson led me to believe. I never saw the entire film or credits.

Gregory Ratoff has sole directorial credit on Black Magic; *however, Barbara Leaming noted in her biography of Welles that Ratoff was "an easygoing director who adored Orson" and who was "perfectly content to let his friend Orson take charge now and then."*[3]

PPT: Did you dub any of Orson's other films?

PW: Yes. Dick Wilson would call me in to different major studios for about a year after we finished with the Scottish play and he would run a scene from Orson's current project on the screen and have me loop from Italian to English or just redo the dialogue, which perhaps was unintelligible or whatever. It was dark and shadowy film mostly.

Although she doesn't remember precisely, Webber believes she may have been dubbing the role of Bianca in Othello *(1952).*

PW: But I did work for Paul Stewart on *Kings Row* at Warner's, playing a leading role (on camera), the doctor's crippled, mentally twisted wife, and

I did dub for Sir Carol Reed on the Tony Quinn picture, *Flap* (1970), where I dubbed the entire leading lady's role. And for Bill Alland, I played the leading mother role, on camera, in his *Space Children* (1958). For this and other jobs, I believe Orson was responsible.

I never saw him petty except with the stage hands. Some of the Republic grips or carpenters or other workers had no respect for what Orson was doing; they were used to working on B pictures or worse, and when he would catch them being lazy or not doing their jobs, he would tongue lash them into oblivion.

He knew how to put on an intimidating attitude. But he never did that with actors.

He was big hearted in his attitude about humanity and the brevity of life, and in the way he would embrace the actors he loved. He took us to dinner every night at James Wong Howe's Chinese restaurant in the valley, near Republic. Dan O'Herlihy did not like Chinese food. He had just come to America from Ireland. At that time, Chinese restaurants were unknown in Ireland. And he would sit with his arms crossed, refusing to eat. Orson was very patient with him, and he ordered all of the food for all of us, getting rare dishes that the public did not get. He reserved the back room so no one could stare at us. He dealt with Dan on the set pretty much the same way. He kept him busy sculpting the witches out of clay and changing them each day as the story became more damning for Macbeth. Dan had been an architect and was a very good artist. Orson understood people. He knew that Dan was insecure performing with such a prominent talent, and that it was Dan's way of hiding it by being petulant or recalcitrant, and so he gave him something to do that was unique, his very own contribution.

But with the Chinese food, which Orson "used" to reduce himself, he could only laugh his big hearted laugh, and order noodles or broth for Dan, which Dan would sneer at.

PPT: Were you ever in touch with Orson again subsequent to the 1950s?

PW: I was a director and producer for a number of theatres. One of the last ones was a theatre in North Hollywood. Sean McClory, my husband, had come from the Abbey in Dublin, and because I prefer Irish playwrights, when we opened the CART [California Artist Radio Theatre] we did mostly the works of great writers of that country. Dick Wilson directed my production of Oscar Wilde's *Importance of Being Earnest,* and during that run it was Orson's last birthday. Dick told me he was going to call him, and I said to please wish him a happy birthday and send him my love, and tell him that maybe someday he would consider directing a play with us. Dick told me that he related the message and Orson was delighted, sent his love, and said he might take me up on it. But he was gone before the year was up. Ironic that Sean O'Casey's daughter called me on the telephone just moments after I heard it announced on the news and I was brushing away the tears. He had loved Ireland and worked in theatre there at The Gate with Michael MacLiamoir, who really, I believe, was a great influence on Orson's style and phrasing, particularly in radio, where Orson did so many narrations.

Webber developed a friendship with George "Shorty" Chirello.

PW: Shorty told me which prison Orson had taken him from. Joseph Cotten (with whom I worked a great deal in radio) and Orson had gone to the facility and Orson paid to have Shorty released to his recognizance. On the set of *Macbeth*, one could hear Orson bellowing, "Shorty!!" and Shorty, who played a role in the film, would come running with a tray of multi-colored pills and a glass of water for Orson, saying, "Yes, boss!!" This shouting happened about every two hours.

He was a sociable fellow and called my house often to gossip or just talk. One story he told me was about Orson taking Rita Hayworth up to Nepenthe, a restaurant on Highway One about two hours from Hearst's castle going north. He said he made up his mind to go one night about one in the morning and when they got near Hearst's castle the fog was so thick that Orson had to get out of the car and by walking, lead Shorty in driving the car, which made the trip take forever. But when he finally got there, he bought the place for Rita as a gift. And I believe he actually named it Nepenthe. They never went back. Rita did not want it.

Several years later, he sold it, about the time they divorced.

Shorty said that Orson would wake him up in the middle of the night and order six course dinners for himself and Rita. And Shorty complied. He loved Orson, but loved to talk about his eccentricities and genius.

I remember when Orson came on the set, how magically the whole tempo and rhythm of everyone and everything changed. I remember that he had six sets of clothing and lost much weight during the filming and took pills to stay awake so that he could see the rushes at night and rewrite. He did continue to make changes and did not have false awe of Shakespeare; where it served the pictorial drama, he put Shakespeare's speeches (from the play) in the mouths of characters not so designated by the bard.

I remember when Elizabeth Taylor visited the set and he remarked that it was a good thing she was under age or he would have set his cap for her. I remember his laugh, his intensity, his theatrical truth. I remember at the beach house where I rehearsed with Orson's daughter, Chris, and little Rebecca was there, that I talked with Roger Hill and his wife from the private Todd School (near Chicago) where Orson was enrolled on a scholarship, offered to him by headmaster Hill from the time he was about ten. They told of how they had given him a magic set, because he did not fit into sports with the rest of the boys, and they told me that he wore the cape from that gift to all of his classes, for a long time. They also said that he directed the other boys at the school, in Shakespearean productions. He knew Shakespeare very well, and had spent his early years studying it, before he got to Todd School.

When he graduated, they gave him his choice of going on with his studies or taking a trip around the world. He chose to go to Ireland and hire a little donkey cart and travel thru the countryside. Probably suggested by the Robert Louis Stevenson story about my little donkey. He worked at the Gate Theatre for a season with MacLiamoir and Hilton Edwards. Orson told us of how he went to the Old Abbey Theatre before leaving the country, and when a worker was changing the marquee, bribed him to put his name on the marquee (which was against Abbey rules, to mention an actor's name on the marquee with a show) and then he had his picture taken as he posed beneath it. When he returned to New York he got jobs with that white lie. He played Marchbanks in Shaw's *Candida* on Broadway, opposite Katharine Cornell, when he was 18.

There was such a feeling of almost a lust for life with Orson and his cohorts. It was a zest that was very youthful and enchanting!

December 30, 2004, and January 2, 2005

4

King Lear

Alvin Epstein

In early 1956, Welles staged a production at the New York City Center of Shakespeare's King Lear. *Epstein, then a young actor, was cast in the role of Lear's Fool.*

Alvin Epstein: I was appearing with Marcel Marceau in his first American engagement. I had just returned from living abroad for quite a few years and the engagement with Marceau was my first in New York. It was a big hit, and when we finished our run at The Barrymore Theatre, we went on tour. I believe we were in Philadelphia when I got a call from my agent to come back to the city to audition for Orson Welles for *Lear,* without a particular mention of any role. I decided to audition for Edmond, and I prepared the opening soliloquy. I came up to New York. I don't remember if it was on an off day or if I had to go back to Philadelphia, but in any case I did the audition. It was at Welles's hotel suite.

There were a few staff people there, also his wife, Paola [Mori]. I did a very good audition, left, took the subway back to my parents' apartment in Upper Manhattan, and when I got home my father told me that I'd received a telephone call from Orson Welles and that I was cast — not as Edmond, but as the Fool. So I was elated and a little bit puzzled, but I guess he thought I would make a better Fool than an Edmond. *[Laughter.]*

I don't remember how long it was before rehearsals were to begin; only a short time, I believe. I gave my notice to Marceau that I was going to be leaving and went into rehearsal with Welles. That's how I got the part.

Peter Prescott Tonguette: Was the audition fairly standard?

AE: It was in his living room. My memory — of course, it could be mixed with my memories of him later on, when I got to know him — was that he was a pretty jovial man. He was having fun, he enjoyed what he was doing, and it was not a particularly cold' or distant, judgmental kind of atmosphere. That might have been because we were in his living room. There was a sense of real contact; I wasn't standing up on a stage, with him watching from a distance.

PPT: Can you tell me about the rehearsal process?

AE: We were rehearsing at the Schumer Warehouse, which was probably just a regular storage facility, but there were large studios. This was a big, big loft room. I don't remember exactly where it was in Manhattan. It was a big production, so there were lots of people there. I don't recall anything about the table work — sitting around and reading the script — which is not to say that it didn't happen.

Once we were on our feet and began to move around, Orson began to stage — *that* I remember very clearly. Every morning we would begin the rehearsal and he would be directing from his place in the staging; he was playing Lear. In the first scene he would be sitting on the throne, starting to rehearse with us and direct at the same time. Every day, as I recall, it would become, after a certain period, very frustrating for him. He would begin to complain, "Oh, I can't do this. I can't see what you're doing, sitting up here, being in it! Pernell, take the book!" That was Pernell Roberts, who was playing one of Cordelia's suitors. Then Orson would sit against the wall, watch, and direct us from there, while Pernell read the role of Lear.

Epstein told me that Welles "could be rather gruff and teasing and demanding, all at the same time."

AE: This rubbed some of the members of the company the wrong way. There were definitely people who really didn't like him — and there were others who liked this way of working. I belonged to the latter party. I liked the way he worked and I got along with him.

He could be very detailed about what he wanted. As I recall, he had designed the set, but was not able to take program credit for it because he was not a member of the scenic artists union. So the man who painted the scenery was listed as the designer, but I think it really was Orson's design. The set required a very specific and precise staging. There were platforms, and they were irregular and at angles. So the staging had to be very controlled.

I asked Epstein to describe the set in greater detail.

AE: He based his design on the Piranesi prison series. It was painted on black velour so that in the light the velour disappeared and you saw this spectral, Piranesi-looking scene hovering in the air. It did not look like painted curtains, which it really was, but like an architecture suspended in space. It was quite a handsome set.

PPT: This brings us to another point. In an interview I read, you said that you felt Welles did too much in this show: directing, acting, and also designing it.[1]

AE: I think he was really under-rehearsed. I remember that when we got into the theatre, the City Center, he then began to light the show and again was not rehearsing. He was sitting out in the house, with the lighting designer.

He was not familiar enough with the actual space when you were on it. Since a lot of it was in the dark, and the lighting consisted of narrow beams of light that did not illuminate the floor, you had to be familiar with the surface of the stage — and he wasn't.

I think he was not sufficiently rehearsed as Lear. It's a very, very demanding role, and eventually you have to give up any objective view of what's going on around you and become totally subjective and be King Lear and nothing else. He was never able to do that.

Part of the design of the set was a narrow platform — a little bit like a diving board — but angled up toward the audience. I would say it was 18 inches to two feet wide and maybe four or five feet long. The front of it might have been two feet high off of the stage floor. He had staged that scene with the two of us at the front edge of that platform, him standing, facing the audience, me crouching and hugging his ankles.

He would then turn and grab hold of me. I was wearing a one-piece costume — tights over my whole body with just two holes for the hands to come through the sleeves and a hole for my face. So he would grab me by the scruff of my neck and, holding me in front of him, would turn at the front edge of that platform, run down the incline on to the stage, then turn to the right and head off into the wings, which were hidden from the audience by a series of loose-hanging black velour curtains. One of those curtains was draped to hide a steel lighting tower.

At one of the previews, we performed the scene, he said the line, "O Fool, I shall go mad," we turned and ran off. I think I must have weighed about 135 lbs and he weighed about 235 lbs! *[Laughs.]* He had me by the scruff of the neck and my feet were paddling in the air, but not making much contact with the stage floor. We came down this incline, which gave us some extra speed, and with his weight behind me, we were heading into the wings fast — he was running and I was sort of flying in front of him. I could see that we were headed toward the black velour that was hiding the tower — not one of the other loose-hanging ones you could just brush aside. He was holding onto the back of my neck with his right hand, and I could see his left arm coming up in front of me to brush aside the curtain. I knew that that curtain was not going to be brushed aside!

You have to realize that this all took place in just a few seconds. I was squirming to avoid hitting the tower, but there was not much I could do since my feet were barely touching the ground! *[Laughs.]* I had no traction. I just managed to get myself out of the way — because I knew the stage better than he did. I squeezed out of the way at the very last split second and he went full force right into the tower.

I remember that he was wearing a false nose which flew off into the dark, and he came down hard onto the deck with a badly sprained ankle. Since we were practically in the wings, his dresser, who was a very attentive and very nice man who probably had worked as his dresser before, helped him up, and together we got him off stage. His ankle was immediately bound up and he was somehow able to finish that performance.

PPT: I understand that he broke his *other* ankle at another point.

AE: That's right. That was opening night.

Opening night was January 12, 1956. Speaking with Barbara Leaming, Welles commented on his performance that evening. He said, "I think I may have been very bad opening night. I was hurt, but the thing that really *did it to me was the applause when I appeared. It was so enormous and so long and so sustained that it completely disoriented me."[2]*

AE: I was with him a lot, being Lear's Fool. Every time we'd go off stage, his dresser would be there with a tumbler, with a half, or full inch, of vodka. He'd slug it down. I don't really know how intoxicated he might have become, because he could absorb a lot I think, but combined with his lack of security with his lines, that really affected him. I remember that when he enters with Cordelia, carrying her dead body in his arms, Lear cries, "Howl," three or four times.[3] Orson went on with quite a few more howls because I don't think he knew what the next line was! *[Laughter.]* When it finally came to him, the play continued.

At the end of the performance, I don't remember if he had told us that he intended to make a curtain speech or if he just decided at the last minute to do so, but he stepped forward. We were all there on stage with him. He addressed the audience and told them — I don't remember the exact words at all — how happy he was to be back in New York, this was his first stage appearance in New York since he had disbanded the Mercury Theatre and gone to Europe in self-imposed exile, and that he was so grateful for the applause of the audience — that kind of thing.

I don't think that he announced, during that speech, that this was really supposed to be the re-establishment of the Mercury Theatre, but the company knew. This was to be the first production of a series, and the next one was going to be *The Playboy of the Western World.*

Then we turned and began to leave the stage. We were walking off into the left wing. There was a double door, leading from the stage to the corridor where there was a staircase and elevator going up to the dressing rooms. In the doorway was a threshold of about ⅜ of an inch high. We were going through it, he tripped over the threshold, fell down, and broke the other ankle.

The next day, there was no performance. We were all there; the whole company arrived. I don't remember exactly how we were notified, but Orson's other foot was in a cast and he was in a wheelchair. The company was invited to sit in the theater. I don't think an announcement was made to the audience. The curtain went up and Orson wheeled himself out onto the stage and told the audience that this was not going to be a performance of *King Lear*— because he was obviously unable to do it — but that he would entertain them with stories and with magic. If they wanted to, they could stay, or they could leave and get their money back. A lot of people stayed, and the cast all stayed, and he did exactly what he said he was going to do.

I think that we had not had any rehearsal that day. This entertainment I just described to you was on the second night. The next day, we all met and had to restage the whole show with Orson in a wheelchair, which meant eliminating the very platform that caused the first injury! *[Laughs.]* And we had to re-stage the whole thing. At least for the first part of the play, as long as the Fool is there, active (because he sort of disappears during the second half of the play), I was pushing him around in a wheelchair. This version could have been called *The King Who Came to Dinner.*

I do recall that before the accident, he had as part of his costume a pair of gloves. I don't know how I knew this, but I remember that the gloves had cost $150, which in those days was a *lot* of money! But he couldn't wear the gloves any more because he had to be able to maneuver himself in the wheelchair when I was no longer pushing him. So the gloves become a museum article! I don't know what ever happened to them.

PPT: How successful was this restaging? Did it look okay?

AE: Well, how successful can it be? It *worked*—it allowed us to do the show and to continue the run, but I was *in* it. I really don't know what it looked like from the front. I cannot imagine that it was a perfect fulfillment of a production of *King Lear*. During a lot of the pre-accident, non–wheelchair staging, I would be at his feet and hugging his ankles. Now I was consigned to the stage floor, hugging the wheels of the wheelchair! *[Laughter.]* He would play little games, in fact. He would rock the wheelchair back and forth so that it would be pinching me! He was determined to have a bit of fun, to enjoy this.

I do remember him at least once talking to me under his breath during a performance, giving me directions. "Get the lead out, Epstein! Get the lead out." It was a way of telling me to go faster!

The play was not a commercial success. Epstein commented, "I don't think that the City Center did good business, and the whole project of the Mercury Theatre dried up."

May 4, 2005

5

The Fountain of Youth

Dann Cahn

Cahn first worked with Welles on Macbeth. *Some years later, their paths crossed again at Desilu Productions, where Cahn was an editor on the classic television comedy,* I Love Lucy.

Dann Cahn: Orson got a kick out of me. First thing he did when he saw me when we were doing *I Love Lucy*, he said, "Well, Danny, you came a long way in 10 years!" I said, "Yeah, I sure did." I was in my early 30s then. He was magnetic, a great magnetic personality.

Lucy and Desi had known him from their days at RKO in the early '40s where they were all under contract. And, like you know some of your high school friends, they contacted him and that's how he got to do his magic act. Desi suggested that they develop something under Desilu Productions and Desilu would finance it, but the negative belonged to Orson.

The pilot Welles made for Desilu was called The Fountain of Youth.

Peter Prescott Tonguette: You're credited as "Editorial Supervisor" on *The Fountain of Youth*.

DC: I supervised the editing. I was involved with him in a lot of pre-production planning and involved with him in the post-production. I was coordinating music and sound effects and all these crazy stills that we did.

In The Fountain of Youth, *still photographs are inter-cut with actual scenes, to very dynamic effect.*

DC: It opens up with a light turning into the camera. We had all these crazy effects at the time. Orson was very open to ideas and one day in the cutting room I said to him, "You know, you've got all these crazy effects. Wouldn't it be interesting if we just started this thing out with kind of a magic lantern with a still projector flashing right into the camera?" He said, "Yeah, you go and shoot it." I used my hand to turn the projector. I literally was in the insert. When you see the lantern turning to the screen, that's me doing it. I'm in *The Fountain of Youth*!

Orson did a lot of innovative editing that hadn't been done before. He had much of it laid out in his head before we shot the film.

On *The Fountain of Youth*, Orson worked exactly the same as he did 10 years earlier when we did *Macbeth*. On *The Fountain of Youth*, I had lunch with him a couple of times and he was still so full of life and energy of what he was going to do in the future. It's a shame that he always had trouble getting financing. This was partly due to his never seeming to want to finish a project.

PPT: Why wasn't the pilot sold?

DC: Well, there were so many reasons, but the big one was that the networks were afraid that Orson would not be able to deliver a show every week. However, it did win an award.

PPT: The Peabody Award.[1]

DC: The Peabody was a prestigious award, still is. But *The Fountain of Youth* only ran once.

For the second episode, Orson had another short story about a man-eating plant by the same guy. His name was John Collier. If you run the picture, at the very end Orson talks about the forthcoming episode. I asked him about it and he said to me, "I got it all in my head, Danny. I'm going to take that short story and that'll be our second show." But he never did discuss it with me. Well, we never got to make the series. Partly, it was so bizarre, non-commercial in a sense.[2]

Bud Molin, the guy that edited *The Fountain of Youth*, had been my first assistant on *I Love Lucy*. When I became supervising editor, Bud became the editor of the show.

November 15, 2004

Bud Molin

Bud Molin: On *Macbeth*, I was just the apprentice. Danny Cahn was the assistant editor and we were all working, it was at Republic at the time. So actually I was not too involved. I was there kind of helping out.

Mainly, that was just taking care of splicing their film and so forth.

Peter Prescott Tonguette: Did you get to meet Orson?

Bud Molin: Oh, yeah, because it was a very small building. Yes, of course.

PPT: What are your memories of him?

BM: Well, actually, at the time I was young and he was kind of the king of the world. I was in awe of him and very impressed by him.

After apprenticing on Macbeth, *Molin went on to edit* The Fountain of Youth.

BM: When I worked on *Fountain of Youth,* he only had one suggestion for one particular scene, which he wanted cut a certain way. The rest of it, he said, "Do whatever you want."

At the end of the show, I showed him what we had and he said, "Okay, everything's fine, except the stuff I told you how to cut! Now take it apart and do it right!" *[Laughs.]* He was actually very, very easy to work with.

It was just like two friends working together. He was real, real loose, real easy. He was actually kind of fun. And he let everybody do their job. He, of course, had the final say. Like when we did the music, for instance, the music was all written and we were recording and he suddenly changed everything. I said, "Well, it's not the way it's written." He said, "Yeah, I know, but it's better!" *[Laughs.]*

PPT: How long did the editing process take on *The Fountain of Youth*?

BM: Oh, God, I don't really remember. It must have been, oh, maybe a month.

Having viewed The Fountain of Youth *numerous times, it always appeared to me that the editing was very pre-planned. But Molin remembered otherwise.*

BM: No, actually, it was not. It was like, "Hey, let's try this! That looks pretty good, let's keep it."

You start out by viewing the dailies, which was kind of fun. Because it was Orson Welles, we were very much in awe of him. He would come in and he'd sit down and then we'd say to the projectionist, "Okay, roll it." And he turned around and said, "You know, the only time of my life that I regret wasting is waiting for the film to start." So from that day on, the minute the door opened, we'd say, "Okay, roll it!" And we'd let him fumble his way through the theatre! *[Laughs.]*

PPT: After you viewed the dailies, what would happen next?

BM: He'd go back to the stage doing what he's doing and I'd go back and cut.

PT: So you were editing as the shooting was going on?

BM: Oh yeah, always, always.

I don't recall that we dropped anything at all. Because, if you remember, everything was pretty tight and pretty concise. It was just fast bits of information, so, no, there wasn't any particular scene that was thrown out.

He found one thing after we were almost finished dubbing. One thing, he said, "Oh, no, I don't like that." And I said, "Well, let me change it." He said, "No. It took me all this time to find it, so nobody else will ever see it."

In addition to writing, directing, designing, and hosting the show, Welles also was credited as music arranger.

BM: Some of it was existing stuff, like, as I recall, the old song, "Get Out and Get Under," and all that. But a lot of it was done, written and then when they were recording it, he would change tempo. Like, for instance, we had a thing with a xylophone. And he suddenly would stop and he'd say to the player, "What happens if you turn the sticks around and hit the keys with just the sticks, rather than the hammer?" He said, "I don't know." They tried that, he liked it better, so he kept it. *[Laughs.]*

PT: Did you know Welles after hours?
BM: No, it was strictly at work and that was it.

PT: But it sounds like you got along.
BM: Oh, beautifully, yes.

He would do things like he would arrive at the studio in a cab and would pull up to the front of the editing room, get out of the cab, and say, "Somebody pay him. I don't have any money," and he'd walk away! *[Laughs.]*

Molin speculated as to the reasons why the pilot wasn't sold.

BM: I think it was because Orson was expensive. And I think everybody was afraid. Because he would change things and it would cost them more than they could make out of it. As a matter of fact, I was working with a director once who knew him and Orson called this director and said, "You know, I want you to work on a project." And the guy said, "With the two of us, one would direct, one would act, and we'd be broke in a week!"

It was just a really fun project to work on and to work with a guy that you really enjoyed.

November 18, 2004

6

The Trial and
Chimes at Midnight

Frederick Muller

Muller edited Welles's adaptation of Franz Kafka's The Trial *(1962) as well as* Chimes at Midnight.

Frederick Muller: I was a film editor. I started in the editing room on films like *Ben Hur* [1959] and *The Nun's Story* [1959]. Then I went to live in New York and I became a film editor there. And then I came back to Rome and I edited for Marco Ferreri and people like that.

Out of the blue, in the '60s, I received a call from Orson Welles's associate producer, a Sicilian prince called Allesandro Tasca, whom I met when I just started. He was the production manager of a TV series called *Captain Gallant of the Foreign Legion*. He asked me if I wanted to go and edit for Orson Welles on *The Trial*. I said, "Yes, of course."

Peter Prescott Tonguette: I noticed that you are co-credited on *The Trial* with another editor, Yvonne Martin.

FM: That is the French version only. You see that in the books. The project was a French national production, if you like, and he needed French people. So, no, I was the only actual editor. If you look in the American version, you'll see that my name is the only one.

PPT: What was your first meeting like? Did he interview you?

FM: No! *[Laughs.]* The thing was this: Orson Welles had a terrible habit of calling the film editor never at the beginning of the production, but always toward the end. In the case of *The Trial*, he had shot 90 percent of the movie when he called me. So he was working in what is today the Musée d'Orsay. At that time, it was the Gare d'Orsay, the railway station. Attached to the railway station, which doesn't exist anymore, was a very important hotel called the Hotel d'Orsay where he was staying and where I was sent.

So I arrived in Paris and I went and asked where Orson Welles was. I was given a ticket by the Italian co-producer, whose name escapes me, and I went. I had no idea what to expect. I really did not know anything. So I went into the hotel, checked in, and it was indicated that he was in the railway station master's office! The railway station by then was half-dilapidated anyway. It was built by Eiffel as a railway station for official visits by dignitaries. So I went there and there was this room which was blacked out because Orson always worked with Italian flat-bed Moviolas. There were two Moviolas and behind one was Orson looking at some material. There were also a couple of assistants in there. And masses of films everywhere, masses of films. There were burlap sacks full of film thrown in there. It's true! *[Laughs.]* So I went in there and he looked at me and said, "Who are you?" I said, "Well, I'm the editor." And he threw me out! "The editor? Get out of here! I don't want to talk to any editor! Get out of here!" So he just threw me out. I paled and walked out. As I was walking in the station hallway towards the hotel entrance, he came out and he called me. He said, "What do you mean, the editor? Film editor?" I said, "Yes." "Oh, you're the cutter!" I said, "Yes." "Oh, I'm sorry, I thought you were the editor of some newspaper or something." So that's how I started with him.

So then we went in. He had two Italian assistants working with him. He said, "Now we need to start cutting the movie." I said, "Well, I need to see some material. I have no idea ..." He said, "Yeah, yeah, you sit down and look at the material." And he walked away and said, "I'll be back in two days." I looked at the material and, of course, he had chopped the material up. Out of every take, he had taken the bits that he didn't like. Normally, as you know, those bits are saved as trims. But he had them all thrown away in the garbage. So I said to the two boys, "You threw everything away?" They said, "Yes, he told us to." I said, "But have you ever worked in films before?" They said, "No." I don't know where he picked them up! To this day I have no idea. *[Laughs.]* Nice boys, because we then worked together and I taught them the business.

So when he came back and we started working, I said, "This isn't going to match. Nothing is going to match here. You threw away a very important part of the takes. We need to re-print everything." So we re-printed everything and we started from scratch, professionally, properly, numbering the film, doing the things seriously. Now Orson always gave the impression that he cut the films, that he knew how to cut the films. He had no idea how to cut a film. He had an idea of what he wanted, like any director. But he had no idea how to actually make a cut work.

Indeed, Muller said that Welles was not always even present during the editing—contrary to what he sometimes asserted in interviews.[1]

FM: In that film, which was the first film we worked on together, after about three weeks, we got into a terrible fight. I actually sent him to hell and walked away. I left the movie. But then he called me in the evening and we discussed it. He said, "You're the only man that knows how to talk to me." I said, "Well, what do you mean?" He said, "Well, nobody tells me to fuck off." I said, "Well, you probably scare people, but you don't treat people the way you treat them." I mean, we used to work 14 hours a day. I said, "You've got to be reasonable. If I tell you something doesn't work, it doesn't work. There's no point in insisting. We'll try if you like, but don't insist it should stay this way if it doesn't work."

So it was sort of stormy initially. After that, we got along just fine. We really got along like a house on fire, as they say today. We did the sound effects together. It was really good.

The challenge of editing any of Orson Welles's films, I suppose, was that he did not like script girls and he did not like the clapper boards. So one had to search and find and create source materials. Normally, you go by numbers and you find a take or something. But in this case, you couldn't. So the challenge was to try to find the pieces and put it together.

But, you know, with Orson you always revisited the reels. Always. He was never happy. As far as he was concerned, the film was never finished — any film of his. The producers had to finally take it away from him, otherwise they would miss their delivery dates and miss the film. He would work on it to exhaustion. Orson had this capacity. When he was tired, he used to go take a very hot bath for twenty minutes and then he could work another five or six hours. Regardless of whether the other people around him could!

PPT: You mentioned earlier that you had 14 hour days ...

FM: Yeah, but actually *Chimes at Midnight* was worse. But, yes, it was 14 hours a day and it was cold and there was no heating in this room because it was a dilapidated railway station. And so in the end, when winter came, we had to work with overcoats, hats, scarves, and gloves! Finally, I said, "Orson, we've got to move to a studio! This is ridiculous. We can't work this way." The whole thing was because he was staying at the hotel nearby. He didn't want to ride to work. Orson was very special. Wonderful man, but very ego-centric.

He shot massive amounts of film. Massive. And that's why — he didn't have the editing in his head. Otherwise, he would not have filmed so much. He filmed every possible angle and every possible shape or whatever, so he had every possible permutation.

PPT: What kind of equipment did you edit on?

FM: They were Italian flatbed Moviolas, which were very good at the time. They had a big screen. And you could sit two people and work and discuss and try again. They were okay.

PPT: Was a lot of the dialogue re-recorded?

FM: All of it. Another quirk of Orson Welles was that he did not want blimped cameras. He wanted light cameras because he used to set the camera himself. And he used to pick up the camera by himself and find the set up. Then the cameraman would do his work. But that meant that the camera had to be light. He did not use a viewfinder, he just used the camera itself. And so you had this terrible motor noise behind all the dialogue. The films were post-synched 100 percent, which was a massive job afterwards to synch it up. And sometimes it was so noisy that Orson himself did not know what he was saying. It's true!

Once we finished editing — well, you never finish editing with him, but suppose you finish editing — we went to do the music. I remember going with him. He made an arrangement with the producer to have an orchestra and he recorded the "Adagio" by Albinoni. And then we went to a sound studio, and he and I started playing backwards and forwards and double-speed and half-speed and created what he called concrete music. I learned a lot then. In fact, the music of that entire film is a single recording of the Alibinoni "Adagio" and then the rest was all created by us — well, by him — in the sound studio, recording it in different shapes and forms.

Do you have the film present in your mind? Remember she has a wooden leg? When they cross the big field towards some buildings and you hear kkkkk-boom, kkkkk-boom — her leg moving — well that noise was me with a washing board! You know the old time wooden washing boards? I'd take a metal thing and go cccccllllllkkk and Orson would go clink with something else. That's, you know, fantastic. One used to do these kinds of things with him which were unusual and very innovative at the time. Nobody else would ever have done anything like that. I have to say that I learned an awful lot.

You know, he never had a script for the films I worked with him on.

PPT: Really?

FM: In the two films I did with him, no, there was no script. There were notes.

In *Chimes at Midnight*, he was already halfway through the shooting when he called me. I was in Africa. I just finished a movie and I flew directly from there to Madrid. There were the usual big hugs and all that sort of thing. Then I said, "Well, I'm going back to the hotel." He said, "No, you're sleeping here, in the cutting room." I said, "No, no, no." He said, "But I have a bed for you here. I made a room for you." I said, "Thank you very much, but I'm going to the hotel! And, by the way, give me a script." He said, "Of course, I'll give it to you tomorrow morning." And the next morning he gave me the complete works of William Shakespeare. He said, "Read *The Merry Wives of Windsor, Henry IV*, and *Henry V* and *Richard III.*" And that was the script.

Muller also worked on Don Quixote *around this time. As Muller put it to me, "I think every editor in the world worked on it!"*

FM: I cut two reels of that movie.

PPT: Do you remember what scenes you worked on?

FM: Don Quixote's interview on television, Don Quixote coming to town and attacking the cars, Don Quixote in a bullfight. Things that were not really Cervantes, and then a couple of Cervantes things. But some other people worked on the same scenes, I'm sure. He shot a bit here and a bit there. He had a close-up or a medium shot of Don Quixote in Spain and the reverse of Sancho Panza, who was played by Akim Tamiroff, was in Mexico. He did that, actually, because he produced it with his own money. So every time he had some money, he would call the actors back and shoot something. But, of course, the problem is that it took, I don't know, twenty years, ten, fifteen years. The girl he tells the story to was, I think, twelve and by the end of her shoot she was over twenty-two.

If anybody ever gets the movie together, that would probably be his biggest masterpiece. It is a most fantastic movie. But, unfortunately, nobody will ever get it together because the negative is lost, some is in Rome, some is in Spain, some was in Mexico. You know, laboratories don't keep the negatives too long. After a number of years, they throw it away.

Several years, Muller edited Chimes at Midnight.

FM: He called me up and I arrived in freezing Madrid from Africa. There he was, a little more organized this time. He lived in one apartment and rented an apartment in a building right across the way and set it up as a cutting room. He had his usual two Italian flatbeds, which he owned, and he was still with his Italian wife at the time. He had two Spanish girl assistant editors. He was doing a bit of the same thing which was running the dailies, and he would mark with a white pencil the bits that he didn't like. The girls would cut them out, but fortunately these girls were professional and didn't throw anything away.

However there was a major problem. They did keep the material, but there were no slates and there were no numbers. It was very difficult to find the bit you were looking for among the thousands of feet of material. He had shot at the time something like 300,000 feet of film, an enormous amount of film. He had not edited anything. He was just "cleaning"—he called it "cleaning"—the bits that he didn't like. By then we had become friends and he respected me. A couple of days later when he gave me the complete works of William Shakespeare and I re-read the plays, I said, "Orson, I think we have a major problem here." He had stopped shooting but he had not completed filming. He needed to film another thirty percent of the movie. For example, the big battle sequence was not filmed and the renunciation was not filmed — several sequences were not completed. I said, "We have a major problem." He said, "What is it?" I said, "You are doing your usual thing. You cut up the stuff, the girls have kept it, but there is no reference, there are no numbers, there's nothing. So I need to speak with the producer"— who was a man named Emiliano Piedra, nice man, but losing his hair with Orson (that's what you did with Orson, you lost your hair)—"and we have to reprint everything, we have to number everything, we have to sync it up, and then we have to create source material." Like: "Hotspur duel" or "Tavern 1," "Tavern 2," "Tavern 3," "Renunciation." "I have to go through it with the plays and put it together, because otherwise we'll never cut this movie." He always did this kind of thing, but on *Chimes at Midnight* he did it in particular. He started a sequence, got bored, and then started another sequence in another location. And then three weeks later, he would go back, shoot a little more, and complete it or maybe not complete it. So the material was all over the place. He never completed a sequence and a set at once. Never. You would have to go back all the time. No continuity and no clapper boards.

So I ended up having to reprint everything, I had to hire a sound editor, I had a cutting room with eight people, which I never had before in my life. At the time, there were no numbering machines available in Madrid, so it was all numbered by hand on a synchronizer. I had a night shift! *[Laughs.]* And then I created the sources, looking take by take, with the assistants, I put shelves all over the apartment (in the corridor, in the rooms, everywhere) and we named each sequence in the film. I would find a piece and say, "Put it in that source." I had said to Orson, "Go away and don't show up for two months." And he did. He went away and didn't show up for two months. I went back to the source material and put it in some continuity order. When he came back, we sat down, I said, "Orson, this time we're going to cut professionally. We're not just going to take the piece that you don't like and throw them away. You're going to tell me the pieces you do like and I'll cut the scenes. Then we'll look at the scenes, we'll correct it, we'll re-cut it, we'll re-form, we'll do whatever we like. But we'll do it professionally, the way it should be done."

And that's the way we did it. Then he understood that it was also much easier for him. We'd look at the entire source material of a sequence and he said, "Here, let's use the long shot and then let's go in to that close shot." So he would go away, I would cut the sequence, he would come back, and we would discuss it and I would put black film in the missing pieces. Now if you look at that film very carefully, you will see fairly often in the various sequences that the swords are sometimes on the left and sometimes on the right. I had to flip over the film, because when he shot it he had no continuity and mixed up the entrance and the exit. Instead of entering screen left, they entered screen right. So I had to flip it over to have them enter from screen left to have it make any sense, but of course the swords were reversed. Nobody ever noticed this. Thank God for that! But if you look at it carefully, you'll find that that's actually the truth.

And after the battle when he's against the big barrel and drinking and telling of his victory, he shot half one day and half two months later. And he had to shoot in reverse because he had all the entrances wrong. So actually what happened was that *Chimes at Midnight* was more complicated than *The Trial*. It took longer to edit, but it was easier to edit because I was organized from the beginning, as it were.

Nevertheless, I fainted once because we were overtired! We used to start working at 7 in the morning, go to lunch between 3 and 4, go back to work until at 9 at night and dine in Madrid at 10:30 or 11. You only slept five, six hours a night. After a while I fainted one day and had to take a couple of weeks off.

But he was never happy with *Chimes at Midnight*. He did not want to relinquish the movie. We then went to Paris to dub the movie and do all the sound work. And then of course the film was too long and we had to re-do it. They finally took it away from him and delivered it because otherwise he would still be working on it if he was alive. He was never happy.

Every scene in that movie has been worked on over and over for a long time and then months later worked on again. For the battle sequence, filmed in a park in Madrid, he filmed a massive amount of material. Orson and I saw the dailies and then discussed the chronology and the impact he wanted to obtain from the sequence. I said, "Orson, I cannot sit down and cut this sequence with you. This is very complicated. Go away, go to see your bullfights in Seville, if you like, and I'll call you when I'm ready." I sat down and it took me about a month to cut it. He never touched that sequence again. Some pieces are only two feet long. He said, "Oh my God, this is wonderful. Leave it alone, leave it alone." We only worked a little bit on the Hotspur/Hal duel, just a little.

PPT: So when Welles came back and saw it, he was very happy with it?

FM: Oh, he was very happy with it.

He really loved the project. He really loved playing Falstaff. He enjoyed it immensely. And, you know, he got all these great actors together. He really nurtured the actors all the time. He was very good with the actors.

He was Falstaff. I used to go to lunch almost every day to his house. We were always about five or six people — actors, some friends of his, or whatever. In the summer, it was in the terrace in the open air. I'll give you an example: there were two big plates of big shrimps. One for himself and one for everybody else. He was Falstaff. He was eating like crazy. He was drinking and eating. He was Falstaff, without a doubt.

Orson had one aspect to him which is not really the greatest. As I said to you before, he was a very self-centered man and he always wanted you to believe that he did everything—that he raised the money, that he did the film, that he did the costumes, that he did the music, like nobody else was worth two cents. But that's not the case. Orson needed professional people around him. In the case of *Chimes at Midnight*, he did have a producer. He bankrupted the producer, but he did have a producer who borrowed the money from the bank. Yes, it was difficult times for the production because Piedra kept running out of money and Orson wanted to do more and more. Piedra didn't know how to stop him.

Another quirk of Orson's was that on *Chimes at Midnight*, he used to make himself up every morning. I used to go up to his house. He had a little makeup room. You know, Orson always used false noses. So he was painting the veins on his nose. He made himself up very painstakingly. Every morning we discussed what he was going to shoot and remind him that he had to do this or that otherwise it wouldn't match. It became a habit that every day I was up there and discussed this and that with him and then he went off to shoot. And often, he would call me to the set to help him out because it got to be too much. And he was drinking an awful lot. But it was wonderful.

> *I mentioned to Muller my favorite scene in the film: the coronation of Prince Hal, during which he rejects Falstaff and says, "I know thee not, old man." It is hard to disagree with what Richard Marienstras said of the scene when he interviewed Welles in 1974: "[it] is one of the most moving scenes you have ever filmed."*[2]

FM: Ah, when he cries. Outside the church, when he comes out and he has to cry, we filmed that in Avila. He couldn't cry, so he drank a whole bottle of vodka at once. That made him cry! True!

But it was wonderful because he wanted it to be so realistic and the only way he could do it was that. I think it was admirable what he did. His passion for his work and his passion for what he was doing was beyond belief. The man was a genius. He really was.

PPT: You mentioned earlier that Welles would go off to see bullfights. I understand that that was a passion of his.

FM: Yes. He taught me about it. He asked me if I had been to bullfights. I said, "Yes, but I don't really understand it." So he said, "Come with me," and we went off! And he took me to the house of [Antonio] Ordonez, who was a very famous bullfighter and a very good friend of his. They took me to a bullfight, right in front, and explained everything to me. I learned to love them and went to the bullfights very often.

After Chimes at Midnight, *Welles asked Muller to work on the television special he was directing for CBS.*

FM: I didn't complete it. He filmed it in London and he was editing it in Rome. I had just come back from South America. By then, I was out of editing, I was doing production. But he called me and asked me if I would go and help him. I said, "Yes." We went to a small studio in Rome. It was a series of sketches that he did for a CBS special. It was a bit of *The Merchant of Venice*, a bit of an English club sketch, a bit of an English stately home sketch. And he played every role — man, woman, whatever.

For *The Merchant of Venice*, we took the regatta in daytime, turned it into night and put fireworks on it. And that was in color. So it was stock footage of the regatta, shot in bright sunlight, turned it into night and then put fireworks on it. It was a nightmare at the laboratory. That idea of his was fantastic.

What happened with that was Orson was already with Oja [Kodar] and you could see that the man was not completely settled. Let's put it this way: you could feel that he was unsettled.

Peter Bogdanovich described Oja Kodar aptly as Welles's "companion, confidante, cohort in conspiracy, closest accomplice, muse."[3]

FM: So we worked on this special for about two and a half months. He had gone back to shoot something and then he came back and we were still editing. It was almost finished — the bit that I was involved with — and then one morning I go to work and he wasn't there and all the material was gone. In the middle of the night, he had picked up the material and vanished. To this day, I don't know where he went. He never wrote. He then ended up in America and, as you know, he didn't end up very well, sadly.

My life with Orson Welles was full of interest and full of experience and full of excitement. I enjoyed it. Although I say that in retrospect. When I was working with him, there were moments when I would want to kill the man.

Nevertheless, Muller does have fond memories of Welles during off-hours.

FM: Some lunches! *[Laughs.]* He loved eating and drinking. Sometimes these things went on for hours upon hours on the weekend. I think that the memorable things with him were on the social aspect. Sometimes we had lunch with the actors or with a musician. And the entire conversation that happened was exhilarating. Those were very, very exciting things to watch. On *The Trial*, sometimes Jeanne Moreau came over and then we all spent a lot of time together having a good time.

On the work side, I can't say it was a good time — except when we were doing the dub. That was very challenging and very interesting. And I used to get into long discussions with him. But, you know, the thing with Orson is that most people were afraid of him. And he made a point of sort of being this character that people would be afraid of. The actors were not, and I was not, but most people were. And I asked him one day, "Why do you do this?" He said, "Well, I grew up in very unhappy family circumstances and this is my defense. I want people to be scared of me." I said, "But you're not a nasty man, so why do you want to give the impression that you're nasty?" He said, "It's my defense." And he wouldn't talk about it.

He always said he grew up unhappily, thrown around between aunts and uncles. So he built this sort of protective mechanism, I don't know.

Filmmaking was his life. He had no other interests. Yes, he did—for art or for this or that—but he was not the man who would often be going to concerts or art galleries. He was aware of everything. He read an awful lot. But filmmaking was his passion. He lived for it. And he couldn't care less about the money. He wanted the money, but he couldn't care less about the money. When he was doing something and he needed some money, he used to go and do a commercial. He'd make a pile of money doing a commercial. For example, we were doing *Chimes at Midnight* and at one point he said, "I'll be away for two or three weeks." I said, "Where are you going?" He said, "I'm going to play a role in *Is Paris Burning?* [1966]" Remember he played the Consul. And off he went and he made a pile of money there. But he used to spend a lot. He had no concept of money at all. But his passion for filmmaking overrode the need for money. So he was perennially bankrupt, really.

He did not want to relent his movies. I remember on *The Trial*, old man Salkind, who was the producer, organized a premiere in the Champs Élysées. Orson said he was going and he said to the press he was going. That evening he called me and said, "Meet me at the Gare du Sud." And I went to meet him there and said, "But we're going to the premiere!" He said, "No, no. You're going to the premiere. I'm going to Rome. I'll take the train overnight." *[Laughs.]* I said, "What do you mean?" He said, "You're going to the premiere and you're going to apologize, after the movie, that I had to go to Rome." And, you know, the reason was that he was scared of the people's reaction. That's why he did not want to release his films. He was scared of the reaction. It's not that he was not satisfied with his work. I think he thought that he could always make it better.

Actually, I had a terrible argument with him one day. It was on *Chimes at Midnight*. He made me cut and cut and cut and cut the sequence when they arrived at Hotspur's castle with the trumpets up on the towers. It's cut and cut and cut and cut. I said, "Orson, stop. This is ridiculous. The scene is so fast that the public will not even know that it happened." That was his problem. Because he knew what was happening, he got bored. And he didn't allow for an audience who saw it for the first and only time to absorb what was happening before going into the next scene. He was on the next step before the first step was completed. I think that that is one of the reasons why his movies were not successful, commercially speaking. The public could not catch up with the story. He was too fast. And it is too fast. That was one of his downsides, I think. He was scared of the public. He never went to the premiere. He actually told me that one day, that once his movie was dubbed and printed, and he saw the answer print, that he would never look at the movie again ever in his life.

He had a lot of insecurities. For as big and as deep voice and an ogre as he was, he was full of insecurities. In that aspect, it's sad. He was a successful man, but he didn't do himself any good. The other thing that he did not have, he had no respect for the producers. He had no respect for the people who trusted him and put up the money. People did not trust him anymore.

Just the cost of the editing for *Chimes at Midnight* and for *The Trial* must have been enormous. I remember a couple of times when the Salkinds had no money to pay us. They eventually paid us, but they did run out of it from time to time. That's where Orson failed a lot, in his respect for the people who trusted him.

PPT: What would you say is the greatest lesson you learned from him?

FM: Actually, not to repeat his mistakes. It's very difficult, there are many lessons that I learned from him. Some are good, some not so good! *[Laughs.]* The creative aspect of filmmaking and film editing that I learned from him is that really a lot of it is impulse of what you're doing at that minute, rather than just a scripted word. But also the fact of not spending so much time on a project. You know, there are so many lessons I learned that I don't think there is one in particular. And it's so long ago.

May 20, 2004

Keith Baxter

Baxter played the role of Prince Hal in Welles's 1960 theatrical production of Chimes at Midnight *and then five years later in the film version.*

Keith Baxter: He was auditioning for a company that planned to take *Chimes at Midnight,* his version of the *Henry IV*s, and *Twelfth Night,* in which he would play Malvolio — to take a pair of plays, opening with *Chimes at Midnight* in Belfast, rehearsing *Twelfth Night* in Dublin and then doing it in Dublin for a long tour which was going to include Athens and Cairo and Paris and goodness knows where. That, of course, never took place, nor indeed did the production of *Twelfth Night.* But the brief that I was given through my agent was that Orson Welles was holding auditions and they were open auditions.

So I had no idea what I was auditioning for. Just the company. And when I got to the New Theatre — which is now called the Albery Theatre — there was a long line of young men — well, men of all ages — and the previous day he'd seen girls. And I hadn't prepared to do Shakespeare. I prepared a piece from a play by Welsh playwright Emlyn Williams. The play was called *The Wind of Heaven,* and I prepared a speech from that and I waited in the wings. Auditions were running late and that was partly due to Welles's good manners. Because afterwards there was a letter in *The Stage* — which is the newspaper of the profession — from somebody simply saying, "Last week I auditioned for Mr. Orson Welles and I would just like to say that, although I didn't get the part, that I've never been handled with more courtesy and politeness at an audition." And that was true. I mean, he had this reputation for this ungovernable temper and whatever. But he also had extraordinary politeness.

Anyway, auditions were running late and I went on quite late. In front of me, actors were doing a lot of *Hamlet* and so on. I went on and Orson Welles — who was then still a huge film star — came down. He was in the auditorium and I was on the stage. And he came down. The stage manager said, "Mr. Keith Baxter." And he said, "Mr. Baxter, my name is Orson Welles. What are you going to do?" And I said, "I'm going to do a piece by Emlyn Williams, *The Wind of Heaven."* I think he rather cheered up at that because I think he'd had an awful lot of *Hamlets* and *Henry Vs.* Anyway, he went back and I auditioned. I did my speech, which was quite long, and he came down and said, "It's been a great honor to listen to you. Will you play Prince Hal?" I had been hoping for a spear-carrier! I thought I could probably get that; possibly the part of Poins. But I had no idea that that's what he was going to do. He asked if I would come back the following week and read him a bit of the renunciation speech — "I know thee not, old man."

I went outside and then I thought, "Oh well, he's asked lots of other people back to audition." I didn't hear for two weeks because he'd gone to Paris to finish cutting *The Trial,* I think. And so I didn't hear anything and so I thought that the whole thing — that I'd sort of dreamed it and it was the sort of thing that you'd hear about Orson Welles. Quite by accident, at the same time — I'd been rather out of work, I'd been very out of work — and quite by accident, at exactly the same time Orson was away, I was offered the part of King Henry V at the Mermaid Theatre. *[Laughs.]* In modern dress, but it was just such a weird coincidence. And I went to a restaurant in Lester Square — Lyon's Corner House — and the actress Joan Plowright was there and Kenneth Williams, too. They'd both worked with Orson in *Moby Dick* in London. They said, "Oh, what are you doing, Keith?" I said, "Well, I've been offered this part of Henry V at the Mermaid and possibly Prince Hal with Orson." And they cried with laughter at all the stories about money running out and all of that. And then Joan Plowright said, "Oh, but you must go with Orson."

Then Welles suddenly turned up and I did go back. And he stopped me halfway through and said, "I don't know why I'm wasting this time. Will you do it?" So that's how I got the part.

The play didn't work in Belfast and it didn't work in Dublin. On my way back, we spent my last day in Dublin with his wife, Paola [Mori], and his daughter, Beatrice. Beatrice is, of course, still alive and living in Las Vegas. Bebe was a little girl then. And we spent our last day, before getting on the ferry, having lunch with Geraldine Fitzgerald and her son, Michael Lindsay-Hogg, and family. It was a very nice day and I was rather depressed. The play was coming to an end and we weren't going to Paris, we weren't going to Cairo, we weren't coming to London. And on top of that, as we got on board the ship, Orson had a row — a meaningless row — with somebody. He went to his cabin and I went on the deck. And I thought, "Oh well, I haven't even said good-bye to him and I'm going back to London and will be out of work." And suddenly there was Welles standing beside me. I could smell the cigar. As we were pulling out of the Dublin port, he said, "When they announced the nominations for the Academy Awards in Los Angeles the year that *Kane* was up, every nomination that *Kane* was in was booed." And I said, stupidly, that I didn't know anything about that. He said, "Listen, you mustn't be disheartened about tonight. It was just a blueprint for the movie. One day we'll make the movie and I'll never make it without you."

That was 1960. And then an awful lot of things happened. As a result of doing that play and playing Prince Hal, a lot of doors opened for me and I was never in any doubt that the name on the handle of the door was Orson Welles. I came to America to play the king in *The Man for All Seasons* on Broadway. And that year [1962], Brenda Vaccaro and Robert Redford and myself, we all won the Theatre World Award as Most Promising Newcomers to Broadway. Then I went back to London and starred in E.M. Forster's *Where Angels Fear to Tread*. It was the first time my name went up in lights on a theatre marquee.

Baxter told me that, in October 1964, at Welles's invitation, he went to work on the film version of Chimes.

Peter Prescott Tonguette: So you were in touch with Welles in the early '60s?

KB: Oh yes, all the time. I was flown over to Rome in 1963. I mean, he was very much responsible for my career taking off, so you always feel a great deal of personal interest, obviously. It's like a school teacher. Like if you have a child who suddenly starts winning awards. So I always heard from him — a telegram, or his wife would send a chatty letter when I was on Broadway.

And when I did the Forster play in London, he and his wife came over from Rome to see it.

PPT: You mentioned that Welles said to you that he was going to go ahead and make *Chimes* on a small budget. Did he originally conceive of the film having a bigger budget?

KB: No, not at all. In fact, the only way he got the money was by persuading the young producer, Emiliano Piedra, who was really a wonderful man of Spanish cinema (and young — I guess he was about my age), and his partner, who was much less interested in film. And Orson was always looking for producers. Of course, Hollywood wouldn't touch him and he wasn't allowed to go back to Hollywood because of the IRS. And he persuaded these Spaniards — in particular Emiliano Piedra — that he would do *Treasure Island* — in color — if they would allow him to shoot at the same time the film of Shakespeare's histories, *Chimes at Midnight.* (They wanted him to play Long John Silver in *Treasure Island.*) And they agreed. The idea that he sold them — and maybe he believed in it himself — was that when they were shooting in the Admiral Benbow Inn, for example, two days would be given up to *Treasure Island* and five days of the week it would be the Boar's Head Tavern.

Anyway, they bought it. When I flew to Madrid for the costumes for *Chimes at Midnight* ... because Sir John Gielgud [who plays Henry IV in *Chimes*] never, never knew that he was also contracted to play Squire Trelawney [in *Treasure Island*]! And I was going to play Dr. Livesey! *[Laughs.]* I don't think that John had ever been told that. Because I think that in his heart of hearts Orson knew that he would never get to it. In any case, John was only able to be with us for three weeks because he was going to do [an] Edward Albee play on Broadway, *Tiny Alice.* So whether he was shooting *Treasure Island* or *Chimes at Midnight,* the producers knew they only had him for three weeks. But the producers were told that he'd been hired also to play Squire Trelawney and I'd been hired to play Dr. Livesey and so on.

And the first day's shooting, when I went to Madrid and got my costumes, I drove with Orson all across Spain to Alicante. That was where the good ship Hispaniola was tied up. It was the same ship that had been used in the film of *Billy Budd.* And they were going to shoot a couple of scenes of Israel Hands — the villain in the film, who was also going to be playing Poins — getting onto the ship. I stood behind the camera and the assistant director set up a shot and the producers were there with wine glasses and champagne. And Orson said, "Acción!" And everybody applauded. And they said, "We've shot the first shot of the film!" Then Orson's secretary, Mrs. Rogers, and I were driven by Orson up to a little place called Calpe to wait for the *Hispaniola* to do two days at sea! *[Laughs.]* And that's when Orson said to me, talking about *Chimes*, "I want to make a film that will call down the corridors of time." That's what he wanted to do.

It was then brought out that they could never afford to make two films in color. And Orson was thrilled.

He believed that film robs an actor of 20 percent of his performance. This was Orson's theory. And the film was to be about performance. He said he was going to use more close-ups than he would normally use in a film, although I don't know if that's true necessarily. But there are a lot of close-ups in *Chimes*, of course. And he always liked working in black-and-white. And it was designed in black-and-white, because the film really is designed by him.

PPT: Since much of the cast of *Chimes* had not been in the stage version, how extensively did you rehearse for the film?

KB: Not at all. He knew that he didn't have to rehearse Sir John. He knew he didn't have to rehearse Margaret Rutherford. I mean, they rehearsed for the camera, of course, but there wasn't time. We all arrived in Madrid and when somebody was there, we shot on them. When Jeanne Moreau came for a week, we shot Jeanne Moreau's scenes.

On *Chimes*, there was no studio. There was no place to do rehearsals. People arrived and learned their lines and I suppose rehearsed a scene of ten minutes or so ... I mean, Orson didn't rush at all. So, yes, of course we rehearsed in that sense. I mean, we were shooting all over the place entirely out of sequence. You had to be on your toes. I actually play — or appear in the film — about ten times. Whenever you don't see Walter Chiari's face as Justice Silence, it's me in his robe. In the battle scene, it was hard to translate through the Spanish first assistant to the actors — who, of course, spoke entirely Spanish — what they wanted to do. They would just say, "Follow El Principe." I was known as the Prince, "El Principe," by all the actors. Orson would say, "Could you walk across there and then start to run?" And I'd do it and they'd follow me.

But nobody felt that that was odd, you see. Filmmaking now is very serious with the amount of grosses ... it's only about grosses and ratings. Otherwise there wouldn't be a magazine like *Variety*. And the films are about the revenue that they can return for an investment. But at heart that's not why anybody goes into the theatre. No actor goes into the world wanting to be Tom Cruise. It's fantastic if he becomes Tom Cruise. But even Tom Cruise must have started once with the sheer pleasure of acting. And most directors do. So when one was working with Orson, one automatically put oneself into his hands because you knew what he was going to do would be at least controversial, possibly remarkable, and possibly legendary.

But meanwhile you were going to have a good time. I don't mean fun, but a good time. I remember when we were filming a scene outdoors and old Margaret Rutherford — who was a very fey, genuinely fey woman and not like Sir John or Jeanne Moreau, who would be horsing around and telling stories — and it was a terribly cold day. And she was sitting under a hawthorne hedge and Orson said, "Look at Margaret — go and get her some coffee and ask if she'd like some brandy in it." And so I took the coffee and the brandy across to Margaret, who was sheltering, and it was an incredibly cold day in Madrid. Early December, I think. And I said, "Would you like some coffee?" She said, "Yes, I would." "Would you like some brandy?" "Yes, I would." And I said, "Are you feeling cold?" She said, "Oh, no, no, no." And she pointed at Orson and said, "Working with him is like walking where there's only sunshine."

Afterwards, I was asked what it was like to be directed by him. I can't remember a single piece of direction that he gave me in terms of changing a performance. Or anybody. I mean, the great soliloquy of Gielgud's about "uneasy lies the head that wears the crown" ... we had Gielgud for a very short time and the locations were extraordinary. That ruined cathedral in Andora — it was so cold there that the breath was coming out of us. That's when Orson said, "You can see why Prince Hal couldn't wait to get down to the warm tavern." *[Laughs.]* Because it was bitterly, bitterly cold. We all had hot water bottles. We all huddled around heaters. Orson had a wind-up gramophone playing old tunes to cheer us up. And then when Sir John was doing "uneasy lies the head that wears the crown," Orson lit it, of course — with his lighting man — because his lighting was wonderful in the film. The use of incense to get those rays of light. I can't go into a Catholic church without thinking of *Chimes at Midnight* now.

When he had lit the "uneasy lies the head that wears the crown" soliloquy — which is one take — he just showed John, he said, "Look, come and stand here and if you look through there there's light in your eyes." And he said, "We'll rehearse on film," which was one of his favorites ... I mean, he knew Sir John would know the lines. And John did it.

He cast, I suppose, very well. Yes, I can't remember him ever saying, "Don't play that scene like that, play it like this." Ever.

PPT: Did he tend to do a lot of takes?

KB: Depends. The take with Gielgud he took two and the second one was purely for insurance because Sir John was leaving two days later to go to New York. And although they said that there was no hair in the gate, he shot a second take as insurance.

There's quite a long take at the beginning of the film. It's in the tavern, when I snatch a piece of paper from Welles and I'm teasing him and running around with Poins. And the camera comes in for a close-up. But before that, the camera has circled us and we had to practice walking over track while the camera came around. And that we rehearsed for quite a long time. That we may have rehearsed a whole day. Probably less. But that's because the camera was moving at the same time as the actors and crossing the actors' path and coming in, and he didn't want to cut it.

And the last scene at the end of the film when he's in that extraordinary house that he discovered in Soria. It's where he learns that the old king is dead and he's sitting in the back in a sort of chair. He rehearsed that a long time. Maybe two days. Because he wanted to shoot that in one take.

But normally he didn't [rehearse]. Normally he didn't. The one he shot of me most of all — which is quite extraordinary, looking back on it — comes right at the end of the film, although I shot it very early. And it's after the coronation. It's when the king turns and says, "My Lord, Chief Justice, enlarge the man committed yesterday." And then I have this line, "We consider it excess of wine that set him on." I must have done about forty takes on that. He wasn't cross; he didn't say, "That's wrong." He wanted a certain look in my eye. And when I see the film, I know what he wanted because it's wonderful. But he never made me feel that I was inept or something.

According to Baxter, Welles didn't block out the scenes in advance of shooting.

KB: The actual movements? No, he didn't. He allowed actors a certain amount of improvisation as to what they were going to do in the scene.

There are about three moments in the film in which Prince Hal — you see that in the end he is going to reject [Falstaff]. One is right after the play scene when he says, "Banish plump Jack, and banish all the world." And it cuts to me saying, "I do. I will." And that scene and that shot was most carefully rehearsed technically. But he never subordinated the authentic dramatic dynamic of the scene, or emotional dynamic, for the movement of the camera.

Like Frederick Muller, Baxter felt Welles related to Falstaff.

KB: Oh, very much. Probably more than even he realized. He thought that Falstaff was Shakespeare's greatest creation. He thought that Shakespeare was not just the greatest playwright in the world — he thought that he was the greatest man in the world. He also thought that there wasn't a human emotion that men are capable of experiencing that Shakespeare hadn't experienced.

There are many things of which Falstaff is culpable that you could not accuse Welles of. His terrible betrayal and dishonesty, which was not true of Orson. But Falstaff needed to duck and dive and to scheme and to plan and always living on the edge of no money at all — but being adored. That's very much Welles.

I never heard Welles criticize another actor or another director. And I was present once in Madrid when a journalist was asking what Welles thought of other directors and Orson — without being in any sense pompous — said, "I don't have anything to say." And afterwards he said to me — not in these words, but what amounted to, "No one who is a professional artist plans to do bad work. There are enough critics out there waiting to savage people, so why should people who work in the theatre or in movies join that pack of wolves?" So I never, ever heard him say a malevolent or malicious thing about another actor or a director.

I think that the last shot of Welles — not the one going through the archway, but the look on Welles's face ... and, by the way, when I did the coronation speech, it was a long time after we shot all the other coronation stuff. Finally, we got to actually saying the speech, which was in the sanctuary of a church outside of Madrid. A lot of water had flown under a lot of bridges from the beginning of the film to the end — and that was a kind of accident. Of course, it helped enormously. It had been six-and-a-half months that we'd been working on the film, and it was four years since I'd known him. And so with that speech — although it's a cruel speech — we both knew that it was the end of our work together as Keith Baxter and Orson.

He didn't much like getting into costume — it was an awful bore and took him a long time — but when I did my speech (and we shot my speech before we did the reverses of him) he wore costume. He looked through the lens and then he wore costume, although it was shot either over his head or in close-up. So I was always looking at him dressed as Falstaff. And he cleared the background behind him. It was not in an affected way — it wasn't "Method." It was something he wanted to do. And then he shot the reverses.

I find now when I see it that the shot on him at the end — right after I finish speaking but before I turn away, there's a shot of him looking at me and there's a shot of me looking at him. And on his face is this incredible look of somebody who has been moved unexpectedly — and hurt by his boy rejecting him — but also an extraordinary sense of pride, saying, "Look at you, you're wonderful." He's looking at the king, you know.

It was just fun. Because it is a great film — and it really is a great film — it's hard to tell people what fun we had. I mean, we delayed for some reason and Sir John wrote from New York — he was rehearsing the Edward Albee play — and he said, "I can't believe you're all running around that old castle where they're no lavatories. I do envy you all. You're having such fun." Everybody had fun.

Jeanne Moreau was hired for four or five days. She was at the height of her fame after *Jules and Jim* (1962) and somebody from *Le Monde* or *Paris Match* asked, "Ms. Moreau, this is a very small part. Why did you come?" And she said, "Because Orson Welles asked me." And people came to the set to pay homage. King Vidor was in Madrid trying to set up a film about Columbus, I think. Omar Sharif came because they were about to start shooting *Dr. Zhivago* (1965). David Lean came to the set — not to pay homage but to say, "Hey, Orson's in town." It was fun, believe me. I bet I had more fun than they did in *Matrix, Reloaded* (2003). But, then, we didn't make so much money.

> *Baxter never acted for Welles again, although at one point it looked as though he might appear in* The Deep, *Welles's adaptation of Charles Williams's novel* Dead Calm. *Shot in the late '60s, the project was never released and many sources claim it was unfinished, though Baxter told me, "There is a finished print of that film." The final film starred Welles, Laurence Harvey, Jeanne Moreau, Michael Bryant, and Oja Kodar.*

KB: After that film [*Chimes at Midnight*], I came back to England to play the lead in *You Never Can Tell,* which was going to the Haymarket Theatre with Ralph Richardson. And we were opening in Brighton and Orson brought Paola and Beatrice over for Christmas. Because we opened just after Christmas and we spent Christmas there. And we saw a lot of them.

I went off to Paris for a weekend and Orson tracked me down and said could I leave immediately for this place because they thought they couldn't get Laurence Harvey and would I be able to go and play this in the film? And I said, "Yes." He said, "Where will you be for the next 36 hours?" I said, "Here in Paris." And 36 hours later, he called me up and said that Laurence Harvey had come through so Laurence Harvey did the film.

And then he and Paola began to go separate ways. He wrote to me when I was doing *Macbeth.* He wrote me a very sweet letter when I was doing *Hamlet.* But the last time I saw him — and he didn't know that I had seen him — was I was going to lunch at Ma Maison in California and he was coming out as I arrived. He was massively overweight. He was all by himself, being helped into the car. And then I guess it was about a year later, I was in Detroit going into a television studio to do an interview and they said, "Orson Welles is dead." I rang Paola and I said, "How is everything?" She said, "Everything is a mess," and then she died in a car crash the following year.

June 15, 2003

Peter Parasheles

Parasheles was sound editor on the film of Chimes at Midnight.

Peter Parasheles: Well, I had just finished a film in Holland — a Dutch film, of all things — and I went to the south of Spain. I was in Torremolinos taking it easy and I read about Orson Welles being in Madrid. He had just gotten out of hospital after over-eating roasted suckling pig. And so I went up to Madrid and within two days I had met Audrey, who was his secretary, and she suggested I talk to an English film editor named Derek Parsons, who had previously worked for him. I went over to talk to him and he said there was an opening as a loop editor, where you re-do the dialogue. So I went and inter-viewed — not with Orson himself, but with his producer Alessandro Tasca. Tasca hired me and I started working on *Chimes at Midnight* in March 1965.

Orson had rented a very large apartment of about nine rooms for edit-ing the film, just outside in the suburbs of Madrid, just across from his other apartment where he lived. Keith Baxter, who played Prince Hal, was living in our apartment while waiting to complete his work.

I was on the film about eight, nine months while we did all the looping of all the actors before they went to England. We did all of the re-voicing at night, sometimes as late as one or two in the morning, after they had com-pleted their scenes with Orson.

Parasheles talked to me about the post-syncing process on Chimes at Midnight.

PP: I had to do all of the voices over again. They would shoot it with guide track. The sound track was just horrendous because most of the time the sound recordist was not properly synced up with the camera. I'd have to take the tapes of the guide track, and resync it with the picture to run at night with the actors.

And every time we'd run it — these actors were mostly from England and had never done film work before — they'd say, "My God, I'm not talking that fast. I never talk that fast." They didn't realize the pace that Orson had put them through. They couldn't believe that they were talking this fast. They'd say, "Well, you're speeding it up." I said, "No, I'm not speeding it up. Just *do* it." But they were very good about it because everybody wanted to work with Orson. They sacrificed a lot, even John Gielgud. His agents didn't want him to work for Orson because he only paid about half the going rate for everyone and they were not sure they were even going to get paid; the English were skeptical of all things Spanish because Franco was still in power.

The famous battle scene was shot in Ritero Park, the general park for Madrid. The producer, Tasca, was mostly in charge of shooting most of that sequence. Orson set it up the way he wanted to and Tasca had to finish it because Orson was always busy rewriting or editing.

While we were dubbing the film in Paris, one of the most violent battle scenes was going on and we're watching and I see this taxi in the top of the frame going by. I said, "Look!" *[Laughs.]* He said, "Forget about it, Peter, just do the fucking work!" That's how he would talk to you if you tried to stop something.

I asked Parasheles about the music in Chimes at Midnight, *which was composed by Alberto Francesco Lavagnino.*

PP: What he did with the music was very unusual. He would get a track and double time it or triple time it or quadruple time it depending on the scene. There's a sequence where Hotspur decides to go to war, to join the forces and leave his wife. I couldn't even keep up with it. And he had this music going on at two, three times its normal speed. *[Laughs.]* I mean, he would try anything just to make it interesting.

Parasheles recalled several meals he shared with Welles after work.

PP: I was working at night on his picture. I was about the last one there. Everybody else had gone home. I did about 2,000 loops because you had to cover every take they did. It wasn't like they do in Hollywood where they would only re-voice to the final edited version.

So, anyway, he saw that I was working late and he invited me over to his house for dinner with him and Paola and Beatrice. It was very nice, a lovely evening, because one thing about Orson was if you were with him socially it couldn't have been a better time. He was a marvelous storyteller. After dinner at about 11:30 P.M., I went back to work and about 1:30 or 2:00 A.M., I got a bus to back to my hotel. The next day, Tasca told me Orson was furious with me because I hadn't stayed all night to work, especially after my dinner with him. He didn't talk to me for another week.

One time he took me out in Paris and it was quite an evening. We actually went to a place called Le Coq d'Or on the Sienne. Because it was crowded, they asked us to sit in the bar, which was a very small little bar. We had some scotch and we talked about the moon goddesses and sun goddesses because he was also interested in the mythologies of Greece. We talked about Robert Graves, who had written *The Greek Myths* and *The White Goddess.*

Finally, we went in and it's a restaurant with different levels of seating arrangement, like an auditorium, and banks of flowers separating the rows. Orson wanted to sit downstairs. As we got in there, of course, there's Darryl F. Zanuck! He introduced me and Zanuck with his cigar and his entourage. So when we sat down to eat, he said, "Let's have American chicken pot pie." Can you believe that? *[Laughs.]* I'm in a French restaurant thinking I'm going to have something French, but actually it was fabulous. The first course was a lobster claw in aspic. That's how it started off—very nice. And he was a wonderful man to be with once work was done.

As Parasheles touched upon above, Welles admired writer Robert Graves (whom Peter Bogdanovich has described as "the moon-possessed poet"[4]) and he specifically alluded to the significance the moon held for him on several occasions.[5]

PP: I was into the moon goddess because I was reading *The King Must Die*. Did you ever hear of that book?

Peter Prescott Tonguette: I haven't, but I know that Welles was very interested in Robert Graves.

PP: [In *The King Must Die*] basically every seven years, or every three years, they had to kill the king in order to re-establish the crops. So the king was killed and chopped up and [they] threw his remnants on the fields so they could sow the new crops for the next year. And this is a story of the change from the moon goddess to the sun god when guys like Oedipus came in; the male society took over.

Orson was more male-oriented than I was. But actually I would think he was both in many ways because he was a very complicated man.

Parasheles later worked as an editor on Don Quixote *in 1966.*

PP: We went to Rome to pick up *Don Quixote* and so we stayed in Rome a couple weeks. We got the prints for it and we got a train ride from Rome, we went to Paris and from Paris we were going to be picked up on the border of Spain. And I made a very bad mistake, which my assistant [Ira Wohl] always reminds me of. I allowed our film and our baggage to go on to the Spanish border instead of stopping on the French border where they were going to meet us and transport us. Because on May 1—which was May Day, a day the Communists celebrated—they were checking everything at the time. Somehow we got out of that problem. But I was considered a little bit of a fool for getting them into that. Somehow we got our stuff back and we just rushed away.

Parasheles and Wohl drove to Madrid and began working on Don Quixote *for a number of months.*

PP: After four or five months, he ran out of money and he sent me some letters, which I still have. He said that he couldn't afford to keep me on any longer but he would hope that I'd be around in order to start with him again. And we had our difficulties because he ... you know, in Spain you worked six days a week, you didn't work five days a week. And he occasionally wanted you to work Sundays, 12, 14 hours a day. I had a wife at the time who needed some attention. I kind of fought back about that. I would like to have my Sundays off once in a while. One time I did go on a Sunday for him and he was at the bullfights and I'm just sitting there with my hand on my ass. So anyway, those were the kinds of fights that we had.

We did a lot of work on that. We did a lot of jump frames. He would ask you to take a scene and take every other frame out or take every third frame out. And poor Ira would be taking this stuff back and forth because we didn't have optical houses to do the special effects. We had to try it for him. And it was laborious kind of work sometimes.

PPT: While cutting *Don Quixote,* how much freedom did Welles give you?

PP: Not much, but he still let you do things. He pretty much knew what he wanted to do all the time.

Interestingly enough, just before I went to Spain, I was in Holland on a Dutch film of all things. I edited the film while my assistant translated the next scene I was to cut.

But while I was on this Dutch film, I met Akim Tamiroff. Now Akim was a wonderful guy. He was a great professional. We kind of adopted him, or he adopted us. He was a very shy man, as a matter of fact. He would sit on his hands because he thought they were too ugly or something. But he started doing imitations and told me about working with Orson on *Don Quixote.* Orson would call him whenever he had a chance to shoot some scenes, as Akim was Sancho Panza.

PPT: For the most part, were you re-cutting old scenes?

PP: Yes. There was some new material, but not a lot. What happened was this: he had shot stuff with Akim. So when I started working on it, I said, "You know, I met Akim up in Amsterdam working on a Dutch film." So he started doing imitations of Akim, like Akim did imitations of him. They sounded like each other because they had these wonderful base voices, both of them. Akim had his accent, of course, as a Russian.

He loved Akim and Akim loved him. But they would go out and shoot and Orson handled the camera himself. He said they'd go out and shoot wherever they could and whenever they could.

He was supposed to make a deal with a Mexican producer, Gustavo Alatriste, who was also Bunuel's producer at the time. Orson was going to do another film for Alatriste and finish up *Don Quixote.* All the scenes that Orson had shot were things that he could do himself with a couple of people, but the major scenes had not been shot.

Orson started *Don Quixote* by telling this classic tale to a young girl staying at the same hotel. It was going to start off as a masked ball. And from this masked ball everybody would go home and change back to reality. But of course Don Quixote is there with Sancho Panza and where do they go? They're still in their attire, so we realize they are in a new time period. We follow them through their adventures.

We were in his living room taking a break. His cutting rooms were downstairs in his house, level with his swimming pool. You know, of course, that he used to walk around with a parrot on his shoulder. My producer friend, Alessandro Tasca, who became a very close friend of mine because he worked in L.A. after a while, he used to go around with a parakeet, imitating Orson!

So anyway we're upstairs listening to some music and I foolishly started whistling along with it. He says, "Peter, what the hell are you doing there? You're ruining the music." So he was teaching me some manners as well. He was always good at letting you know what to do.

The Mexican was supposed to make a deal. It all sounded very promising. Orson always got carried away with deals that he thought were coming through. He thought they were going to happen. He was very optimistic about things like that. Well, eventually, the whole project fell through.

I know one of the reasons. Orson used to make his own budgets up. That was the biggest mistake. He would make his own budgets up instead of getting a production manager who knew what actual costs were; Orson would underestimate the cost of these films. And every time he did that, the production manager from the other side would come in and say, "Orson, you can't do it for this kind of money." And they'd get scared and run off. This happened to Orson I'm sure quite a few times. So his film was never finished.

One of the great scenes was when he [Don Quixote] attacked a scooter, thinking it was something evil. And then he went into a movie house and there's a pirate film going on. And he sees that the woman is being taken away, being captured by the pirates and he goes up to the screen and starts slashing at the screen. Then there was a moon shot, them going up to the moon in a rocket. He had very oddball kinds of scenes in it.

Orson started the film as the narrator and as you're introduced to Don Quixote and Sancho Panza, Orson is voicing both characters. It was truly amazing how well it worked. Orson never cut by dialogue. He always cut by picture. He'd run the picture and never worried about the dialogue that was there. He just cut by the way the picture went.

When the Spanish producers used to come on *Chimes at Midnight,* he told Tasca to tell them to fuck off, I don't want to see them around here, I don't want them anywhere near the place. He was very hard on people at times. And he could be very mean at times, very, very mean. He was threatening in many ways because of his voice. He never physically would touch you, but you thought you were going to be snowed under because when he started hollering at people ... he really scared people.

He was a man who was a powerhouse in many ways; he was a bully, but he could back off very easily. He loved his actors, especially when he had to work with them. As soon as they were gone, he forgot about them. He was concentrating on what he was doing and that's all that mattered to him.

Parasheles appeared very briefly as an actor in Welles's 1968 film The Immortal Story.

PP: He gave me 50 dollars for the day to stand in with a couple other guys. Another American actor, just to go out to work with Orson, he took 50 bucks for the day. He normally would have gotten four times that amount.

So we did our shooting and then we all went to a big dining hall with refectory tables, nothing fancy. And Orson started telling stories and he had everybody going for about an hour-and-a-half. He changed his personality from work to social being. He was very unusual that way.

PPT: Do you have any favorite memories of Welles?

PP: Well, it's interesting. There are all kinds of memories. We were looping his voice in Paris. We had to go to a Paris studio. Usually, on most films when they re-voice, they have a loop, put on ear-phones and they watch the banner that runs down to where the star is speaking. You loop, play it, loop, play it, until you get the rhythm. As an actor, you get to remember what you've done and re-voice yourself and try to do the sync as close as possible.

Well, in Paris they had a different system. They projected a large picture, then underneath they had written out in the way the words were said and when it reached an arrow in the center, you would be talking to that band. You'd be watching the film as you did it and watching the thing below it and you would voice it that way. And then a person with a mic would see what position you were in and he'd follow you, he'd move the mic back and forth as to whether you were in a close-up or further away.

But this was done at the time you were recording it, so it kind of locked you into things so you couldn't use one take for another take. That's what you do many times. You take various takes and combine them in order to get the best performance sometimes. But while I was doing this, Orson had a large 12 ounce glass filled with vodka. Now when Orson gets going ... and I'd say to Orson, "Orson, it's not in sync." He said, "Peter, shut the fuck up. I know what I'm doing." You couldn't talk to him. This happened to me in Paris and in Madrid as well watching him working with someone. He never put up with anything. He did it his own way.

But he was very good at it. The trouble is when he got drunk or when he ate and had too much, he'd start slurring. And he wanted to do voices for all the odd characters in *Chimes*, but at this time, he couldn't control the quality of his voice and it sounded like Orson.

Working for Orson was basically like this: it's a love-hate relationship. You work for him and he's doing you a favor in many ways. You know, you went along with this whole thing. But you did it at half price. But you went along with that because you were working with a guy who's extremely bright and interesting. Once when I questioned him about why he would not pay me what other American and English editors were earning in Madrid, he looked and me and said, "Peter, you're working for 'Orson Welles.'"

October 20, 2004

7

The Other Side of the Wind

Gary Graver

Cinematographer Graver photographed numerous projects for Welles over the course of the 15 years they worked together. "I like to think there are three sections to Orson's life," Graver told me. "Richard Wilson was Orson's right hand man assistant from the Mercury Theatre through Kane, *through the RKO days. He was with Orson right up through, I believe,* Macbeth. *Then Orson left for Europe on his long journey into Europe. He spent more time in Europe than he did in Hollywood until 1970. Then I came into the picture and I was the book-end to the last chapter of Orson's life. It was Richard Wilson; then he didn't have an assistant; and then I came along. I was really Orson's assistant on everything, not just the cameraman. I helped him cast the picture, find locations, and everything."*

Graver told me about seeing Touch of Evil *(1958) before he met Welles.*

Gary Graver: The performances and the camera movement — I never saw anything so creative like that before. I think Orson was one of the first ones to put the camera on the hood of a car. Well, Joseph H. Lewis did it, but [Welles] used it a lot. I know that he used his Camaflex camera that he loved and mounted it and put the sound in later between Heston and the detective, Mort Mills. Orson got five Camaflexes. It's a French camera where you just put the cartridge on the back. You don't thread the camera. He had Universal buy him five cameras. He took one with him as part of his deal and the other four were at Universal. But they didn't know what to do with them, really.

One shows up in a still in the bathroom in the *Psycho* (1961) set. So besides there being so many similarities between *Psycho* and *Touch of Evil,* which came first ... if you notice, Janet Leigh in the motel and all those things, there are a lot of similarities. Mort Mills, the same actor, was in *Psycho* and *Touch of Evil.* They were both at Universal. So I think Universal eventually got rid of the cameras; they didn't know what to do with them, but Orson kept his. And from *Touch of Evil,* Orson used the camera on *The Trial* and *Chimes at Midnight* and eventually *The Other Side of the Wind.*

61

The Other Side of the Wind was a project Welles began shooting in 1970. The screenplay was written by Welles and Oja Kodar (who also co-starred). Kodar has said that the film's "main plot is unfolding during the last day of the life of this great Hollywood director played by John Huston. It's his birthday with a lot of young people and movie buffs that his friend Zarah, played by Lilli Palmer, arranged for him."[1] Huston's character was named Jake Hannaford.

GG: After I saw *Touch of Evil*, I knew that if I ever met Orson that I'd get along with him really good. Once he found out that I could do the sound and do the picture and do so many things, then I was in. *[Laughs.]*

Welles and Graver met in 1970.

GG: I just heard he was in town. I was always saying to myself, "This is someone I'd love to work with." So I called the Beverly Hills Hotel. I was at Schwab's Drugstore. I'd read in *Variety* that he was in L.A. I figured, "Well, where would he stay? At the Beverly Hills Hotel." So I called up and the operator put me right through. He said, "Hello?" Oh, God, I said, "Orson Welles?" He said, "Yes?" I was intimidated. Then I said who I was and that I'd like to work with him, et cetera, and he said, well he couldn't talk to me now, he's too busy, he's going to New York. So he took my phone number. I thought, "That's the end of that. I'll never hear from him."

I went home up in Laurel Canyon and my phone was ringing as I was pulling into the driveway. I ran in and it was Orson. He said, "Get over here at the Beverly Hills Hotel *immediately*. I've got to talk to you!" I said, "Wow!" *[Laughs.]* So I went over there and I met him. Oja was there in the background and she closed the door. Orson and I talked.

I wanted to see more Orson Welles movies and I thought, well, I was the guy who could do it. I helped him put a crew together. I knew he worked independently a lot. After we talked for a while, he suddenly grabbed me by the shoulders and threw me on the floor. He pounced on top of me. I thought, "Oh, God, what am I getting myself in to? What is this? I don't know this guy, he's big, bigger than me, I can't get up." And he held me down there. He kept looking out the window. Finally, he let me up. I said, "What was wrong?" He said, "Oh, there was an actress outside who, if she sees me, she'll talk to me. I had to get out of her eyesight. I want to talk to you, I don't want to talk to her."

Then he went to New York and made *A Safe Place* (1971) with Henry Jaglom. He came back and then we started shooting with Eric Sherman, Peter Bogdanovich, Joe McBride, and Felipe [Herba], the first day, around Christmastime in December. We didn't start big with *The Other Side of the Wind*. We just started with some small scenes with not really an acting cast, just kind of about the documentary crew that was behind the scenes.

I offered my services free. I had an income at the time from a movie I

Welles with cinematographer Gary Graver during the shooting of *The Other Side of the Wind* (photograph courtesy of Gary Graver).

owned a percentage of, so I was financially okay. The first year, I just did it. But to supplement, he would give me jobs when he got assignments.

My arrangement with Orson was, right away he said, "Gary, we got a lot of work to do." *[Laughs.]* As always. He said, "Now if you get a job, if you get a feature or something, come to me and tell me, and I'm going to tell you whether I need you or not." Like I was under contract or something! *[Laughter.]* So I'd tell him. I'd say, "I got a job." He'd say, "We're not shooting, so you should do that."

There are two styles to the film. There's the razzle-dazzle handheld documentary, with all sorts of 16mm, 35, Super 8, video, stills, just recordings, and then the movie-within-the-movie was all shot on a tripod or a dolly, cranes, it's all composed like Huston's character would compose everything. That was very carefully made.

> *In the film, scenes are shown from the film which Hannaford is directing; these constitute the "movie-within-the-movie" sequences in* The Other Side of the Wind.

GG: Orson would say to me, "I don't like to use close-ups." I thought to myself, "What is he talking about? Look at *Ambersons* and *Kane*. What do you mean you don't like to use close-ups?" He was putting me on.

I talked to the cameraman of *The Trial* and *Chimes at Midnight,* Edmond Richard, and I said to him, "Did you have trouble starting and stopping on those films?" He said, "No. We just shot. Especially on *Chimes,* we just went from the beginning and shot the film. There was no waiting to get money or anything like that." Because that kind of stuff surrounds the Welles legend, that films had to be stopped and started, running out of money and stuff. That wasn't the whole situation.

Peter Prescott Tonguette: Sometimes Welles would shoot part of a scene at one time and another part of it later on. Is that correct, and was that a challenge for you?

GG: No, we did it pretty easily. I've got a scene cut together between Huston, Edmond O'Brien, Mercedes McCambridge, and Lilli Palmer, and Lilli Palmer's not even in the same room with them. But we took Huston's costume and the lights and we matched it up. We shot at Lilli Palmer's house in Malaga in Spain in black-and-white. We shot black-and-white in Arizona. And you'd never know they're not in the same room. They all look at each other and Huston's coat passes in front of her and you think it's him. He was very clever doing that stuff.

PPT: How much of *The Other Side of the Wind* was there left to shoot?

GG: Left to shoot? Nothing. Completed. Orson got all the wild lines from Huston and all the voice-overs, he got everything he needed. He was editing on it all the time in his editing room at his house on a flatbed. He was always working on it.

Graver estimated that Welles edited a total of approximately 45 minutes of footage.

GG: I'll tell you a funny story about Orson. We were shooting in Arizona on *The Other Side of the Wind*. I wouldn't turn the camera off fast enough. "You're wasting film, Gary!" He had a guy stand behind me with his hand on the camera switch. Orson said, "Cut," and the guy turned it off. Because it took me a few seconds to reach my hand around back and turn it off. He even had us saving what we call gaffer's tape, so he wouldn't waste money.

PPT: Did you ever shoot any new material for *Don Quixote?*

GG: Yes, he sent me out with some sketches in the car and I went all around Spain shooting windmills. Different angles — in color, because he wanted to cut that in and eventually finish *Don Quixote*.

Welles preferred working in the 1:85 or 1:66 aspect ratios.

GG: I don't know if Orson said it or he repeated it, that CinemaScope was good for parades and snakes. *[Laughs.]*

He was very formal. He liked 1:85. I had to keep reminding him because sometimes the cameras were not scribed that way. Sometimes he would operate the camera and then the heads would be high up in the air and so forth. But basically it's 1:85. Of course, we didn't have video monitors then. They didn't come in until mid–'80s or something, so he just had to trust me. He'd show me what he wanted. He had the camera, he'd look through it, and then

Welles and Graver (photograph courtesy of Gary Graver).

he'd come over and say, "Now, look, start here, then pan, and you end here." And, boy, I had to get it exactly right or I'd catch hell when the film came back from the lab.

PPT: What kind of relationship did you and Welles have when you weren't working together?

GG: Well, if we weren't working together, usually I'd go over to his place if I wasn't working. We'd sit around in front of the fireplace. Did I tell you

A composite shot of Graver, Oja Kodar, and Welles on the MGM Studios back lot, Culver City, California, 1971 (photograph courtesy of Gary Graver).

that story about the time when we were sitting in front of the fireplace and I was doing some low budget picture and he was doing the wine commercials? It was a cold winter day. He kind of sighed and looked at me and said, "Gary, here we are. You and I are sitting here this afternoon in the heart of Hollywood and we're both very talented fellows. And yet we're working in the suburbs of the cinema." *[Laughs.]* I thought that was great: "the suburbs of the cinema."

June 18, 2003; April 15, November 30,
and December 11, 2004; January 6, 2005

Eric Sherman

Like Graver, Sherman (another crew person on Wind*) also met Welles in 1970.*

Eric Sherman: The circumstances were that I had developed a relationship with Peter Bogdanovich, whom I had done a feature interview with at the time that he had directed one film, *Targets* [1968]. He had not yet done *The Last Picture Show* [1971]. I interviewed Peter in the first book that I wrote, *The Director's Event*, which is something of a classic. It's the first book that was written in English about American film directors. It preceded even Andrew Sarris' *The American Cinema*. So I was in college when I wrote that. I interviewed five directors at length, one of whom was Bogdanovich. We hit it off well. Of course, he was a major film fan and film lover. So he next asked me to work on *Directed by John Ford* (1971). I was a cameraman and provided sound and equipment and everything on *Directed by John Ford*.

The next thing was, he called me one day rather suddenly and he said, "Eric! You want to work with Orson?" I said, "Orson who?" And he said, "Welles, of course!" I said, "Sure, who wouldn't?" He said, "Okay, come on over with your camera." At that time, I owned a 16mm I NPR. He gave me the address in the Trousdale Estates.

The Trousdale Estates is a Nouveau Riche part of L.A. It's in Beverly Hills. People in Pasadena consider Beverly Hills *nouveau riche*, people in Beverly Hills consider the Trousdale Estates *nouveau riche*. They're very expensive houses, but all fake modern stuff, or fake classic, I guess you'd say.

So I said, "Sure. What do we do?" And he said, "Well, just bring your camera over and bring Felipe." Felipe Herba is a friend of mine. When I was a student at Yale, he was a student at M.I.T., and we both ran our film societies there. Anyway, I called Felipe and he brought a sound rig over. I think he had a Nagra tape recorder. We drove up to the estate and there were a bunch of people running around. Gary was the main shooter on it. Gary's a good guy and he's a friend. I asked, "So what's going on?" And I was given a thumbnail sketch of what *The Other Side of the Wind* was about.

And that was it. I worked there for about two weeks and I played the part of a cameraman. And I was also shooting. It was a film within the film.

Peter Prescott Tonguette: Were you working on the film within the film portions?

ES: You know, since I have never seen it ... I've seen scenes from it because every once in a while Gary goes to the vaults and shows us a couple of scenes. And it's unbelievable. When it's released — which I predict it will be in our lifetime — it will be like a missing Shakespeare play. It's just ... what a piece of work. So I don't even know what I worked on. I did what I was told.

As Kodar said, a major scene in the film is Jake Hannaford's birthday party.

ES: It was a party, there were a lot of celebrity types walking around. I don't remember too much else. It was a whirlwind and when I tell you about the shooting schedule you'll know what I mean.

PPT: What was the shooting schedule like?

ES: Twenty hours a day. Call at 6:00 A.M., wrap at 2:00 A.M. One meal break, two and a half hours. It was catered by the Beverly Hills Hotel or Chasen's. They'd bring buckets of chili, the famous Chasen's chili that Elizabeth Taylor evidently had shipped to wherever she was when she was working. When we'd leave at 2:00 A.M., we'd all be absolutely wasted, of course, and Orson would be up and sitting in his black robe and black silk pajamas. He would be sitting at a typewriter and he would be there, same position, same clothes, four hours later when we arrived. So I did not see the man sleep for two weeks. Maybe he did, but it was fewer than four hours a day.

PPT: Was this actually Welles's house?

ES: It was a house that he had rented and I believe that he was living in it at the time. There were very beautiful men and women surrounding him at all times, one of whom was Oja, of course. She was featured in the film. What a beautiful woman, oh my God. She's a wonderful gal.

John Huston wasn't cast as Hannaford at this point.

ES: I said to Peter, "Well, obviously Orson is going to be Jake Hannaford." He said, "Well, I don't think so. I think it's going to be Huston." As I recollect, I think it was in the works. But Huston was not there. Susan Strasberg was and Bogdanovich was.

Peter Bogdanovich initially was cast in the role of a film buff. But Sherman explained to me the other "role" Bogdanovich had in Welles's life.

ES: Peter, I think, more than a role, he was keeping Orson alive in many ways. At the time, he was still the only director who had had three hits in a

Welles directing Oja Kodar and Gary Graver (portraying a cineaste in this sequence) in *The Other Side of the Wind* (photograph © Michael Ferris).

row—*The Last Picture Show, What's Up, Doc?* [1972], and *Paper Moon* [1973]. He was a jack of all trades and his main purpose was keeping Orson alive because back then Peter had the clout and interest. So he kind of did some of everything—he production coordinated, he production managed, he gave Orson pep talks, all of that.

[Orson] would set camera position one. He'd say, "Okay, Gary, you start there on 'Action.' Then, Eric, one minute later, you start over there on a second position." So I'd have one more minute of film than Gary. Then when Gary's film ran out, he would reload quickly—which you can do with an Éclair, you don't have to thread anything, you just have to have a magazine pre-prepared. Then Gary would run to position three and set up and he would start rolling. Then I would run out of film, reload, and then I'd go to position four. So we would leapfrog. We pre-lit every room in the house and we shot for about one hour straight. Now can you imagine what the actors felt like?

Oh, it was unbelievable. To top it off—and nobody's ever told me not to tell this story, so I'm going to tell you ... have you ever operated camera?

PPT: Yes, I have operated digital video camera.

ES: Okay. You would, though, be able to anticipate that if you're standing in a position, if it's an awkward position, if you're standing there for, let's say, 10 minutes, your muscles would start cramping up.

So the biggest lesson I learned in all filmmaking — and I would say that almost every technical element of film that I learned, I learned in those two weeks. Enough that I have made features, I've directed and shot features, I've directed a PBS series ... in other words, I got my complete filmmaking hat from Orson in those two weeks. I've never taken a film class in my life, but I teach three classes in two colleges. I've had 7,000 students, 90 percent of whom work in the business. Basically it all came from those two weeks.

So here's the story: Orson as an actor was famous for what we call "the pregnant pause." He would stop mid-sentence and he would look off to the sides. Do you know what he was doing when he was looking off to the sides? He was looking at a guy holding a cue card with his next set of lines. This was a company called Barney Cue Cards. Barney just passed away recently, by the way. Since Orson was a master, he would look at a different position for every pregnant pause. So, as I recall, there were at least six or eight guys employed by Barney Cue Cards to stand in six or eight different places. Now one guy would be standing on a ladder holding it almost straight down, so that Orson could do the God look up to the sky. Then Orson would take a pregnant pause and he would look down — there'd be a guy lying on the floor. There were six or eight guys positioned all over the room, plus the grips and electric pulling all my and Gary's wires. You get the picture. It was like a complete circus.

Now that is the preface to my tale. On the first camera position that I was in, about halfway through the roll, I was bent over because it was too high for me to be sitting on an apple box and too low for me to stand up straight, so I was in a hunched over position for five minutes. And I started getting a muscle cramp in my back. So I straightened up and sort of rubbed my back. Orson said, "Cut, cut!" I said, "Mr. Welles, what's the matter?" He said, "How can I concentrate with all that motion?" I said, "But Mr. Welles, you have eight guys lying all over the place, grips, electric, everything else, what do you mean?" And he didn't answer me. He said, "Just don't do it anymore. We're gonna retake. Start from the beginning."

So my point is, you talk about a control freak and that has a bad connotation. But I made a motion that he did not plan. And though by my standards, it was a simple, uncomplicated motion, it was simply a piece of motion that he had not planned. He cut the whole take and we had to reload the magazines, because each take was ten minutes. Isn't that amazing?

I have never been to a film school, never been to a film class. I learned to make films because, number one, my father is a director; he's the oldest living director, Vincent Sherman. And I used to go to the set every Saturday, but I never shot anything. I was just a kid. When I got to college in the '60s,

I was forced by my friends, kicking and screaming, into filmmaking — although at Yale University, they had no film classes. To study film was beneath contempt. No serious man admitted that he was interested in film. But because I was from Hollywood, my classmates knew more about my dad than I did. So I learned how to make films by making every mistake you could make, literally. But since I wasn't stupid, I made each mistake only once.

I made my first film in 1965. By the time I got out of college, I'd written that book, I'd made an award-winning documentary in which I'd done every technical function, but since it was all by hook and by crook, there was no particular pattern, regimen, policy by which I worked. It was just I did what I had to do to get the shots and I was good, I wasn't bad. But when I entered the space of this absolute genius, everything changed. I could have worked with any other director in the world and I don't think I would have had that experience. So on-the-job training? Only in the simplest definition of that. It was in-the-presence-of-genius-training.

PPT: Welles didn't appear in *The Other Side of the Wind*, yet you mention a scene you were shooting where Welles was on camera and you made the motion that distracted him ...

ES: That's right. At that time, I think he was being a — and this is where my recollection is vague — presence or we'd kind of shoot around him. But he'd be standing there, kind of directing where people should go. So even though it's true that he may not have actually been an actor, he certainly was there. In any event, I distracted him, that's for sure!

He would tell me exactly where to put the camera, exactly what focal length to choose, exactly when to pan and tilt, exactly when to turn the camera off. In other words, it was the closest thing to total control that I have ever experienced, including in dancing or sex — all of which are about control or a willingness to be controlled. He exerted the most control of any artist with whom I have ever worked. Thus, we had about 50 percent crew turnover every day. Many people were just not willing to be controlled. People ask me, did I feel dominated, did I feel suppressed, repressed, anything else. The answer is no. In fact, I did better camerawork for Orson in those two weeks than I've ever done before or since.

Now, in addition to him giving me all these instructions, he never one time looked through the camera. Yet he had absolute certainty on what was being seen when and where. And he would see — I don't know, it was almost as though he had a trick. But it wasn't a trick. You could say, "Well, maybe he's looking at the reflection in the lens." Well, maybe, but I don't think so. He had certainty of all technical aspects of film, though he had never been trained. So I both felt utterly controlled and it was fantastic. Just amazing. And I've done the best work that I've ever done. I don't know why. Just in the presence of that amount of genius, unless one protests it — which half the crew did 'cause they quit everyday — if one opens oneself up to it, I think you can learn an immense amount.

PPT: Did you have any time to talk to him about his films?

ES: Yes, I did. Every two-and-a-half hour meal break. If he wasn't recording Gallo wine commercials or Eastern Airline commercials, I would talk to him. We'd talk about his films. He liked talking about food and music. He loved Duke Ellington and I am a jazz fan. I've made some documentaries on jazz musicians. He just loved to talk about jazz and the good old days and black people. He loved people of all color, of course. He just admired the hell out of anybody who had a career like Duke did. We talked about food. In fact, one night after we'd wrapped the two weeks, he said, "Eric, let's go to an all-night Mexican restaurant. You must know some." I said, "Yeah, I do." I took him to a real funky all-night Mexican restaurant on Sunset Boulevard. I even remember the name of it: Nayarit's. And we all went over there and, oh my God, the amount of food and margaritas we consumed! I'm not a drinker, but, jeez ... we just sat and he was just so full of life. I'm sure you've heard that phrase before with reference to him. But he really was.

PPT: Do you have any favorite memories of Welles?

ES: Yes, I do. It was a comment he made about political wisdom which I thought was very profound. He was sitting there in his black silk PJs. It was during one of our two-and-a-half hour meal breaks. And it was a very difficult time in our country. The Vietnam War was raging, Nixon was president and he's the closest thing to a dictator that we've had, in my opinion. And some kids had just been thrown in jail for slicing up an American flag and wearing it as a shirt. And Orson made a statement that when the time comes that a country and its leadership can't take a joke, the game is over. Somehow that struck me as being extremely profound. He went over the history of all great countries and cultural movements. He sort of pointed out that always, in any country that has anything remotely approaching freedom, you have to be able to poke fun. Otherwise, what's it about? A country is not its symbol. That moment, I remember he said it with such simplicity and such greatness. So that is the favorite moment of that two weeks.

The next time Sherman interacted with Welles was years later when the director was trying to get a project called The Dreamers *produced. Based upon two stories by Isak Dinesen, "The Dreamers" and "Echoes," the screenplay written by Welles and Oja Kodar was never made (although, as we shall later learn, Welles did shoot several scenes from the script with his own money in the early 1980s).*

ES: I think it's one of the greatest scripts I've ever read.

PPT: I love it.

ES: Yeah. I and another man named Doug Edwards — Doug was the head of the Academy of Motion Picture Arts and Sciences Foundation, he was a major fan of Orson's and I think he might have known Orson — and another woman, whose name escapes me, she was the head of publicity for Columbia or something. Anyway, the two of them — this gal and Doug, who was a good friend of mine, he has since died of AIDS, unfortunately — came and they said, "We want you to read this script." I said, "Oh my God, this could be one of the most cosmic films ever made." They said, "We want to produce it for Orson and we want you to be with us." I was the only one of the three who had produced and directed movies. And they knew that I knew Orson's work and knew him personally.

So I had a conversation with Orson. This created a tremendous conflict of moral codes for me. Because you're working with an individual whom you admire as much as any other person, and yet as a producer you're ultimately the legally responsible one for saving expenditure of money and all of that. The conflict was, of course, what would I do if Orson did the famous thing that he did in fact do, which is ask for more money. So I had a conversation with him. It might have been on the phone or it might have been at one of the famous Ma Maison nightly gatherings. This conversation occurred maybe two years before his death. I said, "Orson, you know how much I love you and esteem you as a person and as an artist." He said, "Yeah, yeah, I know all that. What do you want?" I said, "I have an opportunity to produce a film based on *The Dreamers*. I want you to know that this is presenting me with a conflict because if we agree to a budget and you sign it and I sign it, I'd have to hold you to it." And he looked at me with great profundity and some degree of sadness and said, "Eric, I have to recommend that you walk away from the project." I said, "Why?" He said, "Because I won't keep any agreement that I sign if it's about money." I think he even said, "I sign anything I have to to gain survival and then once I get that money, I need more survival." So I said, "Wow. Well, Orson, I really thank you for that honesty. So, sadly, I will walk away from it." Isn't that something?

April 27, 2004

Felipe Herba

"Well, just bring your camera over and bring Felipe," Peter Bogdanovich said to Eric Sherman, as recounted to me by Sherman.

Felipe Herba: Through Peter Bogdanovich, we were asked to participate as actors. I assume that we were a take-off of the Maysles brothers, a sound man and a camera man walking around together, and we were supposed to act somewhat aggressively, I guess, and be very obtrusive and so forth.

The Maysles brothers — David and Albert — were, of course, eminent documentary filmmakers.

FH: After that part was finished, Eric left, I stayed, and became a member of the crew. I stayed working with them maybe for a couple of months and then I left because I had other jobs and it was quite gruesome. *[Laughs.]* Not because of his treatment, but because the hours were long and it was hard work.

I think the first thing that Eric Sherman and I did was the scene with us in a convertible (actually my own car) following the director around. There was this insane thing that happened at a railroad crossing somewhere near the airport. He got a huge train to go by us. He started running around very excited. "Let's shoot! Let's shoot! We have to get this." So I remember that. But the specifics of what we actually did, I don't remember now.

Peter Prescott Tonguette: Did Welles show you a script?

FH: No, he would tell us what to do. "Do this, do that, run around, come in here, get into the camera." We were kind of in the background, coming in and out, that was the idea.

I don't know if I asked or if they needed somebody to help and I said, "Sure, I'll hang around." I figured it would be a good chance to work with Mr. Welles and get to know him and so forth. And it was. I worked on sound on the film within the film. I was assisting Gary Graver with the camera when I was in the crew. As I remember, that was my function. Of course, we would do anything. We would do some grip work if it had to be done and carry things around. There were no boundaries. It was that kind of production.

What I worked on were a bunch of scenes at night and at day that were shot at Century City. Century City was nothing then. It was like three buildings. And he, I remember, brought mirrors and he would start positioning the mirrors to get reflections of buildings so he would actually create an architecture that did not exist. I remember that I broke one of those mirrors and I was very embarrassed. *[Laughs.]* It was like 50 dollars or something.

And then we worked at night I remember again in Century City that we had a big water truck to create rain. Then we shot at the old MGM Lot One too, where all the old streets and standing sets were. There was a lot of stuff in there with Oja walking around dressed very — almost nude, I think. As a matter of fact, I think she was nude, something like that.

At Orson's home here in the hills, there was a lot of shooting with Bob Random in a car and all the night sequences with rain and no rain and so forth. I remember moving the car up and down off camera to look like it was moving. There were scenes in parties that were sort of like part of an orgy or something. Of course, there was no sex involved. We were hand holding 16mm projectors and showing stag films being projected on their bodies on little screens like they had put on. I remember that part. What it had to do with the film, I have no idea.

I remember once we were talking about some guy's film, a student film that Welles had seen and didn't like too much, and for a moment the subject of the cameraman on *Citizen Kane,* Gregg Toland, came up, and he was talking about how Toland came up with all these ideas and building a crane to put the camera up the stage and he had all these very nice commentaries about him. You can see that Welles was very fond of him. That was my impression.

Another time he was talking about *Touch of Evil* and that scene when he walks in and how they shot it. They had to dig a hole in the ground to put a camera underneath so his stomach would sort of pop out into the shot like it is now. But we actually were too busy to have time to talk. It was sort of like a rare thing.

When we were shooting at MGM, we had to be there at 6 in the morning. It still was dark. And we would leave at 8 at night or later. And then at his home, there was a lot of night shooting, I remember that mostly. And we were there the whole day. It was sort of like you go home to sleep and wake up again.... After a while, I said, "I don't really need this." I was getting quite tired so it was pretty intense. Gary Graver has amazing energy, that guy. I was very impressed how much work he put into that thing. He was always *on*, I mean, incredible.

[Welles] would sometimes give us instructions directly, but usually we followed Gary Graver's instructions. In other words, he was like an assistant director also. Very rarely did Welles tell us what to do unless it was like operating one of his handheld projectors in that scene I told you or the mirror or what have you. Then he would directly tell you, "Hey, do this, move it here," and so forth, but he did very little direction of the crew. Graver, as I remember, was the one who did it.

Before leaving, Herba also worked for Welles as an editor.

FH: I did some editing of some 16mm project. I had nothing to do with its shooting. It's something that Orson was doing, he was narrating. One day, I remember Gary Graver told me, "We need some editors in here." I knew a little bit of editing, I could cut. I came in and there were all these Moviolas in this room, facing the pool, and we were cutting 16, but I can't remember what it was. There were several editors besides me working. Apparently there was a rush because he had to get this out.

The whole period, I'm fond of it, even though it was hard work and I eventually got tired of it. He was kind to us, I must say. When you were an actor he would treat you differently than when you were working on the crew. He was much more likable if you were an actor.

October 13, 2004

Bob Random

Random played the role John Dale, the leading actor in the picture Hannaford is directing in Wind. *Kodar played the leading lady, "The Actress."*
For Random, working with Welles was the high point of his career.

Bob Random: I saw a documentary with Sharon Stone in the last year. She said that she worked her way up through *King Solomon's Mines* (1985) and all those little things. She'd always wanted to work with Scorsese. And then she got *Casino* (1995). And it almost killed her or whatever, but after that she didn't have any more huge wishes. That's what happened to me with Orson. I concentrated on Orson.

I first saw *Citizen Kane* when I was 10 on TV in 1955 in North Vancouver. I had no idea who he was, so I wasn't influenced by anything. But I picked up on the visuals of that movie and never forgot it.

Throughout the '60s, Random appeared in numerous television shows, notably Gunsmoke, *and also some films, including Sydney Pollack's* This Property Is Condemned *(1966) and Budd Boetticher's* A Time for Dying *(1969).*

BR: So I was trying to think, "What do I really want?" I got this and I got that. Orson's magical presence kept coming up to me. I went, "Well, that will be my epitome." I think my other one would be to work with Brando, but looking back I'm glad I didn't! *[Laughter.]* From what I've heard, he wasn't particularly fun. Fun to look at, but not to be with.

The '60s were still in full swing and I was sort of trying to get somewhere, but I was tired of the little TV bag I was in. I'd been working for over a decade. I started going to Hawaii and getting very Zen, as was the habit of the day. I was living in little places in Hawaii and then went back to Hollywood and try to scrounge money and then go back to Hawaii and live for 30 bucks a month.

There was this period where I'd gone back to Vancouver for some reason and lived there for a winter and then come back down to do a TV show. And I got an interview for *The Last Picture Show*. It was very cool because it was just Peter [Bogdanovich] and me. I liked those one-on-ones. Almost immediately, he was kind enough to say, "Well, you're really not right for this, but I'll tell you who recommended you to me." And he said, "Orson Welles." My little mind went, "A-ha." *[Laughter.]*

I was living in this teeny little flat in Ocean Park. In those days, I had no furniture, a turn-table, and a phone to keep in touch with my agent. I answered the phone one day. "Hello, Bob, this is Orson Welles." And, you know, I wasn't that surprised. In my '60s little mind, I thought, "Oh, well, I have summoned this guy just by concentrating on it so much."

So I said, "Oh, hi, Orson." *[Laughs.]* And he is so cool — and always was, every minute. Once I got on the set, people would say, "Oh, Mr. Welles, Mr. Welles ..." And he would always say, "Oh, call me Orson." There he was, this legend, with all these 20-somethings fawning over him, and he was very informal.

He goes, "I want you to be the lead" — or something — "in my new movie." The lead meaning I was the young actor that the old guy, who was coming back to Hollywood after being an expatriate, had hired. So it was a pivotal character. And I didn't even care. He said, "You have the part." Right on the phone in my empty flat.

I went up to his house, carrying a bag of figs and a gallon of carrot juice. *[Laughs.]* I was what they call now a raw food vegan. I didn't eat anything at all. So he made fun of that. He said, "You clutching your macro-biotic treasures." He had a wonderful way of describing things. I didn't mind if he made fun of me at all. I didn't mind anything.

Once I'd been sitting on the set for a while, I did say, "Well, why me?" He had seen me on this *Gunsmoke* that I'd done that summer, which, incidentally and coincidentally, I just saw three weeks ago on the Lone Star Channel in British Columbia. There was this shot where I was playing a harmonica and my hair was curly for some reason, because it's crazy hair and does whatever it wants, and the bottom part of my mouth is covered up because I had the harmonica. I was looking up and it was shot from above — I was sitting on a chair and looking up. For that minute, I looked like him. He had a wider face, but the eyes were very similar. I have a little Indian in me. He's got the Nordic slant.

> *It is interesting to note that it was also on* Gunsmoke *that Welles saw Dennis Weaver. He was such a fan that he cast Weaver as the motel clerk in* Touch of Evil.[2]

BR: I think that was it. I never asked him to extrapolate or forced him to have conversations or anything. *[Laughs.]* I'd been working for so long on so many things that I knew that the name of the game on a set was just waiting. I was good at it. I could wait *forever* and not necessarily have a conversation or need to know what was going on. I was just happy to be in his presence on his set, a tremendous feather in my cap for the rest of my life.

It began as a non-union picture. The subject of coin came up immediately. "I can only afford to pay you $10,000." If he'd said nothing, I would have said fine. "But I can only give you $2,000 at the beginning." He said,

"You're going to be on a motorcycle. Don't worry, we'll get you a scooter, a Honda or something." And he gave me the check for two grand.

Throughout his scenes in The Other Side of the Wind, *Random is seen on a motorcycle, presumably following the girl played by Kodar.*

BR: Well, I immediately went down to the Triumph place where I'd had a motorcycle years before, where Steve McQueen used to get his. I bought a Triumph because I wasn't going to be in Orson's movie on a Honda. Typical movie thing. Although everyone in *The Wild One* (1953) drove a Harley, Brando drove a Triumph.

So I purposefully blew the whole two thousand on this motorcycle. The next day I went to his house and drove up on the motorcycle. I said, "You don't have to buy me one. This is mine." I didn't say that I'd bought it. *[Laughter.]*

Random shot his scenes over a three month period lasting from September to December 1970.

BR: The first day of shooting was we were supposed to go to the destruction derby, which is now monster trucks and all that. But it used to be

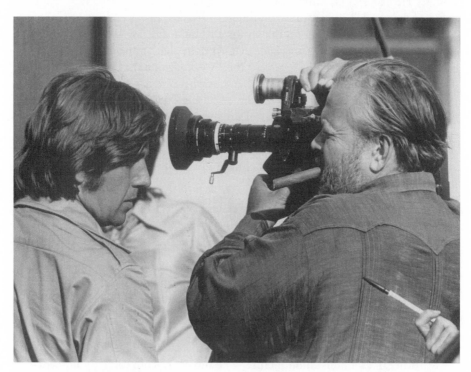

Graver and Welles shooting scenes in Los Angeles for *The Other Side of the Wind* (photograph © Michael Ferris).

different. They just mashed cars into each other, like the coliseum — stupid. I'd never been to one before or since, but I showed up at this destruction derby. Orson said, "Look for my cameraman, Gary Graver." I didn't know what Gary Graver looked like, he didn't know what I looked like, I don't think, but somehow we found each other. But Orson wasn't there. He couldn't make it. So the first day of shooting he wasn't there. *[Laughs.]* So Gary's got the Arriflex and takes some pictures of the destruction derby and then takes some pictures of me supposedly reacting and walking around. It was very strange. There was nothing to it. There was no content. After a couple of hours, we went home.

As Felipe Herba told me, Welles shot in Century City as it was being built.

BR: So he was able to get futuristic mirrored skyscrapers in 1970 — and no people in his way and nobody questioning him and no permit. The crew was like five people and the truck was small. All my stuff was shot MOS.[3] So there was no need for big blimps and covers. There was a sound guy, but I think it was just for guidance.

I remember being out there in Century City one time and he had me dressed in this denim outfit. He wanted this generic outfit, so it was kind of like Ralph Lauren. Denim shirt, denim pants, and kind of used and worn — and I had those. And then some raincoat, to make it look like I was wearing a cape. Probably to make me look like him or something.

He did to me what he had done to Rita [Hayworth], which I didn't know.[4] My hair at the time was very dark brown. He wanted it to be blonde. Whatever you see in that film is blonde highlights basically, by his request. So I went to the Pacific Palisades for some reason because I used to live out by the beach. I figured they had the richest women and I'd get the best 'do. So I'm sitting in there with all the women, the ladies, with the tinfoil on my head, under the hairdryer, with a magazine. *[Laughs.]* I'm this 25 year old *guy* with a motorcycle and it just was not normal.

Oja was great. I remember this one thing. She was so cool. I was sensitive to the way I looked. I wasn't really saying much — or anything. So I figured, "It's Orson and he did describe that he wanted the movie-within-the-movie to look really spectacular and perfect." The other thing is going to be cinéma vérité. One day, I get on the bike and I was at the beach and he's in Bel Air. I get there with the blonde hair and the locks and everything. Oja was from behind the Iron Curtain, so that made it even more international and juicy and interesting in every way. She was a woman of very few words. She didn't go on and on. She had a lovely stern-ness about her and she was like Garbo in *Ninotchka* (1939). I got there that one day and the first thing she said to me, just off-the-cuff, no schmooze, was, "You look like a god." I went, "Oh, this is good. This is what I'm shooting for."

The next day, I get on the bike again, maybe I put a helmet on or my hair was tangled, but I get to the set and find my place, mill around, talk to Orson. Oja comes over and says, "You look like a boob." Within one day! *[Laughter.]*

Here's what it mostly was: "Okay, Bob, stand over there." "No, back a little bit." "No, over there." "Okay, roll." "Okay, Bob, now look around, you're a little agitated and you're looking for the girl. Remember you've just followed her." But, of course, I hadn't because we hadn't shot that yet. "Okay, walk over to the door to the building." "Okay, cut." This went on and on and on. "Okay, now you see the girl. Go after her. Courageously now, Bob. Okay, all right, cut."

Of course, I took editing as part of my curriculum at UCLA Film School and I knew about Orson's methods. Nothing fazed me at all because I'm a director's actor, always was. I never saw a script. There was no script. I didn't care. He could have told me to stand on my head, anything.

Much of the time was taken where he'd just get one of these accidental ideas and then the crew would spend half a day building whatever ridiculous thing or holding things in such a way that he would get the visual that he wanted. For the three months that I was there, a lot of it was in his house, him stalking around in his jammies. It was sort of like living in his house, which was great. $35,000 Arriflexes on the floor. It was remarkably hip. *[Laughter.]*

I do know, by the way, that he had an entire roast turkey for lunch — I saw that. He drank lots of wine, as I remember. He smoked many cigars, as I remember, almost constantly. Cigarettes, too, and took lots of pain killers, over the counter — Nyquil and stuff like that. I think he had gout or something, whatever he had, and he had a cold for a while. And 20 cups of coffee a day. I was counting because I was like this vegan guy. And here was this otherworldly person, consuming mass quantities like a Conehead. *[Laughter.]* He never got drunk, nothing affected him, he just kept going.

I remember once he said, "Okay, Bob, now I'll see you tomorrow at 5:00 A.M." He could have said anything. He could have said, "Sleep on the floor. I'll wake you up." So at 5:00 A.M., I show up on my motorcycle in Bel Air in complete pitch black. There's no crew truck, there's no crew, there's no lights on, there's nothing. It was impossible for me to remember him wrong. I knew it was the next day and it was 5:00 A.M. So I went, "What the hell?" I went up to the front door and knocked on the door. Nothing. Nothing. Knocking and ringing the door bell. Finally I hear in the background, "*Who is it? Who's there?*" Finally, the door opens and there he is, just huge, right out of bed, big black jammies, looking like he's still asleep. His eyes rolled up in his head, hardly able to focus on me. *"Oh!* Oh, Bob, yeah, come on in!"

And then Oja got up and they started to mill around. I'm still sitting there. Then they called Gary and the crew. I don't know if they knew that they were going to come or if their call was later. But he completely forgot. So that was a lovely moment.

> When it came to accidents, Welles "knew what to do with them when they happened," a crew member on Wind, Michael Ferris, told me. Welles also expressed his views on them to Random.

BR: He said, "If there's any talent to being a director, which I *doubt,* it is the ability to take advantage of accidents, things that happen."

As the movie progressed, in the three months, I guess one of the accidents he took advantage of was that we [Random and Kodar] were both willing to take our clothes off. So it became less and less clothes. When they were ready to shoot, he'd go, "Okay, everybody. Pants off, Bob." Literally.

I didn't care. I'm in this European Orson movie taking off my clothes — that's fine, I'm an exhibitionist anyway. I never got to do this on *Gunsmoke,* so let's go.

At some point probably in the last two weeks, he rented MGM Lot One. That's the one that Debbie Reynolds and all those people were so sentimental about when they made *That's Entertainment!* [1974], just before it was all torn down and sold for real estate. He was able to get MGM Lot One for like $200 a day or something, remarkably inexpensive. It all had gone to seed. It was dusty. I even remember tumbleweeds, but I don't even know if that's in my mind or not. It was disheveled, dirty, filthy, ramshackle, falling apart. It'd been *abandoned* for years.

Somehow in that three day thing — and I don't know if this is going to end up in the movie — but Oja and I, more or less separately, end up doing some wandering through this entire MGM lot completely starkers, like we've lost each other. But the impact was surreal for me because MGM was always my favorite studio because they were the classiest.

For me to be in this sort of legendary — and, I didn't know, doomed — lot (which I wanted to preserve, I didn't want everything to turn into casinos and parking lots and junk), walking around with Orson directing me with no clothes on, it was like being Adam. It's like a better version of being Adam. This is Adam 2,000 years later, or 5,000 years later.

Now I was being the actor, so I sort of had to look rested and I didn't have to lug equipment around. But the other guys were lugging equipment around and being the crew. He didn't go take a nap. He was hands-on with the whole thing, holding things, making orders, sitting there thinking up, sort of 24 hours a day, all the time.

Graver and Welles photograph Kodar in *Wind* (photograph © Michael Ferris).

Peter Prescott Tonguette: Did you shoot any scenes outside of the movie-within-the-movie?

BR: I think we shot maybe two takes of me storming into [Hannaford's] house, down the halls, pounding on the bedroom door, because Jake was having an affair with my girlfriend. Or something like that. It never went anywhere because I didn't *have* a girlfriend! *[Laughs.]*

> *Author Joseph McBride wrote that Hannaford "has always been a Don Juan, with a penchant for seducing his leading men's girlfriends."*[5] *But it's impossible for Random to know the full context for this scene, since the role of Hannaford hadn't been cast yet.*

PPT: To the best of your knowledge, was your role finished when you stopped shooting?

BR: To the best of my knowledge, it wasn't done. That was another Orson-ism. We started in September and as I said I had chosen to spend dry time and hiatuses in Hawaii. I was from a forest and I didn't want to go back to North Van.

Consequently, I generally had a sun tan. So in the ensuing time, getting into late December, a sun tan fades even in L.A. He said, "Okay, Bob, you go to Hawaii and get your tan back and then we'll finish." It was sort of almost like, "We'll finish the movie." I still don't know anything, but I'm going, "That's fine." So I went to Lahaina for two weeks, ran into a bunch of windstorms, but managed to get some color, came back, called Orson, and the phone was disconnected. And that was it. *[Laughs.]* He was gone.

So I waited for a month or so. But it was typical. I knew enough about him to know that he was quite mad in that way and that he would change on a dime. I don't think I minded, but I was completely in the dark. Somehow I got a hold of Gary. "Oh, he's in Europe now shooting with Marlene Dietrich or Mercedes McCambridge or all these European people," hypothetically. Finally, through skillful husbandry, I managed to get his telephone number in France. I don't know how I did it, but through the grapevine and film guys like you, I *slowly* extracted this treasure. That was difficult.

I call this number in France from whatever little flat I'm living in. I asked for Orson Welles. And I hear the secretary say, "Orson, there's a call for you." I hear in the background, *"Who is it?"* I said, "Well, it's just urgent that I speak to him." *"Who is it?"* I said, "If you would just have him come to the phone." I didn't tell them who it was. I could hear his voice getting louder as he walked towards the phone. His curiosity was piqued or something. He says, "Hello?" I go, "Hi, Orson, this is Bob ..." I started a little sentence and he goes, "Oh! Good to hear from you. Busy, Bob." Click. *[Laughter.]*

Two years passed.

BR: Now I'm married to this thing which was sort of like my *Casino*. I don't know what's happening and really nothing else is going on in my career. In fact, while we were shooting he told me, "Don't tell anybody about this." So I didn't tell anybody *ever* for years.

I found out that Orson was in fact back in Bel Air and he was shooting more of the party scene. There was an open extras casting for this mysterious Orson Welles movie that I got wind of. I showed up in a gaggle of stubbly extras and stood there for the entire day's shooting hidden from him — on purpose, because I'm dramatic too. Then when it was over and everybody signed their voucher and started to filter out and all these people left his house, there was nobody left but me standing there, looking at him. *[Laughs.]* I'm standing there with my arms folded, like "What's going on?" He holds out his big, huge arms and gives me this great big, huge hug. "Oh, Bob, so good to see you ... Yes, we're still making it and it won't be long ..." I was completely diffused at that point. I got this sweetness because he was so good.

So I was satisfied and went home and never heard from him again. *[Laughter.]*

February 25, 2005

Curtis Harrington

Harrington, director of such visually brilliant films as Night Tide *(1961) and* What's the Matter with Helen? *(1971), appeared as himself in the birthday party scene in* Wind. *His first encounter with Welles, however, was during the shooting of another scene in the film: the sex scene from Hannaford's film which featured John Dale (Bob Random) and "The Actress" (Oja Kodar). It took place in a car.*

Curtis Harrington: Well, the driver of the car in that sequence is my friend Robert Aiken. So I said to Robert, "Oh, God, I'd love to watch Orson work." They were shooting that sequence in what is called poor man's process. In other words, that car wasn't even moving. It was just jiggled and had water being sprayed on it for rain. And then there were lights that kept turning. It's an effect. That's how they were doing it, at a top of a hill where Orson was living at the time in the Beverly Hills area.

So a friend and I climbed up the side of the hill, just to peek; Robert had told us where they would be. And I can't quite remember how, but at some point we were discovered. *[Laughs.]* And it was all very embarrassing. But because I was a friend of Gary Graver's, instead of being told to go away, we were welcomed, and Orson said, "We need someone else on a light. Will you work on one of the lights?" So the next thing I knew, I was on the crew doing one of those turning lights to give the effect of lights going by as the car moves along.

Peter Prescott Tonguette: Had you ever met Welles before?

CH: Well, the first time I met Welles was when Gary invited me to join the two of them for dinner. So I'd had dinner with Mr. Welles. But that's the only contact I'd had with him, that one dinner.

In regard to my appearance in *The Other Side of the Wind*, it happened mainly through Gary, but Orson wanted me. There is a sequence in the film where the John Huston character interviews a number of younger directors at a party, in the big party sequence. And I'm one of the directors.

He was interviewing me as myself. And at that time, John Huston had still not been cast. So, in the curious way that Orson had been shooting in those days, he'd shoot one side of a scene and he played the John Huston part off-screen while he was shooting me. Then, eventually, when he found someone to play the role — which he finally found in Huston — then the other side of it would be shot and then it would be intercut.

So the night that he did that scene with me, interviewing me, playing the John Huston part off-screen and directing me, was the very night before I started to shoot *What's the Matter with Helen?* Ordinarily, I wouldn't have thought of doing anything like that on the night before my very first day of shooting. But it was such a privilege and honor for me, and I was so flattered that Orson wanted to do it. And it was the only time [Welles could shoot the scene], really, so I agreed to it.

I remember that evening, I told him that I had engaged Michael MacLiamoir to appear in *What's the Matter with Helen?* and he was very pleased. He mentioned "dear Michael" and how much he loved him.

When I was shooting *What's the Matter with Helen?,* whenever Michael was working, I had two lunches brought to me in my dressing room trailer (or, when we were at the studio, I had a little room), so we could have lunch together.

PPT: I imagine he had a lot of stories.

CH: He did indeed. I wish I could remember them all. I didn't write them down.

I admired Welles deeply. When I've watched his films, I often studied how he shoots and cuts very carefully. I've tried to duplicate that at moments in some of my films.

I wasn't in the Welles circle, as it were; I wasn't close to Welles, like Peter Bogdanovich was. In his later years, Welles was in the habit of having lunch every day at a restaurant called Ma Maison in Beverly Hills on Melrose Avenue. I also ate lunch there often in those days. Welles always ate inside and often he would be in a corner with Peter Bogdanovich or whomever. He dined there virtually every day and so sometimes he would be eating alone. Always inside. I always ate outside. It had a garden area outside and I liked that the best, so that's where I always ate. But Welles always ate inside, possibly to avoid the crowds staring at him and so on.

Anyway, so one day I had to go to the men's room inside. I would not have had the temerity — even though I had met him — to interrupt his lunch. It was just not my nature because I consider that to be rude. So I was coming back from the men's room and walking past his table, but at some distance from it. And suddenly the great voice boomed out, "Curtis!" *[Laughs.]* I said, "Yes, Orson?" He said, "Come here." So I went over to his table. He was sitting, having lunch alone. He said, "Now Curtis. When you come to Ma Maison to have lunch, I expect you to come to my table and say hello to me." Of course, I was deeply flattered. I said, "Well, thank you. I would love to do that and I will!" So from that moment on, whenever I saw him there, even when he was with other people, I always made that effort, to go to the table and say hello. He was always very gracious towards me. I think that gives a wonderful insight to the sort of person he was. His generosity of spirit.

I just wanted to tell you this wonderful story about our very last meeting, just a few days before he died. I was in the restaurant to have lunch. And I had some kind of an appointment with somebody. So I was all dressed up. I had a coat and a tie and you know. So he was in the corner table with Peter and two or three other people. But, as usual, I went over to the table to say hello to him. And I can tell you exactly what he said to me. He looked up at me and he said, "Don't you look splendid!" And it was so nice, you know. My last words to him, in return, which I also remember, were, "You look pretty splendid yourself, Orson."

Isn't that a nice good-bye?

He was a great man. I think there is absolutely no doubt about that. And the fact that he had such a hard time keeping it together in later life is very, very, very sad. But he couldn't really get any proper backing. And it's very hard to make films with no money. I just made one called *Usher* (2002) and I know how difficult that is.

Obviously, he was indulgent. He ate too much, he drank too much — I don't mean that he was a drunkard, but he loved his wine with his meals. He was overweight and got more and more and more overweight. And I think on that level, he was never able to discipline himself. Also, I think he did have a complex about finishing things. I wouldn't presume to do an amateur psychological analysis of his fear of completion, but I think that it did exist. In some ways, I suspect that it was because of that overwhelming success and brilliance of his beginning work. My theory — and it's only a theory — is that weighed on him as time went by. And he wanted to create, he wanted to keep working, but at the same time, I think he realized — in fact, I know he realized—that a great deal of what he was doing was not up to his own standards. And what better way to cut that off than to be unable to complete it?

I've seen now all this footage of *Dead Calm*[6] and I think it's very poor. It's no wonder that he didn't want to finish that film.

But I would love to see *The Other Side of the Wind* completed. It has all kinds of brilliance in it, and I think the whole idea of the film within the film is very fascinating. And the difference in style of the two.

I remember that first dinner with him was very amusing for me. He spent most of the evening talking about the Irish theatre. And, as you know, I got to know Michael MacLiamoir and his partner, Hilton Edwards, very well. And I did ask them about the story of Welles coming to their theatre in Dublin and announcing that he was a well-known American actor. *[Laughs.]* I said, "Did you really believe that?" Michael said, "Oh no, we didn't believe that for a minute. But we let him think that we believed it. And we also thought that he was absolutely brilliant and we wanted to put him in a play right away."

April 28, 2004

R. Michael Stringer

R. Michael Stringer: I was an actor with him, I was a key grip, I was a chief lighting technician, I did sound at some points, and I operated the camera. Over the years, the relationship matured and towards the end, if Gary Graver was not available, Orson would call me and I would go shoot an interview or some portion of one of the many projects we did.

Early in 1970, I was working with Gary Graver as his assistant cameraman on a little, low budget, non-union feature. He came to work on the second day of the show and said to me, "Michael, Orson just telexed me. I phoned him back and he wants me to come to Paris to meet with him; I have to leave in the morning. Do you think you could take over shooting this picture for me? I'll lend you my light meter." I said, "Sure, I can do it," but I was terrified at the prospect of lensing my first film. Graver left the next morning and met with Orson Welles, and within a few months, Orson had come here, rented a house, and we started filming *The Other Side of the Wind*. The first few days, it was just Gary Graver and myself working with Mr. Welles. I let it be known that we really needed some manpower to help out, and that I couldn't be expected to do all of the tasks that needed doing by myself. So I would hire this person or that person to come in and help out. After a while, you realized that whoever comes in to work with this "master of the cinema" must truly be a dedicated film person himself. One couldn't arrive for work just because he wanted to meet Orson Welles, or come in to work so that he could say that he had worked with the film legend. Orson could sniff out that kind of character, he would brutalize that person without mercy. *[Laughs.]* He was very capable of being quite ruthless verbally. But then on the other hand he had the absolute princely generosity, and was gracious beyond words. So how one was treated depended on mood or circumstances surrounding any specific event.

Like Graver, Stringer was practically "on call" for Welles.

RMS: We (Graver and I) made a joke about that very thing. We would get a call, a VISTOW alert — Volunteers in Service to Orson Welles. Gary would call and say, "Michael, VISTOW alert!" I would make some calls and a small group of cineastes (*pronounced: cine-ass-ts*) would show up for work.

We did some very long days, and they were all flat rates. Whatever the market could bear is what we earned for that day. The money was coming out of Orson's pocket, so Gary would say, "You can't ask for that much." The rates escalated over the 15 years. I'd make $50 a day, $100 a day. I remember — painfully remember — that when my rate went to $150 a day, Orson *flipped. "My God, he wants how much?"* Like I said, these were flat rates for unlimited commitments. We worked anywhere from 14 to 18 [hours a day]. Sometimes we did very long days, 20-hour days more than once. Once in a while we'd show up and just sit around for four or five hours, hiding out while Orson would walk through the house puttering around. Finally, Gary would come up to me and say, "Go home. He doesn't want to shoot today."

Some of my greatest memories surround events with Orson and his personal friends. When Mercedes McCambridge showed up one day to work, or the time we visited Joseph Cotten in his home, or when Paul Stewart and Edmond O'Brien arrived — these people came when Orson called. They worked with us, laughed with us, ate with us, and were there until the last dog was dead. Each of these Hollywood film stars adored Orson Welles personally, and they relished any chance to share old school stories about his early exploits and naughty behavior. They thanked Orson for remembering them, and thanked those of us on the crew for our support of him. When their portion of the project had ended and they departed, we all realized that we were the better for the experience — those were really the gems, the real memories. Mercedes was so much fun. She said, "Ah, that son of a bitch. Let me tell you what he did to me." This is in reference to *Touch of Evil.*[7] She said, "I get this phone call, this cold phone call, from Orson. 'My God it was wonderful to hear you, Orson.' He says, 'Mercy, come, let's have some lunch.' 'Okay, that'd be grand.' 'Do you still have that black leather jacket?' Orson asked. 'Bring it.' 'All right.'" So she shows up at lunch with this black leather jacket. They dined together and laughed, when finally he asked, "Want to do this little

From Left to Right: Cameron Mitchell, Paul Stewart, Mercedes McCambridge, and Welles, conferring before filming a scene in *The Other Side of the Wind* (photograph © Michael Ferris).

scene with me?" So that's how he got her to come in and do the hard female thing. She just loved Orson. She would do anything for him.

I learned from Orson my set etiquette, to allow the actors their complete space, never to interrupt, don't make eye contact — just courtesies. "Don't whistle on the stage, it's bad luck." He explained all of these superstitions. He was a very superstitious man. Oja Kodar said, "Well, life would be very boring without superstitions." He respected the *essence* of what the superstition was. You don't walk under a ladder because you *could* get hurt. Never put a hat on a bed. "Oh my God, it's bad luck." Well, of course it's bad luck — someone could sit on it and you'd ruin your hat. He understood the birth of these superstitions. Superstitions were likened to mythology to him.

He had several little idiosyncrasies and quirks. There was a period where he didn't like sunsets, like the transition time from day to night. He would go into his room and nap. We would sit there and wonder what's going on. Gary would kind of say *[in a quiet voice]*, "He's taking a nap." We would have to occupy ourselves for two hours and then he would get up and we would work for another eight hours. *[Laughs.]*

I was a dolly grip for a while. And doing handheld camera as a dolly grip, you support the camera operator. You are their eyes when they are walking backwards. They are completely in tunnel vision and as they are walking backwards, you guide them, you direct them, and you move them. And when you're shooting and you have young knees and all, the operator will bend at the knees and go down really low and sit there for a while and then he'll have to stand up and move again. So as the grip for the camera that's moving, I would tend to grab the waist of the operator. As he went down, I would take some of his own weight so that his knees don't get fatigued and he shakes. As he stands up again, I assist with some of his weight. You learn to work with your camera operator.

I remembered the first time I realized just how big Orson was — I don't mean heavy, but I mean *big in stature*—when he was operating. Just out of instinct, I immediately got behind him in case he moved. I would keep him from tripping or going down a step or something. I put my hands on his waist. The thing I noticed first off was, "My God, he's huge!" He was so tall — I don't know, well over 6 feet — he towered over me. I was never in that proximity with the great man before; that is, in someone's personal space, and you never really get in a person's personal space. So if you're a few feet away from them, you're still looking eye to eye even if you're looking up a little bit. But if you're inside their space, the man towered over me head and shoulders. I thought I'd steady him and I realized, "This man is not moving. He is rock steady." The camera looked like a little toy up to his face. He cut, then he turned and looked at me and said, "Michael, please don't do that." *[Laughter.]* We sometimes referred to him as Awesome Welles.

One of my favorite memories working with Mr. Welles happened one day in June sometime in the Seventies. Orson wanted to share his favorite holiday with his extended film family, so he invited us for a Thanksgiving dinner after some shooting he had in mind for *The Other Side of the Wind.* We began working at eight o'clock sharp; Orson was a stickler about tardiness. We plodded through each handcrafted shot, massaging to perfection every angle the audience was to see. As happens during a day of shooting, the task of making a movie tends to frustrate those involved. As frustration mounts, the tensions build, tempers flare, and (violà) a typical day of filmmaking has begun. If music sooths the savage beast, then what can one say of the smell of fine cooking. As the day progressed and the house filled with the aroma of the feast to come, a calm settled over a normally chaotic atmosphere and we laughed more often than usual as we worked each set up. Around 3 o'clock that afternoon, with table set, Orson announced, "Dinner is served." It was a marvelous sharing of fine food, great stories, and good companionship. Mr. Welles held court that afternoon with his captivating charm and incredibly sharp wit.

May 5, 2004

Michael Ferris

Michael Ferris: When I was four-and-a-half I sat on my mother's knee and saw my first movie. I was what was known in that era as a "navy brat." We were at an open air theatre in Key West, Florida, where my father was stationed. It was the kind of a thing a kid doesn't forget. The air was thick, warm and balmy, the sun had set and darkness was slowly stealing the day. These theatres were common to the navy bases at the time. The screen was made out of plaster with matching benches and chairs. People would also bring their own fold-up chairs and sit wherever convenient. You'd sit there out in the open, having a wonderful experience even before the movie started. There was an anticipation when a movie is about to begin and there was mystery in the air.

The movie comes on. I had no idea what it was about but it was in black-and-white and I am quickly hypnotized by its images. The film was *Lady from Shanghai* [1947], as I find out later on in life, and I was hooked. I am not smart enough to explain the psychology of that time except to say that from that memory on, movies have always been a part of my life in an important determining fashion, something I wanted to become a part of.

It's funny because when you're young you have no idea what it means to become a part of something unless it's a boy scout troop or a baseball game, but for me growing up to "be in the movies" became something real, something I verbalized; not just a dream but was something I carried with me throughout my formative school years. People would look at me and say, "What do you want to do when you grow up?" I said, "I'm going to be in the movie business" or "I'm going to make movies" or "I'm going to go to Hollywood."

I grew up, went to college, did all the things expected of me. I was a kid in the '40s, grew up in the '50s, '60s, and saw everything. Movies were how I learned about life: what adults were, why they did the things they did, and about dreams. I went into the service, spent four years in the air force, got out, lived in New York City, purposefully picking work that was un-involving. I worked on Wall Street at a job I had absolutely no interest in. I gave them a day's work and they paid me a salary.

I had connections from my experiences living in a wealthy suburb of New York. I could have worked at CBS News or a number of places that would have interested me, but I consciously avoided those. After two years I said, "It's time." In 1970 I packed up, quit my job and left for California.

I met Michael Stringer and became instant friends. From my friendship with Mike Stringer came everything else. Mike was the person that brought me to meet and work with Gary Graver, which led to meeting Orson. Stringer was essential to any success in this business I have ever had, and he's the kind of blessed friend that you keep forever if you're lucky.

I met Gary within the first month or two. He and Stringer were making low budget movies, little action pictures that they'd been doing a while. I became a part of that group. All I did was support them. I put stands on the ground, lifted equipment, did anything I could to be useful. That kind of grew. I was also a full-on film buff with a very strong memory for films and a fascination for it and a film scholar. Gary and I started to match movie memories and trivia and it became clear we were both encyclopedic about movies. That was probably one of the strongest things that drew us together, because we clearly saw in each other a real love of movies. I would come up with the names of actors in little obscure films — and he'd name the cast and crew and describe the film's themes.

Now it's 1970, which is when Orson began *The Other Side of the Wind*. Gary was Orson's cameraman, but shooting hadn't gotten into full swing yet. I was living in a little kitchenette, a room the size of two closets, it was March, the phone rang. Gary and Stringer had been in Arizona, in Phoenix, working with Orson for a while. I had just been kicking around, trying to do what film work I could find. I had worked on a few films with them prior to their leaving. They called and they said, "Can you come out here?" "Yup." *[Laughs.]* I think I got [that call] at night and the next morning I left. I pulled in to Orson's and immediately went to work.

I was just stunned by the fact that I was going to be working around Orson Welles. But not so stunned that I didn't move rapidly to accept the invitation. Very quickly I found out that you didn't work around him. You worked *with* him. His style was literally hands-on. And over my career — which is 35 years now — some of the greatest cameramen, directors that I've worked with all get deeply involved. They are totally hands-on. Directors will come onto the set and pace out the movement of the actors with them or they'll direct the scene from right next to the camera. A big shift in the business in the last ten years is to find everyone glued to the monitor. It's comfortable, easy, and you see literally what you're going to get. For today's film-makers it is the place to be. It's part of the TV generation of making movies. All the greats, John Ford, Alfred Hitchcock, William Wyler, Orson Welles — we've all seen the books and the pictures — they're standing next to the camera or they're seated next to the camera, watching the performers speak their lines as if they're watching a play live. I like to describe my meeting Orson as, "I got the call at night, the next day I was in the middle of the desert, on one side of the camera lens with Orson on the other side of the camera lens, throwing dirt at me and yelling at me to throw it harder and faster in front of the lens at him." Literally! He was on his hands and knees. The camera was low, he was creating some kind of a storm. We were throwing dirt and dust and little twigs, anything we could in front of the lens to make this action. That was my first exposure to Orson Welles. *[Laughs.]* It was quite something because he was so down to earth. Involved in the moment and sharing with you whether he had known you for years or minutes. He was funny and loved what he was doing. This playful quality made him laugh and you could feel the joy he felt in what he was doing. I always thought that this made him, in some nonliteral way, light on his feet. His humor made him in some way more physically nimble despite his larger-than-life size.

Like Stringer — who told me, "I was an actor with him, I was a key grip, I was a chief lighting technician, I did sound at some points, I operated camera" — Ferris wore many hats when he worked with Welles.

MF: At that point I was utterly green about filmmaking. I had a vague sense of where I was going when I met Orson. That everything revolved around the camera and that seemed like the place for me to be. It didn't take me long to decide for myself that my personality belonged somewhere in that realm.

So with Orson I was a cameraman — not first, not last, but I was a cameraman because of my association with Gary. He was hugely generous and helpful to me. You couldn't get into the union, it was a closed door. Fortunately, there was a huge, very active, and very productive non-union industry in those days. And Gary and Michael Stringer made me a part of that. I was a grip, I was an electrician, I was a prop boy, I was whatever was needed for Orson. When we were in the desert Orson needed a car to get around in, but he didn't fit in most cars. So we went shopping. I think Frank Marshall or Gary or Stringer or somebody found this Chrysler convertible with this huge backseat. An old one. You remember in the '50s they made cars large. It was maybe a '60s Chrysler convertible and we bought that thing. That's where Orson traveled, with the top down, he took up the entire backseat. We used it for lots of other things too, but it was most practical for transporting Orson. That was an example of the kind of things we would do.

One of the memories I have was after I got to know Orson well (which took a little time), he would use everyone else's name according to what he wanted done. As Gary was our leader I remember you'd hear from the other room, as he would be talking to Gary, Orson would instruct Gary as to the rest of us. Orson would say to him, "Have Polly draw this schematic." "Send Glenn to find that antique door." "Give that job to Michael Ferris. It's something he'll do well." So he had a read on people's personalities. He used that.

I remember I was on my way to do an errand once when I got into this truck which was parked too close to the garage. It was a stick shift, an old pickup, perfect for the desert, and as I put it into gear instead of going backward, it went forward. It punched a hole in the wall of the garage. *[Laughs.]* Well, that was a big deal because we had to spend money to fix this leased house. Nobody made a big issue of it. Certainly not Orson. He took it in stride. He knew we were giving him the only thing we could give, our time and selves. It was very special.

We were all working for free, yes, but I always thought Orson recognized in all of us a strong and youthful commitment to film and especially to him and he appreciated it, in his own way.

Ferris was to meet his future wife on The Other Side of the Wind.

MF: Orson was out in Cave Creek, which was a 25 mile ride from Scottsdale and Phoenix proper. You drove through the desert — nothing but saguaro cactus and rocks and old dead Apache bones. *[Laughs.]* You'd get out to his house. I don't know if you ever saw *Zabriskie Point* (1970), but when they blow up the house that's the beginning of where Orson's house was. Those rocks carry on and further down into those rocks was Orson's house, built into the boulders, very dramatic.

We would drive from Scottsdale, where we lived in a motel, in the morning to Orson and then back at night. Often, because Orson was an insomniac, we'd get called in the middle of the night, and go running out. So we were there at all odd hours, but by and large we had a routine of breakfast in the morning at the local Coco's Restaurant and then out there to work and back for dinner, depending on Orson's requirements. There were a group of girls and some guys there from the local high school who had heard that there was an Orson Welles movie being made. They just started to hang around and we got to know them.

Orson heard about our social club and one day said, "Invite all your friends, tell them to dress up for a party, and have them come out at 7 o'clock on Thursday night and we'll shoot it for the beginning of the party sequence." So that's exactly what happened.[8]

I'll always remember, I was loading an Arri IIC, a handheld camera that belonged to Gary. I was busy in the living room when this beautiful woman came walking into the room, totally dressed for a party. I tripped my way over the furniture getting across the room to initiate a conversation. That is how I met my wife. Thank you, Orson! And that is how the party sequence came to be. The word had spread and there were a lot of people that were excited to be a part of Orson's movie. That's the way Orson worked. There were no releases signed or extras paid or anything like that.

The script was Orson's and meant to be followed, but if he saw something that fell into place or was extraordinary and felt right, of course he would go with it. There was something we were doing with a couple of actors. I forget what it was, but there was crockery involved. Gary was shooting past Orson. Orson wasn't part of it, he was just there directing. Something happened and they spilled a cup or dropped it and broke a cup. Gary let the camera go and then Orson said, "Cut." Gary said, "Look, we can set this up real fast to re-do that because I know you hadn't planned." Orson said, "Oh, no, no, Gary, that's a wonderful thing that happened. Let's leave that. I want to see what the critics are going to make of that in 20 years." *[Laughter.]* And, of course, accidents occur in life and in movies, which are part of life, all the time. Orson knew what to do with them when they happened.

I spent a lot of years — all of the '70s — working with John Cassavetes, and I watched him do that all the time. He set it up. Every one always says that Cassavetes's movies are all improvised. *A Woman Under the Influence* (1974) is a script of 250 pages. It's all written. He would set things up so that when actors were a little helpless or didn't quite know what to do, he used that and wanted to see them kind of paw around to find the right foothold, verbally and emotionally. He was searching for an unscripted bit of humanity that could not be predicted. If they got the words right, fine, but if they added or subtracted their own words and got the feeling he was after, then that was better. Orson was absolutely of the same mind.

You don't work through a day waiting for accidents to happen, you just keep working and they occur along the way.

Orson and Gary would talk, Gary would disseminate information to the rest of us. "We're going to put the camera over here, you be over there." We brought in a couple other cameramen from L.A. One in particular was David Nowell, who is now a very successful director of photography. Another was Bill Weaver, a documentary cameraman who was very good at his job. We shot every format there was. We shot 8mm, 16mm, and we shot 35mm. We didn't shoot 70, but he would've if he could've afforded it. 70mm is so expensive.

Orson was waiting for the release of a camera called the Éclair XL5, but it was new and it had been much anticipated. It arrived while we were shooting. It came out of its case and we gave it to Orson. What was great about it was that it was the size of a video camera, but it's a film camera —16mm — and very compact. We started shooting. Orson sat in his overstuffed chair, in his pajamas and terrycloth robe, and he photographed while we photographed.

We moved around, we got different angles, we shot, say, two or three other cameras, we would try not to do the traditional Hollywood style, which was you shoot, you cut, you shoot again, you change angles, you relight, you shoot again. Everything was lit and we shot documentary style. Orson never moved. He pointed in different directions, but never moved. It had a zoom and an on-and-off switch. And a battery that kept the camera running.

When you saw his footage, it was cut — in the camera. So he had a mastery of the camera quite unlike anybody I've ever seen! The point is he never moved, he didn't get up or change positions as we did, no changed angles or relit scenes. He zoomed, he found this and he found that, but his footage was phenomenal.

Peter Prescott Tonguette: How did you have the opportunity to see the footage? Were there dailies?

MF: There were dailies, simply not on a regular basis. I got to see them because I was with Gary a lot. Some in L.A. There were no formal dailies that we saw while we were on location that I recall. I saw them somewhere in Los Angeles.

Orson didn't have problems spending money, but I wouldn't call him profligate. He would do what performing he needed to support his filmmaking. He didn't live a meager lifestyle nor did he live lavishly. When it came to his films, I think that he knew how to use money well. When it came to his own life, he lived well, but didn't choose to live like a king. I thought Orson was adaptable. I'm sure that he could spend money. His cigars cost $25 in an era when a $10 cigar was a major deal. He didn't deprive himself in that area. *[Laughs.]*

The stuff that we built for the set out in the desert [was] all hand built by us or Orson would design them. They were made out of chicken wire and canvas coverings and parallels. There wasn't a major company building that stuff. There weren't carpenters building for months as the studios do it. They were built by us. We were in the process of using all of it.

Who was it — Napoleon? — who said that when his generals would bring other generals to him to be interviewed for his staff, he would say, "Do not bring me their resumes. Just bring me the generals who are lucky." And luck is an extraordinary thing and some people have it. Orson had extraordinary luck in the beginning of his career, as we all know, and for whatever reason the gods decided he had had so much luck at such an early age that they were going to take it away for the rest of his life! *[Laughter.]* What happened to Orson in Hollywood may be unfair or deserved, I am no one to judge, but one thing is certain, we're all diminished by not seeing the films he might have made had he the support of the system throughout his career. Imagine what he'd have done with the kind of creative power of a Steven Spielberg or a Jerry Bruckheimer? Spielberg has talent of his own, but to me these are commercial talents, especially Bruckheimer. Bruckheimer is great at what he does — you've heard this before — but if Orson had had a quarter of that access

... because he didn't need the kind of money that most people need. He could do things with tables and chairs that other people would have to spend millions of dollars to do.

I remember him holding forth at a huge dining table with all the actors, Mercedes McCambridge, Cameron Mitchell, Paul Stewart, Norman Foster, John Huston, Peter Jason, and they would talk about old times. I remember being in the next room and just kind of easing up closer to the door or sitting down on the floor if there wasn't a chair — and just listening. And we all would do that. We knew where we were and it was special. Orson's dialogue — you've seen film on him, you've seen him when he's in a natural state — he's a man who never used the word, "Uh." His sentences sprung from his mind fully formed. That's the way he spoke always. And he spoke with a grandeur and an awareness. He certainly was not someone who thought little of himself. He had a grand ego, but in a good sense of the word. I have nothing but good things to say about Orson Welles.

I came there as a volunteer. He didn't know me at all. There were many ways he could have treated me. He treated me like a human being, he treated me well, and with respect. Orson made you feel as though he was drawn to you, in a human sense.

Ferris's involvement in The Other Side of the Wind *lessened after his collaboration with John Cassavetes began.*

MF: What happened to me was that in '72 I met John Cassavetes and he became a direction that I went in — in the way Gary followed Orson. The thing was, there was plenty of time between pictures for me to work with Gary and Orson and I did, but my creative and professional energy was with John. I was on all of the films John Cassavetes made during the '70s. There was a lot of pre-production involved, and as I became a personal friend I was at his house for social occasions and we shot in his house on many of these films. It was a great opportunity and I used it to get Stringer and Graver work on these films. It was the best experience of my film career, working with Orson and John.

January 5, 2005

Rich Little

Little, the renowned celebrity impressionist, was cast by Welles as the young film director named Brooks Otterlake in Wind.

Rich Little: The first time I met him was when I was doing a show called *Copycats* in England, with other impersonators. And he was a guest, on for the week. He arrived one afternoon while we were shooting and he came over to the studio with his black cape on. I hadn't met him at all and I was in the middle of shooting a routine of famous celebrity sneezing. I did Louis Armstrong sneezing, Jimmy Stewart sneezing. It was just kind of a silly bit, but it was funny. Cary Grant sneezing.

I didn't know it, but he was watching me — just out of my view. And he was quite amused by it. Because he was going to be the guest of the week, I said, "And now I'll do Orson Welles sneezing." And Orson just came right on camera, just right next to me, and just looked into the lens with that poker face and said, "I never sneeze." *[Laughter.]* And he walked off.

So he did *Copycats* and we spoofed him. We did a take-off on *War of the Worlds* and all kinds of stuff. He had a great time. We hit it off great and ended up talking about movies and got along great. I thought he was a fabulous storyteller and had total recall of almost everything and knew everybody in the business so you could ask him almost about anybody. He had quite an opinion on everybody, so we got along great.

I guess he was working for the second time on *The Other Side of the Wind,* which I think they started years ago in Spain or somewhere, and never finished the picture, which was typical of Orson. I think there were a lot of pictures not finished. But he was going to shoot it again, or pick up where he left off, and he asked me if I would read the script and would I be interested in playing a part in it. Of course, I jumped at that. I'd never been in a film in my life.

So he said to me, "I'll fly up to Vegas and we'll discuss the part." We picked a certain day he would fly up. He didn't show up, which was typical. *[Laughs.]* And the next day I didn't hear so I thought, "Well, something else came up." So then about a week later he phoned me back and he said, "I'm sorry but I couldn't make it. I was flying up on America West and the seats are just too small for me." So I started chuckling inwardly on that. He said, "I'm driving up." I think he owned a house up here or something. I don't know whether he did at that time or not.

During Little's time on The Other Side of the Wind, *Welles was shooting the picture in the Phoenix area.*

RL: Orson had rented someone's home up there, beautiful home up in the mountains outside of Phoenix. We shot a lot of stuff there. He told the owners, who were going to Europe for the summer, that he'd just like to quietly come up there and write his memoirs by the pool. And then as soon as they'd left, he brought in a whole crew and people and they took walls out. *[Laughs.]* I think they cracked the swimming pool. He just took over. He had a producer who he was yelling at all the time.

But Orson surprised me because he had a marvelous sense of humor. Sometimes you had to be careful because if you really made him laugh, you thought he was going to keel over and die, he was so heavy. His whole face would light up and he'd just roar with laughter. "Take a breath! Take a breath!" He used to walk around with his shoelaces undone. One day I said to him, "You never do up your shoelaces." He said, "I've only been down there twice in my life!" *[Laughs.]*

And then he propped himself up in bed every night and re-write the script. I don't know when he slept. I don't know whether he could lay down or not, but he just propped himself up and would re-write every night. He gave us fresh pages in the morning and then tell us if he wanted boards, which are cue-cards. "It's not an embarrassment if you need the cue-cards"—the "boards" as he called them. Nobody ever used them, but they were always there.

He was charming. The thing that really amazed me about him was, with all his success and everything, he listened to everybody. He wasn't stubborn about anything. If somebody had an opinion, he would listen to them. It was unbelievable. One time he said, "Hold it, everybody. One of the grips has a suggestion." And the guy was so embarrassed! *[Laughs.]* He took suggestions from everybody. Jokingly, one day he said to me, "I listen to everyone because you never know when you might get a great idea from someone. If it wasn't for one of the lighting men in the rafters, I would have named the sleigh in *Citizen Kane* 'Sam.'" Which was totally made up, but it was a funny bit.

Welles seated poolside contemplating script revisions on *The Other Side of the Wind* (photograph © Michael Ferris).

Nobody really understood what the hell it was all about because it would change everyday. I never made a film before and everybody said, "Just do your part and keep your mouth shut." But one day we were having a cocktail party, and the scene was a cocktail party with Mercedes McCambridge and Susan Strasberg, and Norman Foster was there. And we were having this cocktail scene. We shot it and Orson said, "That's a wrap." And then I just happened to say — and everybody looked at me like, "Don't say anything" — but in my naivete I said, "Orson, if this was a cocktail party, wouldn't we be drinking or eating or wouldn't there be trays of drinks or something?" And everybody looked at me. Orson went, "Oh my God, you're right! How could I ever forget such a thing? You're absolutely right!" He went nuts and he got drinks and we had to do the scene over. I mean, a little thing like that he forgot and he was very grateful to me. But it was so obvious. His mind was racing ahead — and sometimes he overlooked things.

The thing that I thought was extremely funny was one day when we were shooting this scene. Everybody went through their dialogue the way we were supposed to. Then we came to the end and we were waiting for "Cut." Orson said, "Look down at your feet in total disgust." And everybody went, "What?" Orson said, "Don't ask any questions! Look down at your feet in total disgust!" So we looked down at our feet, not knowing what the hell this was, in total disgust. "Eww, gosh, oh my God!" He said, "Keep it up! This is excellent!" So we all went, "Ohh, aahh, mmm, God," not knowing what we were doing. Then he said, "Cut! Beautiful! Let's move into the dining room." And everybody just moved into the dining room.

I remember I said, "Norman, what the hell was that?" He said, "Don't even ask." I said, "Don't even ask?" He said, "No, there's some purpose." I said, "I know, but what were we doing? What would be at our feet?" So once again I asked Orson during the break, "What were we doing? Why were we looking at our feet in disgust?" *[Laughs.]* He said, "Midgets running between your legs. I'll put them in later in Spain." "What?" "Midgets running between your legs. I'll put them in later in Spain." And I thought, "Ah-ha. Midgets in Spain running between our legs. For what reason and what the hell does that have to do with us?" But that was all I got from him. We kind of accepted it.

Then as the shooting days progressed, once in a while we'd be in the middle of a scene and he'd yell, "Midgets on the roof!" And we'd look up! I never found out what the midgets was all about. The picture was never completed, so I don't know if there were midgets or not running between your legs or on the roof. But I used to tell this on talk shows, kind of jokingly and lovingly, and Orson said to me later, "Everybody enjoys a good joke and a good story and everything, but I just worry if in telling that story you make me look like an idiot." *[Laughs.]* I wanted to say, "Well ... sorta, but it's too good to refuse." He said, "No, I understand, but there is a reason for the midgets." And then he never told me!

He loved to joke. He would say to me sometimes just before doing a scene, "Do these lines again as Johnny Carson." I said, "*What?*" He said, "Do the lines again as Johnny Carson." I said, "Johnny Carson?" "Yeah, just do the lines"—talking to whoever I was talking to in the scene—"and do them as Johnny Carson." So I did them as Johnny Carson. Then he'd say to me, "All right, now let's do them again and this time do, I don't know, Andy Rooney or Walter Cronkite." "What for?" And then he finally told me why he did that. He was going to submit those scenes to be edited in Spain and when they went to dub it in Spain they would go nuts trying to figure out who this Johnny Carson was or Walter Cronkite was. They wouldn't know who it was and they wouldn't know how to dub it. It was a joke. I guess he got a laugh out of it and gave them the original print, but he thought that was funny. "Who else do you do that's just American?" *[Laughs.]* Just to put some people on. He loved to pull pranks on people and laugh and have a good time. So there was no tension on the set at all.

We started sometimes very early in the morning. For shooting something where he wanted the sun coming up, God, we'd get there at 4 o'clock in the morning. He wanted the sky looking perfect coming up and the light and the reflections on our faces and everything, so he timed it. We had to start shooting at 6:22 for the perfect light. Of course, the way they worked with the crew and everything, we finally shot it at 11 o'clock! "Oh, well," he said, "We'll put a filter on it." *[Laughs.]* So sometimes we started early, sometimes I think we started at about 8 o'clock in the morning. Orson looked like he just woke up, which he probably did, with his shoelaces dangling. It was a very pleasant atmosphere to be in, though, because everybody was in such a good mood and no pressure. If you flubbed a line, no problem. You didn't feel that he was like God, although he sounded like Him.

Peter Prescott Tonguette: What was the actor-director relationship between you and Welles?

RL: Excellent. Excellent. He was so kind with you. "Do it again, I think you can do it better," or "Relax a little more." I remember I did a scene once and we were in a bathroom. John Huston and I were having some conversation in the bathroom. I was very upset in the scene. I remember I was really upset and he was trying to calm me down. We're in this little tiny bathroom and Orson was kind of wedged in the corner with a hand-held camera. We didn't think we could get him out but we did. I think we greased him with butter and pulled him out ... joke.

But anyway he was just complimenting me on how emotional and how convincing that scene I did was and the tears were genuine and I was really upset. I never had the heart to tell him that the reason was that the two of them smoke cigars that you didn't need to put a screen on the camera or anything to tone the light down. The smoke was unbelievable. And the reason I was crying was I was gasping for breath! So it made me look like I was upset. It had nothing to do with acting. He was very complimentary.

I mean, he'd get into the back of a car, a convertible, and shoot us in the front, talking, and I don't know, it'd take him about a half hour to get in the damn car. We were driving along and he was shooting in the back. John Huston said he couldn't drive a car and I said, "What? Let me outta here." We nearly went into the canal. "Don't worry, Rich, if we go into the canal ..." John said, "With Orson in the back, there's no chance to survive. It would be over quick. We'll be sucked down immediately." I said, "I want out of this car." Orson said, "Rich, just think, in Army Archerd's column" — who is a columnist in *Variety* trade paper — "you'll look so good between the two of us. Drowned in a canal in Phoenix, Arizona! John Huston, Rich Little, and Orson Welles. You might even get top billing, so don't complain."

Little remembered John Huston.

RL: That was a thrill to meet him. I didn't know what to expect with him. When Orson introduced me to him, he said, "John, I want you to meet Rich Little. He's probably the world's greatest impressionist." John said, "Oh, well then, we're going to get along *fine*. I have a lot of paintings and that's one of my hobbies and we'll have many great discussions. I'm thrilled." *[Laughter.]* And Orson said, "No, not that kind of impressionist!" I'll never forget that.

It was terrific working with those two. Those two — Orson and John Huston — they just idolized each other and they agreed on almost everything. At lunchtime, I was very privileged to have lunch with them every day. I was amazed at how little Orson ate, so I figured a man of that size has to be eating Ding Dongs and Twinkies all night while he's propped up in bed, because he didn't eat that much during the day.

But they would sit around the breakfast table at lunch break and just start discussing everybody in Hollywood, who they liked and who they didn't like. And I just listened, I didn't say anything. They would discuss Errol Flynn a lot. He was one of their subjects that they'd discuss. I think they were intrigued by his whole lifestyle because he was such a rogue. And then Orson said, "I remember the time, John, when you whipped the tar out of him!" John said, "Not really, Orson. Thank you for that. That's a nice compliment, but I didn't really whip the tar out of him." Apparently they were at a party in Beverly Hills and he and Errol Flynn got into a skirmish. They actually went out onto the front lawn of these people's home and they had a fist fight. John was a heck of a sportsman and a boxer, I guess, and Errol Flynn used to be a boxer too. And they went at it with bare fists. "It was a draw," John said.

But they would go through so many people. *[In Huston's voice:]* "I never liked James Mason!" — kind of out of the blue. And Orson said, "But I did like him in *Odd Man Out*, Carol Reed's movie." John said, "That's right, that was probably his best, but the rest of it ..." And Katie Hepburn — now you'd think Katharine Hepburn, with John Huston and Orson both, would be like number one in their books. But by this time they were saying *[again, in Huston's voice]*, "You know, Katie Hepburn has become a caricature of herself. She's over the top and all the tears and all that, it's too much, you know?" Orson would say, "My thoughts exactly! She's become a *cartoon!*"

Every day I looked forward to lunch time because we'd talk about Charlie Chaplin or we'd talk about Errol Flynn. And I'd just absorb all this. I think now about a lot of things that I would have liked to have asked them both.

At a certain point, however, Little was obligated to leave the production due to a prior commitment. Several years later, Peter Bogdanovich was re-cast as Brooks Otterlake.

RL: We had a wonderful time on that shoot except that I never finished my part. When I went into that, I said to him, "I got three weeks and then I'm committed to do a live show in New Orleans. I've got to be there for it or I'll be sued. So I've got three weeks with you." Well, he was way behind time and the time came up and I said, "Geez, he's not finished with me." I said, "Orson, you know I've got to go. And then I've got another date right behind that." That was our deal. He said, "I'm working as fast as I can!" I said, "Well, I don't want to let you down or anything but I don't want to get sued. I've got a commitment here."

I felt real bad about that and I didn't really know what to do. I think he thought that I would just forget about doing the show because he was one of the great film directors of all time and I would just bite the bullet and do it. But my agent said, "You're going to be in big trouble if you miss that show. I have a lot of advertising on it and everything, and the show after it." So I told him the morning, "Orson, I gotta go." And he wasn't too pleased. I said, "Look, I'm not being difficult. I've been telling you this about every two or three days." He said, "I know, I know. Well, can we shoot you on the way to the airport?" I said, "Doing what?" He said, "I don't know. Just make up some dialogue." *[Laughs.]* So we're going to the airport to catch a plane, sitting in the back making up dialogue about I don't know what — nothing, really. But he had to be shooting it and he shot me right going up to the gate. Then I left and I felt *bad* about it. He decided to do my part all over again with Peter Bogdanovich.

I wonder if they started all over. I did a lot of stuff there. He must have been more pissed than I thought. But he did call me a few times after that and he was very friendly and everything.

PPT: Percentage wise, do you have any recollection of how much of your role was completed?

RL: I think I completed at least three quarters, maybe more. He didn't waste too much time going over it and over it and over it. As soon as everybody got their lines right and what he wanted, he didn't keep doing it over and over. And he didn't go for a lot of close-ups; sometimes he'd do no long shots because in his head he knew what he wanted on the screen, a lot like John Ford. So it saved a lot of time because a director who doesn't know how he's going to cut it will protect themselves by shooting it 17 ways. So it was all in his head, but what was in his head I'll never know. I don't know what the midgets were.

PPT: When were you next in touch with Welles after your experience of being in *The Other Side of the Wind*?

RL: I'd see him at the Dean Martin roasts quite a lot. I don't think we ever discussed *The Other Side of the Wind*. It was sort of like a closed chapter. He had told me about the problems he had and about the producer, and the whole thing was a mess. But he didn't hold a grudge against me leaving or anything. As a matter of fact, we got along great on the roasts. He loved to do those Dean Martin roasts because he marveled at Dean's ability to ad-lib and have fun and thought that was a real gift, which it is.

I think those roasts were some of the more enjoyable things that he did. The last time I saw him was when we finished a roast up in Vegas. Most of the cast was flying back to L.A. I don't know how much luggage Orson had, but I was leaving the terminal going out to get into a car and I looked back and there was Orson sitting on top of 15 bags. I said, "What are you doing up there?" *[Laughs.]* First of all, I wondered how the hell he got up there. I still don't know! He said, "I'm waiting for my driver."

And then one time he was coming over to my place in Malibu. A friend of mine from Canada — because I'm from Canada — was doing interviews with famous celebrities. And he said he'd come over and give him an interview. We had a terrific storm in Malibu at that particular time and I remember he phoned my friend to say that he wouldn't be over because he was wedged between the canyons. *[Laughs.]*

October 19, 2004

Peter Bogdanovich

Peter Bogdanovich: I don't think there's anything original about it, but when I first saw *Citizen Kane*— like everybody else, particularly people who would ultimately make films — I was blown away by it. It's sort of a cliché, but it's true. It was amazing to me. It was the first time that I was aware that somebody directed a movie. I don't know why — probably because Orson was in it. That was probably the obvious reason. "Oh, he's in this and he also directed it." So you could sort of picture him behind the camera. Whereas people like Ford, whom I knew about by that point, you had sort of a vague idea of what they were like and what they looked like. You didn't really picture it. But with Orson, there he was and you thought, "Well, this is the guy who is behind the camera too."

My parents never talked much about *Kane,* but had remembered *Ambersons* as a film they had particularly liked when they came to America. They saw it in the first three years of their being in America. It seemed to them a great piece of Americana. The first time I saw it was on a very dim, lousy TV in the middle of the night, somewhere in New York. Even then, it was extraordinary. You could hardly see it because the dark stuff was un-viewable. The television would tend to make dark scenes invisible. Nevertheless, it impressed the hell out of me even then, even under those circumstances. Everything I saw that Orson directed had an equal impact on me. I sort of sucked it in and it became part of my life.

I had written a program note about *Othello* for the New Yorker Theatre in which I'd said that it was the best Shakespeare film ever made. Now this was a very controversial opinion in 1960, hardly the general consensus. In fact, it was just the opposite. So it attracted the attention of Richard Griffith, the curator of The Museum of Modern Art, who called me out of the blue and said he wanted to know if I'd like to curate or put together the first Orson Welles retrospective in the United States at The Museum of Modern Art, and write the accompanying monograph. I was flabbergasted and said that I would, but why wasn't he doing it himself since he often wrote the monographs for the retrospectives? He said that he wasn't a particularly big fan of Welles, but many of the members of the museum were and his colleagues in Europe were. He thought that a retrospective was justified, but he didn't have the passion to write it. Since he read my program note on *Othello,* he thought that I did.

So I organized it and put it together. I think I got paid $50 or $100 for the whole job, which took a while. We pulled everything we could that existed. We found *Mr. Arkadin.* Orson at that moment was shooting *The Trial* in Europe, so I had no contact with him at all. The monograph was published.[9] The series went on in the spring and summer. It was quite extensive and it was very popular. I was out of the city for most of it, directing summer theatre. Two copies of the monograph were sent to Orson at some address in Europe. I never heard a word about it until seven years later.

It was sometime in August or September — if not later — of '68. I get a phone call. I'm living in Los Angeles by now. I have a daughter and am married and so on — first wife. And the phone rings and a familiar voice asks for me. I said, "Speaking," thinking, "Could it be?" He said, "This is Orson Welles." I said, "Oh, hello." He said, "I can't tell how long I've wanted to meet you." I said, "That's my line. Why?" He said, "Because you have written the truest words ever published about me ... in English." I was bowled over by that statement. He was rather brief. He always hated talking on the phone. He said, "I'm staying at the Beverly Hills Hotel. Can you meet me tomorrow at the Polo Lounge around 3 o'clock?" I said, "I'll be there."

I drove over the hill to Beverly Hills in a Chevy station wagon that I put in the wrong gear because I was so apprehensive and nervous. The car overheated and I arrived with steam coming out of the hood. He was waiting for me in a large black caftan or something — he was wearing something loose. But he was very warm and we spent a couple or three hours together. He was so disarming, as Orson could be — enormously disarming — that I felt that I could say anything to him. I even had the nerve to tell him that there was one film of his that I didn't particularly like, which was *The Trial*. He said, "I don't *either!*" Which turned out to be a lie, but nevertheless it made me feel like, "Wow, I can say anything to this man."

Peter Prescott Tonguette: I suppose that Welles knew you were an actor before becoming a director.[10] Is that why he thought to cast you in *The Other Side of the Wind*?

PB: He knew that, but by the time he started shooting *The Other Side of the Wind*, which was in the fall of '70, we'd spent quite a lot of time together in Rome when I was there preparing a [Sergio] Leone picture that I didn't make and Orson was cutting. So we spent quite a bit of time in Rome. We spent time in Guyamas, Mexico. I was doing the book with him. He'd agreed that we would do an interview book together.

Actually in Guyamas, when we were there, we had a long talk about directors, certain directors being considered over the hill and not bankable anymore. He was very upset about that. I remember we had a very late night conversation about that and the next day he said he hadn't slept for thinking about that. He said that there was a movie that he'd been thinking about making for years. It was about an older movie director and a young filmmaker. It was originally going to be a young bullfighter and an older bullfighter, but he'd decided to make it about two directors. He said that he must make that film now. Well, this was in early '69. I said, "Do you have a script?" He said, "I've written four scripts" — or something — "I know this by heart. I know how to do this." He was talking about it a lot.

But I didn't know he was starting to shoot what turned out to be *The Other Side of the Wind* until he called me. I think it was in October of '70. He was in L.A. We'd been talking and he didn't like the script of *[The Last]*

Picture Show. He didn't like the whole subject matter. He thought it was grim and thought it was a dirty movie. He referred to it as "that dirty movie." But he called me up and said, "What are you doing next Thursday?"—or whatever day it was. I said, "Well, I'm leaving for Texas that day." "Oh, really, what time?" I said, "Well, I don't know, 2 o'clock in the afternoon or something." "Good. Can you meet me at 11 at the airport? You know where the planes fly low over the street?" I said, "Yeah." "Well, there's a fence there and we're going to be shooting there." I said, "Shooting? What are you shooting?" He said, "I'm shooting a dirty picture." I said, "What?" He said, "Well, you're shooting a dirty movie, so I'm going to be shooting a dirty movie." "Oh, okay. What do you want me to do?" "I want you to be in it." "Oh, okay." "I want you to do your Jerry Lewis impression and you're going to play a cinephile named Charles Higgam"—which was an inside joke—"and I want you to do it like Jerry Lewis." Orson loved it when I did impressions. "Let me hear Jimmy Stewart, let me hear Jerry Lewis, let me hear Howard Hawks." He was very keen on the impressions. He'd laugh and the room would shake.

So that's how I started in the movie. It was me showing up and asking questions like *[in a Jerry Lewis-esque voice],* "Mr. Hannaford, do you believe that the cinema is a phallus?" Stupid things like that. Well, Orson thought that was hilarious. *[Laughs.]* We shot for a couple of hours and then I got on the plane and flew to Texas to make *Picture Show.* I was there until December and he kept shooting. Then when I came back in '71, we did shoot some more of me playing that character—not that much, but enough.

> *Although it wasn't the role he was first cast in, Bogdanovich always felt that the character of Brooks Otterlake was, as he told me, "sort of based on me because it was a young director who'd had a couple of hits, very successful pictures, and who also did impressions and was friendly to Huston's character. They cast Rich because Rich did his impressions and he had a similar complexion to me, so I assumed he was sort of doing me in a way. And Polly Platt, my first wife who I was divorced from by now and she was the mother of my kids, had been involved in the picture briefly and had visited him in Carefree or in Beverly Hills. She said, 'Well, he's doing you, you know.'"*
>
> *Bogdanovich and Welles were talking on the phone after Little left the picture when Bogdanovich made a suggestion:*

PB: I said, "Well, why don't I play it?" There was a long pause. He said, "Well, that never occurred to me." *[Laughs.]* I said, "Orson, the guy does impressions, he's had three hits, he's friendly with the director. I mean, how could it not have occurred to you?" He said, "No, no, it didn't occur to me because you're in the picture. You're playing that other role." I said, "Well, that's not a big part. Get somebody else to fill in those lines." He said, "My God, you're right. Of course you could do it. Of course we could get somebody else."[11] I could hear him cottoning to the idea in a big way. He said, "Would you come down?" I said, "Sure." "Oh my God, you've just saved my life." He was very, very happy about the idea. Whether he'd had the idea anyway and was waiting for me to have it, I don't know.

Welles asked Bogdanovich to bring two suitcases of his clothes to the shoot in Carefree, Arizona.

PB: When I got there, I had these two suitcases full of stuff and I said, "Do you want to see the clothes?" He said, "No, sit down, let's talk." And we talked for an hour, just talking about things, laughing and having a good time. I said, "Don't you want to shoot?" He said, "Yes, but I want you to be comfortable." I said, "Well, I'm comfortable." He said, "Well, let's just talk." So we talked for another 40 minutes or so. Finally I said, "Well, Orson, aren't you shooting?" He said, "I want you to be *very* comfortable and relaxed." I said, "Well, I am. Do you want to see the clothes?" He said, "Yes, let's look at the clothes."

So he looks through them and in about five minutes picks out pants, shirt, sweater. I said, "Geez, Orson, it's weird — these are my clothes, but I've never worn them in this combination." He said, "Well, there you see. Now

Welles photographing John Huston, in character as Jake Hannaford, for *The Other Side of the Wind* (photograph © Michael Ferris).

you know how a successful young film director dresses!" Those were the clothes I wore: cotton turtleneck, a wool sweater, and a pair of slacks.

I think we shot with John Huston for about ten days. It's hard for me to remember the exact sequence of events. I should have kept a journal, but I didn't. I was there for a while, for a couple of weeks, and he was shooting John for some of it. Then John left and I shot some of it with Orson. I think that was the only time I was in Carefree. He shot at my house later quite a bit and I worked in that stuff too. But the most intense stuff was a period of about ten days.

When Bogdanovich discussed how he'd sometimes "play scenes to Orson off camera," I was reminded of what Keith Baxter told me about the shooting of the coronation scene in Chimes at Midnight. *Baxter said that Welles was in costume when Baxter delivered his lines: "... I was always looking at him dressed as Falstaff."*

PB: In a way, it made it easier. There was the last scene that we did that was supposed to be taking place in a drive-in. I don't remember where he shot it. I think it was at my place, outside. I was playing it to him. It was very much the end of the relationship between Hannaford and Otterlake. He wanted me to think about him and to play it like we were talking about our relationship. At one point, he's being very cold to me and dismissive and I say something like, "Our revels now are ended?" That was a tricky line and he had me say it many times. [Hannaford's] line was, "You bet your sweet cheeks," and he drives off. It was the end of the relationship, so he said, "Play it to me."

He did everything in little pieces, little short takes, a lot of it, and I kept saying, "Can't we do a long take, like from *Ambersons*? A long scene, play the whole scene out?" He said, "Well, I haven't got actors. It's very difficult to do it because I haven't got all the actors at one time." I said, "I know, but it'd be fun if you could." One day, he said, "All right, you're going to get what you want. We're going to do this in one, with you and John." I said, "Really?" He shot this two or three page scene in one shot, putting the camera in the middle and I think we walked around. The camera stayed in one place, but the staging was elaborate. It involved Huston exiting at one point and me kind of trying out sitting in his throne-like chair — it was clear what was going on, that I was thinking about being him.

It was all sorts of stuff that I didn't think existed in my relationship with Orson at all, but I guess it did as far as Orson was concerned. I didn't feel that kind of thing with Orson. It would be absurd to be competitive with him. But I think he basically fictionalized our relationship and a lot of other relationships that he'd known, and used stuff of me and so on to make it closer to some sort of reality.

I never read the script at the time. I just learned the scene.

PPT: Even when you were cast as Otterlake?

PB: I didn't really read it all the way through because it wasn't necessary. Maybe I skimmed it. But it was a long script. He told me what I needed to know. A lot of the lines he'd make up just before you shot it.

We would get together often socially. He lived in my house for three years off-and-on, so of course we saw each other socially. We had dinner or breakfast or lunch or we'd just hang out. When we were both in New York, we'd go to dinner. We did a lot of socialization in Paris when we were alone together there.

PPT: How did it develop that he moved into your house?

PB: I asked him if he wanted a place to stay and he said, "Yes."

PPT: What was that experience like?

PB: It was kind of marvelous. I miss him. It went on for a couple of years off-and-on. He'd come in, he'd leave, he'd come back. Oja was there at times, with him. He sort of took over the house. *[Laughs.]* He had a room and a bathroom that were his, but he liked the room that was outside his room which had a big long table that he liked to sit at. He also liked to sit at the dining room table, which was all the way across the house. He didn't use my office, but he did like that dining room table quite a bit. It was big. It could seat 12, so he used to spread out his papers and work there.

Left to Right: John Huston, Welles, and Peter Bogdanovich during filming of *The Other Side of the Wind* (photograph courtesy of Gary Graver).

I asked Bogdanovich about his memories of Kodar.

PB: I never saw Orson with anybody the way he was with Oja. He was very unbuttoned with her and very much smitten by her. It was easy for her to get her way with him. He would give in easily with her. She sort of knew how to handle him. Being Slavic, we both spoke Serbo-Croatian. She spoke it and I spoke it and she would speak it in front of him. Serbo-Croatian, and generally people from that part of the world, are sexually kind of candid, which Orson *wasn't*. It was funny because she would tease him. He would really get embarrassed. He'd be amused, but slightly scandalized by her. She could get away with things that nobody else could. He'd shake his head and say, "These Balkan people!"

PPT: Did you ever meet his third wife, Paola Mori?

PB: I met Paola once at the AFI tribute. He was very formal with her — very nice, but he was formal. She was quite formal. She was very warm to me and very nice, as was Beatrice, but there was a certain formality.

Bogdanovich wanted Welles to direct a film for The Directors Company, which he founded with Francis Ford Coppola and William Friedkin.[12]

PB: There was one based on a Joseph Conrad novel, *Victory*, and I think he wanted to call it *Surinam*. He wrote a script on it and we were going to do it, but then we found out that somebody else owned the rights to the book. He thought it was public domain and it wasn't. That fell apart. He did get some money from Paramount on that, through The Directors' Company, but it never happened.

There were a number of things we talked about, but I don't know if we actually tried to get money on anything besides *Surinam*. We got money on that. That was really the last money he ever got from a studio, but then The Directors' Company fell apart. We had plans to have Orson do pictures.

I remember a project I really wanted very much to do with him was one about Alexander Dumas. It's a wonderful idea. It was based on the relationship between the father and the son, the father aging and being the writer of *The Three Musketeers* and all those great novels, and the son writing *Camille* and having a big hit with that. And the irony of the fact that the son asked the father to stop having an affair with a young actress/dancer because it was ruining the son's reputation. He loved the irony of that. He was going to play Dumas, the father, and I was going to play the son.

Welles recommended that Bogdanovich read the work of writer Robert Graves.

PB: He said, "You should read Robert Graves." "What should I read?" "*The White Goddess* and *The Greek Myths*." I remember getting them and giving them to Cybill [Shepherd] and telling her to read them and fill me in.

Left to Right: Welles, Bogdanovich, and Huston (photograph courtesy of Gary Graver).

[Laughs.] She did zip right through them. Looking back on it, I don't know how she did it.

In *The Other Side of the Wind*, I've seen some scenes where some of the things that Huston's character talks about — somebody says, "You know what the old man says ..." — are definitely taken from Graves. Definitively. They're Robert Graves kinds of things about the mother goddess and things like that.

PPT: In your new introduction to *This Is Orson Welles*, you write that you feel Graves had an influence on Welles's work.[13]

PB: I think it was very strong, starting in '48 with *Macbeth*. That's when *The White Goddess* came out.

Welles and Bogdanovich's relationship "faded," Bogdanovich told me, towards the end of the 1970's.

PB: It was compounded by two things. One is that he was going to be in *Nickelodeon* (1976) and play the Brian Keith part. We couldn't work out the deal with the studio. They didn't want to pay him what he wanted. Then Ryan [O'Neal] and Burt [Reynolds] both put up some money for Orson. He found out about it and wouldn't take it.

I think he was a little bit afraid of doing it on a certain level because it would have meant my directing him. I think he was having trouble with remembering lines and I didn't think he wanted to go through it. So I think he created an atmosphere where he'd have to get out of it, but it sort of screwed things up for me. Then he gave me some bad advice on *Nickelodeon*, which was good advice but bad advice, if you know what I mean. It was good artistically, bad from a business point of view. He suggested that I don't do it unless I do it in black-and-white, which he was right about, but it sort of fucked up things.[14]

We had gotten the rights to *Saint Jack* (1979) for him, but it was Cybill who really owned them because she got them in a lawsuit against *Playboy*. Part of a settlement was that she would get those rights — it was the reason she settled, to do it for Orson. He said he wanted Jack Nicholson, we got Jack for him, and then he decided he didn't want Jack Nicholson, which was very embarrassing. Then he wanted Dean Martin, and Cybill and [Hugh] Hefner, who also had a piece of the action, didn't want to do it with Dean Martin and started not wanting to do it with Orson because he wouldn't let himself be pinned down as to when he would do it or how he was going to do it. We had this terrible thing when we had to tell Jack that now he didn't want him to do it.

Eventually, Bogdanovich directed Saint Jack.

PB: I had to make the picture and that didn't exactly sit too well with Orson. He was pretty pissed off. So the relationship faded, but we still saw each other a few more times and we still talked on the phone. It was not the same.

It was strained. He invited me to a few things that I went to, but we never quite regained it. Although the last couple of phone conversations, as I wrote, were almost back to normal.

March 5 and 30, 2005

8

F for Fake

Gary Graver

Gary Graver: We shot [*The Other Side of the Wind*] from, really, 1971 on-and-off for a year, and then we took a year off in '72 to and made *F for Fake* [1974].

And so we come to F for Fake, *an essay film made in the midst of* The Other Side of the Wind. *Peter Bogdanovich wrote that "it began as a documentary by Francois Reichenbach on art fakery through the ages. But one of the people interviewed—along with Orson—was Clifford Irving, the man who faked Howard Hughes' autobiography."*[1]

GG: [On *F for Fake*] Orson started with the Reichenbach footage and then we were just adding some things to it. All of the sudden, this thing broke with Howard Hughes exposing that the book was a fake. So we went into that, we went into Hughes, and every day whatever we read in the paper in Paris we adapted that. Orson just built on what was happening in the news. That sort of dictated the way *F for Fake* was made.

Basically, the thing was this: Orson did all the lighting because he wanted to do it. He designed everything. It was all Orson. I was there to make sure that it would work technically. If it wasn't, I'd say, "We don't have enough light or that's not going to work or the lab can't do this," or something like that. So I was basically the technical part that he needed to make sure everything was okay.

We collaborated, but I just basically was there to serve his vision, really.

Then as it got along, he would trust me more and sometimes send me out by myself to do things. He would do sketches, little storyboard things. Like in *F for Fake,* he sent me out to do the church. He would just look at the stuff when we got back and then send me out again, something else he wanted, or something.

There's a sequence in F for Fake *in which Welles discusses the great Chartres cathedral of Notre Dame. I asked Graver about filming the cathedral.*

GG: The funny thing was I went there three times and we miscalculated. Orson sent me out late and for three trips it was dark when I got there. *[Laughs.]* The traffic and stuff. So finally I said, "I've got to leave earlier." "Okay, go ahead." So the fourth time was it.

Peter Prescott Tonguette: I heard that you and Welles would go into churches and film them.[2]

GG: Basically it was in Venice, Italy and in France. Orson would want to film in a church inside. The security guards would always tell me that I couldn't bring the camera in. Anyway, we bought this little Canon Scoopic camera. It looks like an amateur camera. It's 16mm, but looks like an 8mm. So I was able to go places with that and get what Orson wanted.

PPT: Why did he want this footage? Was it for any particular project?

GG: We were doing *Filming Othello* (1978) and some other stuff, whatever he wanted.

Orson would get stuff and just file it away. He didn't know where it was going to go exactly, but I think this was for *Filming Othello* or something.

Towards the end of F for Fake *is a fictional sequence involving Oja Kodar posing for nudes supposedly painted by Pablo Picasso.*

GG: We shot all that in Orson and Oja's house in Orvilliers, outside of Paris, where they lived. We used the whole living room as a big studio. I

Welles and Kodar pose for camera assistant Michael Ferris on location in Arizona during filming of *The Other Side of the Wind* (photograph © Michael Ferris).

brought in all the easels and everything. I was the only crew member on that. When they were walking around, when Orson was walking around, I had to pull my own focus. What I'd do is I'd set the first focus and then tie a little string to the lens and pull it down and hit a toothpick and that would stop it where the focus was. So I had to be very creative on that.

I was in it as a newscaster and then Orson would get behind the camera.

As he told me, Graver appeared briefly on screen in F for Fake; *indeed, Welles was aware that Graver's original aspiration in the movie business was to become an actor.*

GG: He was offered a series called *Nero Wolfe* at Paramount. He wanted me to play his assistant in the series. Nero Wolfe sits in his apartment and tends to his orchids. They eventually did it with somebody else. I don't know why, but he wanted to do it because he didn't have to run around, he could stay in one set. He was going to do it, but it didn't come to fruition for some reason.

Orson always had five or six things going at the same time. Like we were shooting *F for Fake* and I was staying at the house there. One morning I came down and Orson had assembled on the stage there in the house a whole bunch of pots and pans and food and everything. I said, "What is this?" He said, "The *cooking* show!" Like I should know about it! He wanted to do a cooking series. We never did it, but he was setting up for it. Like I was supposed to be a mind-reader or something.

Marie-Sophie Dubus and Dominique Engerer Boussagol

Dubus and Boussagol began editing F for Fake *in 1972.*

Marie-Sophie Dubus: Orson Welles started to cut his film with two different editors and they didn't fit to him, or him to them. I don't know. It didn't work. So he was looking for someone else and a friend of mine said, "Would you like to cut for Orson Welles?" I said, "You are joking." He said, "No, not at all."

So I met Orson Welles with the big cape and his big hat and, well, you know the person. And he said, "Okay, we're going to try," because he wanted to have his cutter. He had an American cutter, an Italian cutter, and an English cutter. And the producer said, "No, I'm sorry but I'm not going to have them here in France because I have to pay for the hotels and everything. So I want you to try another cutter." So I was there and I started with him and it was a wonderful show. We went through the film all together. At the end of the film he said, "I didn't want to have a French technician and I didn't want to have a *girl* technician." But he had both.

He was very intimidating to meet, of course, because Orson Welles is Orson Welles and there's only one on the Earth. So what shall I do? A little French girl like that with such a man, but at the same time I said, "Okay, well I have to try and see if it works or not." So we went in the cutting room, we had a machine called Kem, which was a German editing machine, and this machine had three different speeds. You could run normal speed, double speed, or four times speed. We were looking at the stuff which existed and he pushed the four times speed button and then it was going very, very, very fast for the machine. He said, "Okay, this in, this out, this in, this out, this in, this out." So we have, of course, no time to write anything. We were there for about two hours, I suppose. He said, "Okay, I have to go now. I'll come back tomorrow. Do you think you will be ready?" I said, "Yes, I think so." So he went and I stayed in the cutting room. Just before he left, I said, "Well, is it the picture or sound and picture that you want in and out?" He said, "No, both. In and out is for picture and sound."

In the editing room along with Dubus was Dominique Engerer Boussagol. Boussagol explained her role to me: "I was helping her and when she was very busy I was working directly with Welles (for example, I edited with Mr. Welles all sound effects.)"[3]

M-SD: She was my assistant and she was in the room when Orson Welles was working. So he went and we were looking to each other and said, "Now we have to start something." We went back to the machine and we kept what he wanted and we didn't keep what he didn't want. It was perfect. We didn't miss anything, we didn't forget anything.

When he came back there the day after, he said, "All right. We're going to work very well together."

For certain things he was very precise and for other things he said, "Well, try something ..." So I tried something. He sat just behind me in a big armchair because he was very fat. So he sat behind me and from time to time he used to say, "Marie-Sophie, you have the most *eloquent* back that I have ever seen." Because he knew that if I didn't agree with what he was asking, he could see the reaction on my back. *[Laughs.]*

Then we discussed very much. "Why don't you like that? Why did you do that?" It was always listening, listening, listening, listening. Of course, he didn't agree every time, but he was very listening.

Peter Prescott Tonguette: So he was open to your ideas as an editor?
M-SD: Yes, always. Always.

Boussagol had a slightly different memory of Welles's working methods in the cutting room. She said: "Welles was in the editing room all the time. Every cut was

his decision.... [He was] very, very demanding, very impatient to have the result
he asked for. Very hard worker."
   Dubus told me about her recollection of the genesis of F for Fake.

MS-D: At the beginning, he was supposed to make a short film of about
25 minutes or 30 minutes. Then he discovered that Francois Reichenbach,
the producer, had shot a documentary about Elmyr de Hory and it had been
edited I think in England somewhere. He said to Orson Welles, "Well, you
see I have quite a lot of stuff which has not been used at all, so if you want
to look at it ..." And Orson Welles, of course, said, "Yes." He found very nice
stuff and he said, "Okay, I'm going to now make a long picture."

So he had to shoot more than he thought. He started to come into the
cutting room and started to cut what we had. Then he was thinking of the
rest of the script and from time to time he said, "Okay, I'm going to stop cutting and we are going to shoot a new sequence or two new sequences or three
new sequences."

Orson was inventing the story every day. He tried many different things
for the same sequence. And sometimes he said, "We have to go in the Francois Reichenbach rushes or we have to go to what I have shot or we have to
go what existed before." It was all day long, we had to go to all the sources
we had in the cutting room.

The cutting of the picture took nine months, and then three months on
the sound.

PPT: Talking about the sound, was a lot of the film re-dubbed?

M-SD: Yes, he had to dub quite a lot of things because it was never perfect for him. All the narration he did many times because he wanted to ame-
liorate the narration every day. And then when he was recording the narration,
we went to the cutting room, tried to put it on the film, and said, "No, it
doesn't work." So we had to take over again all the cutting to make another
film. It was not one thing, it was hundreds and millions of things. "Millions"
is too much, but there were a hundred different versions.

It was, for sure, the greatest time I had in my cutting life.

When I asked Dubus — who was by no means a novice when she edited F for
Fake *— if she learned anything from working with Welles which she has carried*
with her in her subsequent career, she emphatically said that she had.

M-SD: The way of thinking of film, the way of building a film. To re-
do every day another film. It was really a great, great job he had done. He
was never satisfied. He was a perfectionist. Of course, it's easier to cut fiction
than cutting a film like that because every day you had to invent something,
you had to find something in the back of your mind and in the back of your
heart, which is completely different than in fiction.

I asked Dubus about the editing of the scene at the Chartres cathedral.

M–SD: There were a lot of shots, but he was very sure of his choice. For what he shot himself, he was very sure of his choice. When he was shooting something and then we were looking at the rushes in the cutting room, he knew what he could use and he knew what he couldn't use.

For everything, we had a very big discussion. When we were looking at rushes, for instance, and he wanted to have, say, 10 shots out of 100, but then I said, "No, look, there are two more shots I would like to keep because they are wonderful." He said, "Okay."

Welles occasionally claimed in interviews that he personally cut his films,[4] but Dubus said otherwise.

M–SD: It was always me at the editing table. Always. He was at the editing table only for the shooting.[5] I know that he had an editing table at his place outside of Paris and he was still working on different films, let's say on Sundays or something like that. But it was other films, maybe *Don Quixote and Sancho Panza*[6] or *The Merchant of Venice* or *The Deep* or films he had not finished and he had all the stuff in his house.

I saw some material of *The Deep*. I didn't see anything from *The Merchant of Venice*, but I saw two or three reels of *Don Quixote and Sancho Panza*.

Don Quixote and Sancho Panza was a film edited. Just some sequences were missing, but the film exists. The film is there in 10 or 11 reels or something like that.

Dubus wasn't involved with these projects, though she did work with him again. She told me, "After F for Fake, *I worked with him again for six months on another film which was* The Other Side of the Wind.*"*

M–SD: We cut about an hour or something like that. Then he went to the States and he said, "I have to finish my shooting because my actors start to be old and not very well and so on." But he went to the States and he never came back to France. Or almost never.

It was completely different. The way of working was completely different because he knew what the script was. He didn't have to re-think the script every day. So it was completely different, but nevertheless he was never satisfied with the cutting. It was always very long because he didn't want to change the scenes, of course, but nevertheless he changed them because sometimes he cut with a lot of close-ups, sometimes he re-cut with very wide shots. So each time was a different film, a different feeling of the sequence.

I think he enjoyed working with me. Really, we were very close in the cutting business. Very, very close.

Boussagol remembered their lunches with Welles fondly, saying, "Some days he noticed that we were very tired and he invited us for lunch. It was a rare moment. He was more relaxed and telling us lot of stories about films, shooting, with a good sense of humor."

M-SD: We used to work from 9 o'clock in the morning up to 11 about every day, including Saturdays and Sundays most of the time. So around 11 o'clock, he said, "Okay, girls, we are going to have dinner," and he took us to the restaurant and he was very proud. He was very proud of his cutters.

In my mind, he knew that he couldn't shoot for long years because he was very tired and he couldn't move very easily and so on. So I think that what was more important for him was to shoot, to shoot, to shoot and then wait for the cutting because the cutting could be done years and years later. That's what I think because he must have known that one day he wouldn't be able to shoot any longer but he would be able to come to the cutting room, sit in a big armchair, and make the editing.

He loved the editing. He loved it. I didn't know him in the shooting section because I've never seen him shooting anything, but I can tell you that he was in love with the editing, that's for sure.

January 1, 2005

9

"The Company of Magicians"

Abb Dickson

Abb Dickson: I think Orson really was bothered a little by the usual Hollywood suspects and tended to want to hang out with magicians — as he had for years and years.

The world of magic is a universe unto itself ... and if you are lucky enough to know the ins and outs of how to create it, you have total power to suspend the disbelief in an audience. Orson was very fortunate to know and combine the secrets of two mysterious worlds: the world of magic and the world of film. As "magicians together," we shared those secrets with each other.

Orson often would rather have the company of magicians, I think, because it's a fantasy world we live in. It was simply a way that he could just relax his own mind and get it out of the day-to-day rut of Hollywood and back into, "Let me clear my head and let me work on another project."

This chapter contains the recollections of a number of the magicians who knew and worked with Welles during the 1970s and early '80s: Abb Dickson, Don Wayne, Mike Caveney, Don Bice, Allen Bracken, and Jim Steinmeyer, as well as cinematographer Tim Suhrstedt.
Dickson met Welles in 1976.

AD: In 1975 I had put together a show in Atlanta, Georgia — an illusion show called *Presto!* We had a number of large stage illusions — 39, in fact, of the big boxes that you can crawl into and be sawed in half or shot out of cannons or whatever. At the time, there was only myself, Doug Henning in New York with *The Magic Show*, and Harry Blackstone, Jr., on tour. We were the three biggest shows. I had to pick a couple of magic tricks that were different from the ones in *The Magic Show* on Broadway and some that really hadn't been seen by audiences in a number of years. I ran across a picture of a prop called "The Disembodied Princess" — sounds wonderful. It was a prop that I copied from a photograph that showed Orson performing it with Rita

Hayworth years ago when he was doing USO shows for the troops in Holly-wood. So this magic prop had really fallen out of favor with magicians for many years perhaps because of the performing constraints, number of assistants needed, etc. Fortunately, I had the rare opportunity of having a cast of performers large enough to perform it properly. It turned out to be one of my favorites. I had it reconstructed from that photograph and film of Orson performing it.

In 1976, our show was to be at a bicentennial event in Washington, D.C., and I was to do my first USA tour. (*Presto!* was to stay out on the road for twelve years doing forty weeks a year all over the country.) Just before we were to take off to go to Washington, I was in Atlanta in the Alliance The-atre, and we had finished our run there and were rehearsing packing the show in and out of theatres and setting up and so forth ... putting it in the truck and taking it out of the truck.

One of the secretaries from the theatre came running into the rehearsal hall and she said, "There's a man on the phone who says he's Orson Welles — and he must speak to you." And I said to her, "Have him call back." Because I had no idea who it was. I do a lot of comedy magic and I had a lot of funny friends around the country, so there was no telling who it was calling. Well, in about five minutes she came back and she was white as a ghost. She said, "I think I recognize this voice on the phone and the man says he's Orson Welles and that he must speak to you." So I said, "Okay, have him hold on!" I went back to the phone and this voice said, "Hello! This is Orson Welles!" And I said, "And this is the Queen of England!" And indeed it was Orson. Of course, I dropped to a chair nearby when I recognized the voice as well. Orson explained that he had seen a review of my show in a magic magazine and had come across a picture of this "Disembodied Princess" prop. He wanted to know if he could rent it for a film that he was doing. I explained to Orson that we were to be in Washington, D.C., at the end of the week. We had only five or six days before we were to leave town. And he said, "Well, that's enough time. Do you have control of the theatre?" I said, "Certainly I do. It's still under my contract, we're moving in and out and we're doing rehearsal." He said, "Good. Then would it be possible for me to fly to Atlanta and bring a film crew with me? I will hire your assistants and we'll put together, from what illusions you have in your show, a short film that I want to do." I said, "Sure. When would you like to be here?" And he said, *"Tomorrow."*

The film that Welles was doing was The Magic Show. *Never finished, it included illusions performed by Welles, such as the Gypsy Thread (which we'll learn about later) and a long slapstick sequence starring Welles and Dickson.*

AD: So I went to the powers that be at the theatre — which is in the High Museum of Art in Atlanta — and I said, "Perhaps you may want to close the balcony doors tomorrow and put on a little bit more security because Orson

Welles is coming here to film." And they went, "Yeah, sure." So the next morning, I drove to the Atlanta airport in a station wagon and picked up Orson, Oja, Gary Graver and Gary's son. And one more person, who I think was a light person. That was the whole entourage. I had gotten them hotel rooms right across from the theatre. At 8:30 in the morning, into the theatre walks Orson Welles and all of the rest. After the formalities of introductions, we sat about figuring out what Orson was going to do. Now this took about an hour. As I said, I had 39 stage illusions in the show and all this scenery and all these costumes. So in that hour, he sat down and just looked. We paraded the costumes by him and he just looked. About 45 minutes into this, he said, "Okay, give me some paper, I'll type the script." He had brought along a manual typewriter and a bunch of oversize paper. For the next fifteen or twenty minutes, he typed away and wrote the script. We broke, he told us what illusions he wanted to do, what costumes he wanted to set up, and he went about giving us a little bit of direction as to what was to go on.

A still taken during the shooting of a sequence from *The Magic Show* at the Variety Arts Theatre in Los Angeles, 1982. L–R: Allen Bracken (seated), Dave Egan (third from left), Don Bice, Orson Welles (seated), Bruce Gold, Oja Kodar (with dog Kiki), Abb Dickson, and a female magic assistant (photograph courtesy of Abb Dickson).

I was the stand-in for Orson. He would rehearse things along and give me direction as to what he was going to do. He would talk me through it and make his decisions, saying, "Yes, no, okay, do it this way, do it that way," and so on. Later on, he fitted himself into a turban and caftan that he had made. Oja had become the star of the show. And we began filming. We were rehearsing and just getting some things down that first day.

The second morning, Orson said, "Now I want your lighting director and I want all of the lights lowered down to the theatre floor so that I can re-aim what I want to. I'll light for about half the day and we'll begin shooting in earnest." We had already gotten him a pail full of sand to be used as an ashtray for his cigars. He went through three boxes of those a day. We got him a cooler to hold his Fresca, because that's what he drank at the moment. So he began to tell my lighting director exactly where he wanted pools of light and how he wanted things done and this and that. Orson trusted Gary Graver completely. Orson would sit on a chair at the front of the stage, with Gary behind him, with one camera that Gary was operating, and one that would be operated remotely. And so he would constantly go, "Have you got this shot? Have you got this shot? This is what I want ..."

Graver doing lights, camera, and sound during filming of *F For Fake* (photograph courtesy of Gary Graver).

If you've seen this footage, one scene begins with a squad of policemen coming through a loading door at the back of this theatre. Now this was legitimately three to four hundred feet away from the camera. The light person, of course, was going, "This isn't going to work. There isn't enough light here to even make this happen." Orson's going, "Nope, nope, just do this. Okay, Gary have you got that?" Gary says, "Yep, looks fine." Now I must admit that I had (and continue to have) a lot of gall ... and that was the fun part of it. So on the second day I said, "Mr. Welles, why is it that you never look through the camera?" He said, "Because I know exactly what the camera sees. I designed the lenses, you know." And I went, "Oh." Not knowing that indeed he had! So he was shooting more depth-of-field stuff as he had in *Citizen Kane* and several other films. And he knew that this would work. He just knew it. And Gary did too. He never ran dailies while he was here, trusted what he had in the can.

The scene Welles was shooting at the Alliance Theatre was the aforementioned slapstick sequence in which a group of policemen (Dickson plays the police chief) happen upon a magic show which has gone very wrong.[1] *After performing a trick involving a woman being lifted to the sky by some balloons, Abu Kahn (Welles, who notes in the episode's prologue that he bears a "vague physical resemblance" to the old magician) encounters a heckler in the audience. The magician invites the heckler up on stage, positions him directly in front of the curtain, and begins "hypnotizing" him. Unbeknownst to the heckler, a stagehand behind the curtain has been cued to whack him on the head with a mallet. The heckler, knocked out, falls to the ground as though he was hypnotized.*

Several moments later, the heckler awakens backstage. He picks up the mallet and whacks Abu on the head. Disoriented, the magician fumbles about, trying to salvage his routine. By the time the policemen arrive, they stumble upon such sights as a woman sawed in half and not put back together (or, as Dickson's character puts it when he recalls the event, "bits and pieces of them pretty little women strewn out all over the theatre"). It is an extremely inventive sequence.

AD: A few years later, we were still shooting more bits of this same scene one night in his Hollywood home ... a continuation of these policemen sketches. As the chief of police I stumbled upon a handkerchief in a bottle and I picked up the bottle, took the cork out, smelled the bottle to see if there was any booze in it, and that handkerchief popped out of the bottle and hit me in the nose. The handkerchief began to plague me like a fly — as he said — flying around my head and eventually wound up scurrying into my jacket. Now I'm tickled by this thing running around under my coat. I begin to pat myself and the handkerchief kept popping out of sleeves and necklines and so forth. Eventually, a hundred handkerchiefs come flying out of every orifice in this coat — lots of them just zoomed out. It looked like something from *Ghost Busters* (1984). During the course of this I was to grab the original handkerchief and shoot it with a blank pistol. Well, he thought it would be funnier if all of the policemen — like Keystone Cops — were shooting this poor handkerchief, which eventually died and had death rattles and all of this business.

Orson said to us, "Now, we're going to have one time and one time only to shoot this handkerchief. After you shoot it I want you to go and everyone remove their wardrobe and hide the pistols and we'll take a break after this shot." So indeed we shot the handkerchief and we all go flying off in directions and hide our policemen's wardrobe and things. Then came the Beverly Hills police. We were all sitting innocently eating pizza by then. The policemen said, "We've heard shots in this area." Orson said, "No, I've heard something, but I don't know what it was." We didn't realize but we were two houses down from Sharon Tate's parents, so naturally gunfire in the house would attract quite a bit of attention from the neighbors! But we finished shooting and it turned out to be great footage that eventually found its way into this film.

There was to have been no "vocal sound" during the policeman sketches; Orson envisioned it as almost a Keystone Cops kind of piece ... with only music underscoring the piece. Like a silent movie, there would have been dramatic music, comedy music, sound effects, and Old Tyme Hand Drawn Title Cards. He thought that the characters' actions would speak for themselves.

Being "out on tour," my show was going to be out on the road for forty weeks. But we spoke frequently and, of course, anything that he wanted to re-shoot — since I was on the road, in theatres, with the same people, the same costumes, the same lighting — Orson knew that he could come back in and shoot if he needed to. We took off to Washington, D.C., where we opened at the Warner Theatre and got wonderful telegrams from Orson on our opening. And Orson and I became fast friends after that.

It became a wonderful telephone relationship after that. I would send Orson my route sheets ... my schedule of cities, and I would be in a hotel somewhere or another and at 2 in the morning, I would get a telephone call like this: "Abner, do you remember an illusion Thurston did in 1935 with a bucket of water and a sand pail?" "Yes, it was blah blah blah ..." Because I carried my library with me, I was able to research things. But I had one of these memories of old illusions that just gelled greatly with the great man. So he would call and ask me a question. He would never say thank-you, he would just hang up. That was it until another phantom phone call would come.

So after I would finish my tour, I would always go to Hollywood and spend a little time with Orson back-and-forth in any of the number of homes that he rented out there. We became fast friends and I would supply Orson with whatever props that he needed or remembered. Because he had been doing things since the '30s it was helpful that one of the things that I do is collect antique magic props, especially the larger ones.

Orson was a terrific magic nut, by the way. He never got over his wonderful suspension of disbelief and childhood wonder. He just loved magic tricks. From a couple of the larger magic companies in the United States, he would get their sale flyer and he would order one of each! They would be sent to him and he would keep these in boxes. When I would show up — or sometimes he would call Jim Steinmeyer to come over to his house — and we would open these boxes and perform these things for him. He wanted to see if they're good or bad or if he could use it for something. And most of the time, Orson would take something that was for one purpose and use it for another. So it didn't matter what the routine was; he wanted to see what the effect was and then how he could use it. And several of these things popped up in various film pieces over the years and in a lot of television performances at the time. He and Johnny Carson were good friends, and Johnny had such a love of magic. He knew that Orson would take the least thing and turn it into some raving miracle. Or he could lead you on and on and on to the point that you didn't care whether the trick worked or not! It was just Orson doing his thing.

Many times when Oja was out of town, he would call me — when I would know he was lonely or tired of talking about Hollywood. The unspoken rule between Orson and I was that I never asked him about Orson Welles. I never asked him about the great film career. I didn't want to ask him any of the questions that he'd been asked all of his life. We were *magicians together* and that he loved. And that's why sometimes I found myself playing his lawyer, playing a film producer from Germany — because I can fake a fair German accent, a business representative, an advertising executive. He would put me on as various things.

I would go with Orson to the "Company Cafeteria," which was Ma Maison. Whenever he would meet anyone there, the procedure was this: if you were to meet Orson at two o'clock, when you arrived, he would already be there and seated in his favorite table, which was right next to the kitchen door. During your meeting with Orson, certain timing devices happened. A script would arrive at the table from someone. "Oh, I'm getting scripts from everyone, you know." He knew that was 30 minutes. At 45 minutes, I would show up sometimes, just passing by. And then he would sit me down to sort of cut short the meeting and we would have dessert, at which point he would say, "Abner, come with me into the kitchen, we must thank the chef for this marvelous meal." And he would leave, leaving the person there of course with the check — Orson would go back and make his hasty exit through the kitchen.

And the reason he went through the kitchen is because literally he was having a very tough time walking and so we would go through the kitchen and out the door to the waiting car and speed away before the person could get out of the restaurant. No one would see him having this physical difficulty moving around. Legitimately, although he would never want it known, Orson was practically in a wheelchair by the time the end was near. He could hardly get around. But it was my job many times to go and plan the entrance and exit for him and plan various alibis to get him in and out of places gracefully, shall we say.

I asked Dickson about Welles's black poodle, Kiki, a pet Barbara Leaming discussed at some length in her biography. Several of Welles's magician friends mentioned seeing Welles with Kiki.

AD: Kiki. He loved that dog to death. Why that dog didn't die of overeating, I have no idea. That dog had the finest cuisine! Orson literally loved that little puppy.

Dickson was to play Lear's Fool in Welles's film adaptation of Shakespeare's King Lear.

AD: He sent me a copy of the script and I — never being Shakespeare trained — it was a bit of a hassle to begin to understand and go through. But one night at his home, we were finishing shooting something and he puts me in this wardrobe and he is in his and we're sort of like shooting an interview back-and-forth — a two-sided interview. So he says, "All right," and he starts with lines from *King Lear*. And I answered him as the Fool! So we continued and then he said, "All right, now we go to the ending!" And he picks up a line and I knew it and I said it back to him. So we shot some conversations back and forth between Lear and the Fool towards the end. Boy, I wish I knew who had those.

Sadly, we didn't do this ever again.

But Welles had, apparently, been doing some shooting of one kind or another for Lear *over the years. He told Dickson that he had been "working on this for a long time ... almost as long as* Don Quixote.*"*

AD: Literally, he had been shooting *King Lear* for so long that you could see the king age all the way through! I've seen this footage so I know that it exists.

Gary Graver confirmed to me that he shot what he described as "lighting and makeup tests" with Welles as Lear; the purpose of these tests was to determine the quality of videotape to film transfers, for Welles wanted to shoot significant portions of his Lear *film on tape.[4] Graver explained, "He wanted to do all the acting on video and then the pageantry scenes — big scenes with lots of extras and stuff and costumed people — he wanted to shoot in 35. Because he wanted to shoot on video so he could shoot lots and lots of acting, without spending a lot of money on film."[5] Unfortunately, this footage — along with whatever else Welles may have shot for* King Lear — *is presently unaccounted for (and Graver believes the "lighting and makeup tests" to be lost).*

AD: There were other times that — as I say, I've been an attorney, I've been this and that in his life, and one day at his home we were opening up boxes and doing magic tricks. And he looks at me and he says, "You want some Chinese food?" And I said, "Yeah." So he goes in and makes a phone call. About an hour-and-a-half later, a truck pulls up and a captain, a waiter, and a maître d' from some wonderful Hollywood restaurant come up. And here comes just a banquet of Chinese food. They came in with banquet tables, table cloths, silver services, and set up an entire buffet. They said, "Oh, Mr. Welles, thank you so much for calling. There will be no charge whatsoever, just call us when you want everything cleared and we'll be fine. We hope you and your film crew enjoy your dinner." And they left. And there were just two of us. I said, "Orson, what did you order?" He said, "One of each."

Peter Prescott Tonguette: Just like the magic flier!

AD: Just like the magic flier. So we called every starving actor that we knew of to come and enjoy what was there and also all the magician friends. He was such a kind person. He wrote for me several reviews and several articles on me just out of the goodness of his heart.

There were times when Oja might be out of town. And Orson would call me up and say, "Let's go and raid Cantor's!" Now Cantor's was a well-known delicatessen in L.A. in the Jewish district, and they have a pastry counter right in front of the window. Well, I drove a big red convertible that was easy for Orson to get in and out of. Business associates would always send a limousine for him and he hated that because it was physically hard to get in and out of, so he would often call me to take him to various places. He also had a friend who drove a pizza delivery wagon ... and would ride with him.... Anyway, here we are in an open convertible, and we're going to raid Cantor's. We would drive to Cantor's, which had a friendly parking space right in front of the pastry window, and he would sit in the car while I would go in and point at things in the counter. And he'd go, "Yes," "No," "Yes," four fingers, two fingers, whatever. We'd wind up with all of this stuff that we probably shouldn't have had. We went home and made a wonderful feast with a quart of milk and all of this pastry.

For those people who said that Orson was a cantankerous person, the person never to be worked with, awful to his crew and cast — they probably never really worked with the man, because legitimately he was the kindest soul to everyone in the business. People would be there, they would finish their filming, they would take down the curtains, they would roll up the cords and get the tape off the floor, they would do this and do that. Orson would sign any autograph, sign any script pages or whatever, made sure that every crew person had their very own "memento." One evening, Orson finished and he looked at me. We were the last two there — Oja I think had gone to bed.

Just worn out. And Orson looked at me and he looked around the house. There are pizza boxes and flotsam and jetsam and tape and this and that. He says, "You know, I'm Orson Welles but now I must clean this up before I go to bed — or Oja will shoot me." So literally I got on my hands and knees and we cleaned up the house. I let Orson smoke all the cigars he wanted to and we just cleaned up eventually.

Oja was a terrific gal to be with too. She was a great "minder" — as we want to say — of Orson. She was very strong-willed and took care of him very well. And, of course, put up with all of us silly people doing various things. She could con me into conning Orson into doing something back and forth. She was just a delight to be with. But there at the house at Stanley, which was the last house I think, she was perfectly at home out in the yard with a grinder and a big block of wood or granite or something, whacking away at some statue.

Oja was a great light in his life. He loved her so much. It was a mutual thing. They were very good together. I never met the real Mrs. Welles, but I can say that the relationship with Oja was a wonderful one and you can't say anything bad about it — they were just terrific with one another.

And she was a wonderful princess! We have floated Oja in the air for hours on end. She never issued even an annoyance. She was wonderful at playing the magical princess. She just had a ball doing what we could come up with.

Dickson's involvement with The Magic Show *continued until 1982, when the last portion of the Abu Kahn sequence was shot. But that film wasn't his only professional collaboration with Welles.*

AD: During the course of being on tour, we wound up with offices in the Sardi building in New York, and we were booking our show out of there. I was with a producer named Joe Butt. Joe had a company called Maverick Productions and it was the beginning of music videos at that time. Somehow Joe had a contact with Columbia Pay Television. I had written a piece that was a tour of the Magic Castle in Hollywood.

So I'm sitting in New York and I said, "Well, I have this Magic Castle special that I'd like to do." No one had ever done a Magic Castle special. Joe said, "Well, it's great, but I don't think they're going to buy it because it doesn't have a star attached to it." I said, "Well, how about Orson Welles?" He said, "You couldn't get Orson Welles to do this!" I said, "Give me your phone." I picked up the phone, I called Orson, I said, "Look, I've written this Magic Castle special ..." Joe Butt is standing there with his mouth open. I said, "I need for you to do the introduction and the in-and-out. It will probably be one day of shooting, at the most two, and I've only got, I think, $25,000. Will you shoot this?" And he said, "Sure! But I get the extra film."

I said, "Okay, great." I hung up the phone and said, "Okay, we got him." Joe Butt was truly amazed.

We go running across the street to Columbia Pay Television and in less than an hour we have sold — at my age, 24 — a pay television special to Columbia Pay Television called *Orson Welles at the Magic Castle*. Well, of course, they wanted to send a line producer out to Hollywood to supervise the footage and that was fine. Orson and I worked out all of the intros and outros. So he showed up, we did our tape, we did our intros, we shot for that one day, and the next morning we were to finish the outside shots where Orson arrived at the Castle — full of fog — and he gestures and the doors open and he walks into the Castle. Well, Orson called me at about 7 o'clock in the morning and said, "I'm not coming. I've shot everything they need, you can shoot the rest of it. I'll send you my wardrobe, but you're going to have to have a hat made at Western Costume Company because your head is smaller than mine and my hat won't fit you." So I go flying over to Western Costume, where they take a Cavalry hat and somehow magically reblock it, pull it, put this thing together until it's a marvelous looking hat that looks exactly like Orson's. So I'm the one outside, gesturing in the cape and wandering through the fog, and I was the one who finished the shot. Well, of course this would drive the producer crazy but we knew what we're doing, we're both familiar with this way of working, and this is going to be the way it is.

So we shot the tease. One of the things that Orson wanted to do was this trick that a magician in the 1930s had done called the "Duck Tub." Now the trick is this: you show a barrel cut in half, you tip it up and show that it's empty. Then you fill this barrel full of water and you crack a dozen duck eggs into the barrel, and suddenly a dozen ducks come out of the barrel — quacking. So he asked me, "Do you know where this barrel is?" And I said, "Yes, I know what collector has it, but you don't want to know, it's probably got a plant growing in it. It hasn't been used since the '40s and it's just rusting somewhere." He said, "Can you get it and put it back into condition?" So I went out and I managed to take the man's plant out of this prop — which was rusting away — and I went up to one of the magic maker shops in California and attempted to get this prop working again.

The trick worked like this:

AD: The ducks were placed in a rather tight hidden compartment within the tub. At the push of a secret button, the ducks would be released from their hiding place into the water filled tub ... and as you can imagine, they were pretty mad!

Well, Bill Smith performed an act with a duck. So Bill knew where ducks came from. We needed a dozen ducks and this prop. And if you need a duck in Hollywood, you might as well hire Bill Smith to be the duck wrangler. So

I got the prop but it was badly in need of caulking. The wood had shrunk over the years. This barrel was literally going to fall apart in a while. So I called Orson and said, "Well, I'm sorry to tell you that we have the prop and physically it works, but the barrel is in bad condition." And he said, "Doesn't your hotel have a swimming pool?" I said, "Yes." He said, "Sink the tub down into the swimming pool for a couple of days and it'll swell up." I said, "Okay." Now the producer from Columbia is pulling her hair out because she doesn't know what the hell is going on. We're all waiting for Orson, who is off filming something else — but he really wasn't, he was across town. So now we have this thing in the swimming pool of the hotel and people are going by, saying, "What's that? We don't want to swim with this thing in the pool!" Well, we finally get the prop up and running and it was time to rehearse. Our hotel had an underground garage, so in a distant corner I set up a temporary cage — a dozen ducks living in a small container, smelling up the joint and people trying to park their cars and going, "What are these ducks doing here?"

Finally one afternoon, Orson calls and he wants to rehearse this. Well, where are we going to rehearse it? Behind the Magic Castle. "I'll just drive up in the car and you do the trick." Well, we go up and we sit this behind the Magic Castle. Then we realize that even with a fire hose we couldn't fill up this barrel fast enough ... we needed buckets of water.... So I go running down the street to the Burger King, where their pickles come in a plastic bucket.... I buy a dozen of these empty pickle buckets and go running up Highland with a dozen buckets on my arm. Meanwhile Bill Smith, a fellow magician, is trying to wrangle these ducks from the parking lot at the hotel next to the Magic Castle up to where the barrel is. He's trying to squish them all down into their little compartments — of course they don't want to be there, because they've never been there in their life. But suddenly we have all of these ducks in the bucket and I'm standing there covered in pickle juice with buckets and barrels of water. Suddenly the producer from Columbia, Angela Shapiro, is standing there; "What the hell is this going to look like? How's it gonna work?" We'd been hiding this from her so she won't see the ducks and she won't know how this works, trying to maintain the secrecy of something. So there I am, sweating like a whatever ... suddenly, Orson arrives in the convertible. And he stands up like a potentate in a parade, puts his hands on the windshield, and commands, "Show the tub empty!" We do. "Pour the water!" We do. "Produce the ducks!" We do. "I'll call you in the morning!" And the potentate sits down and rolls away. Now here stand six people and we have just produced a dozen ducks who don't like to be in this tub. So they're escaping up the Hollywood Hills, around the corners, anywhere in the world. And we're looking at each other like, "This is the Twilight Zone. This is not happening. This is amazing."

Well, we wrangle most of the ducks, we put them back under the hotel.

The next morning, Orson calls and says, "No, it's too messy. It's not as I remember it. We'll cut it from the show." *[Laughs.]* So that was it. But do we have something else we can put in? Yes, we can do this, blah, blah, blah. We went over to his house, it was shot, we brought the film back, and Columbia thought it was perfect.

And so that is what you see at *Orson Welles at the Magic Castle.*

Orson and I had this kind of wonderful relationship. Here was this man who enjoyed a practical joke, enjoyed putting someone on to the point of tears, and he could just do this to you and then be so nice and so good and so giving that everyone would just roar with laughter over a good joke. He was that kind of guy. It was as if we were children, playing in our own land of make-believe.

Orson had such a great sense of being able, in the middle of a scene, to turn his eyes towards the camera and get the attention of that one theatergoer in the seat, letting him in on the scam. And everything was a culmination of this magical misdirection and control of the audience and control of the situation. He used that many times in many places.

I know in the film *Black Magic* that he did some wonderful close-up magic and in *Casino Royale* [1967] he also did some magic tricks and so forth. And many times he would do things and just have things happen, he would have a scene in which something would happen that would catch your attention — you weren't aware that it was a magic trick at all, but it was just some little device. Like — Orson had a habit of unbending a paper clip into a straight piece of wire. He would insert this down the middle of his cigar ... the wire then becoming invisible. I've seen him do this in meetings many times. He would be sitting there with a lit cigar, puffing away, and suddenly the room would be absolutely staring at this cigar because the ash wouldn't fall off. And the ash would be like three inches long! Everybody was waiting for it to drop and it wouldn't drop! *[Laughs.]* And he did this in films sometime. He would do things that were, let's say, impossibly balanced or something just happened — well, it was a magical technique or a magical effect or something like that that he would use to either grab the attention of the audience or lead the attention away to something else.

Orson also liked to do things as a bit of a joke ... just to see if people were paying attention. Orson had a love of fake noses, for example. He used them in various things. In *The Third Man* [1949], he would reshape the nose all the time between scenes — just to throw people off. They'd be looking and think, "There's a shadow I've not seen."

A magician may not be a screenplay writer, but the medium of movies is essentially related to the art of magic. (Georges Melies, one of the first directors in movie history, was originally a magician. In 1888 he bought the theatre of one of the most famous magicians in France — Robert-Houdin's theatre in Paris — for his own performances. Twelve years later he renovated his theatre into a movie theatre to show his own films.)

Perhaps it was Orson's background as a performing magician that brought him to do take after take, shot after shot ... sometimes shooting the same scene for years until he was satisfied with the material enough to add it to his repertoire.

One of the best ways performing magicians find to go through the process is to find some fellow magic friends with whom you can honestly share advice and criticism. Each respects the other for his own achievements and style, but nevertheless uses the opportunity to improve certain routines and their presentations. That's what Orson did with his closest magic friends.

The times that we did talk about the studio system and how it worked, he said, "We simply got up in the morning and got on the streetcar and we went to the studio and we made whatever it is they want us to make, Monday through Friday, and then we shot sometimes on Saturday, then we got a day off, and then we came back. Friday we were a cowboy, Monday we were a detective, Tuesday we were something else." It was just a factory. We did talk a little bit about *Citizen Kane* and where the group came from, because they hired Orson and he insisted that his troops — the entire Mercury players — come with him. So after they made *Citizen Kane*, then they came to him with another script and said, "You're going to make this next." He said, "No, I'll make what I choose next." They said, "Well, see on the contract it says that we've hired you and this entire bunch of players so if you don't want to play the game, then we'll continue to use the rest of the people and you're out." And that spoiled it. He did get to make *Ambersons* the way he wanted to, but after that it was simply that they'd taken the wind out of him. They'd told him what he could and couldn't do.

He preferred the freedom of being able to do it himself with his own group of happy little players.

March 25, 2004

Don Wayne

Magician Wayne met Welles through Abb Dickson. Dickson recruited Wayne to work on Orson Welles at the Magic Castle *and a friendship with Welles developed.*

Don Wayne: It was basically that Orson was just looking for someone to help do little things. His hobby was magic and he had an ongoing TV special that was in development, actually. When he would perform on some other TV special, he'd often film an extra trick for his own special. So that's how he was putting some of it together.

Wayne is referring here to The Magic Show. *Along with Dickson, Wayne appeared in the Abu Kahn segment of the film as a police officer. He remembers the scene in which Abu's memory loss has caused a handkerchief to spring to life.*

DW: It was kind of based on a 1950s science fiction film where all these handkerchiefs would attack people.

There was a whole routine on film. At one time there was more of it, but he kept trying to work at it, trying to make it better and better. Because it was film, pieces would get lost or misplaced and it became choppier and choppier. It just slowly got worse. I think what happened was that Orson was too close to it. He had watched the routine so often that it seemed boring to him. It was good when I first saw it and to me if he went back to his original version he would have a really good routine.

I never saw a script. I was at the editing studio a few times with him where I saw the completed routine. He seemed to do most everything himself and [with] some help from Marty Roth.

Marty Roth edited Welles's Filming Othello. *According to Wayne, he also worked on* The Magic Show *at one point.*

Peter Prescott Tonguette: How close to being done with the film was he?

DW: At one time, I thought he had close to enough material because all he needed was something like 48 minutes if he did it as a network TV special. Now if it was going to be a film, I don't know that.

He was a likable guy. On the surface, when you'd see him, he would sometimes be gruff and apparently demanding and all that stuff. For the most part, that was just for the public, it was just a show. And I'm not sure why that it is, but it was. *[Laughs.]* One-on-one, he was just a likable guy and had funny jokes, stuff like that.

When I first met him, we didn't hit it off at all! Which was over the phone. Abb Dickson could do an impersonation of Orson Welles, so Abb would call up saying, "This is Orson Welles." He had done this maybe six times or so. Finally, the real Orson Welles calls and he says, "This is Orson Welles." I said, "Sure it is!" And started throwing all kinds of remarks back at him. Sure enough, when he hung up, I realized it was Orson Welles! *[Laughs.]* So I called Abb immediately and told him what I had done, thinking it was Abb's impersonation. So Abb told Orson, then Orson said, "We'll just meet this afternoon and we'll pick up from there."

Orson hates the telephone. He would call up and say, "Don, come over." Click. Wait a few minutes and he would call back and say, "Bring the so-and-so trick." Click. Then calls back and says, "By the way, do this and this." It'd be one sentence conversations. *[Laughs.]* He hated the phone for whatever reason.

He was the originator of numerous tricks that many magicians don't know that he created. There's one trick called Orange, Lemon, Egg, and Canary. His original version dealt with a grapefruit, orange, and an egg, or something like that. But it's now a classic trick in magic.

He never brought up the past —*ever*. I would have to bring it up, asking him about Houdini, asking him about *Citizen Kane*, and a few things like that. I would have to pry it out of him. He just wasn't caught up in the past and didn't care to talk about it. It wasn't the future.

He loved magic. He made a comment that he always wanted to be on the cover of *Genii* magazine. *Genii* magazine was the leading magic magazine at the time. Then a few years back they put his picture on the cover, which I know would have pleased him. I think it was in the 1940s or '50s Orson had a magic show in Hollywood with a few top movie stars in it, and he did not see a mention of it in *Genii*. He was disappointed in that. I looked at this guy who won lots of awards and everything else and had critical acclaim, wanting to be on the cover of *Genii* magazine. It was just amazing that that was his dream. *[Laughs.]*

We worked briefly on a Las Vegas magic act. He didn't go through with it, although he did have offers in Vegas.

We were shooting for a show where Orson was in a big black hat and a black cape. We were shooting somewhere in Laurel Canyon. He was doing this thing and the dialogue was going to be dubbed in later. So we're shooting inserts at the bottom of a large cliff. At the top of the cliff was someone's backyard. It must have been a good 30 to 40 foot drop. So Orson was doing this thing and two kids were looking over the fence from above and saying, "Hey! Hey, you! Hey, down there! Who is that?" And then one of the kids says, "Are you John Wayne?" Because Orson was backlit you couldn't see his face, but you saw him laughing. His body started shaking and all that. He thought it was pretty funny.

Orson was a very interesting guy; I miss him.

July 21, 2004, April 14, 2006, and April 27, 2006

Mike Caveney

Magician Caveney met Welles in 1980.

Mike Caveney: Orson used to be a very fine magician but, unbeknownst to me, still had a great love for magic. He had worked with a couple friends of mine: Don Keller and Don Wayne. It was Don Wayne who suggested to Orson that I might be able to help him. The first time that Orson Welles calls you on the telephone, you think it's a friend playing a joke on you. Eventually you realize that it's actually Orson Welles on the other end of the line and he's saying, "I need your help." It's very exciting, you can't wait to meet with him, and you are anxious to make the project run smoothly. And then Orson calls again and again and again. His calls could come at any time and when he called, he was not calling to make an appointment. In that booming voice, he would say, "Mike, this is Orson. Come over." You would say, "Okay, Orson. Let me see, I'm right in the middle of something ..." And then you realized you're talking to Orson Welles. And you say, "Orson, I'll be right over."

But many of the projects were frustrating for various reasons. I think that's the point that Don Keller and Don Wayne had reached, and they said, "Orson, we've got a great idea. You should call Mike Caveney. Mike is a magician who knows about magic history and does an act himself and he's up to speed on what's new in magic." So I think they were passing Orson off to me. One afternoon at home I got the phone call — what I thought was a prank phone call — saying, "Mike, this is Orson." I dropped everything and drove over to Orson's house on Stanley Avenue in Hollywood for the first time.

At that time, Orson was a frequent guest on shows like Merv Griffin and Johnny Carson. And for Orson, the whole reason for doing these shows was not to sit and chat about something. It was to perform. He couldn't perform something from a movie or radio show but magic, something he had been well versed in early in his career, was perfectly suited to the situation. So that's what he did.

He always needed help getting these routines together and he would never do the same thing twice. It always had to be something brand new, so that's what he would call about. He would have an idea and wanted to see if I had any additional thoughts. I would round up the props, go over to Orson's, and we would talk it through.

I worked with Orson for a couple of years — and I say "worked [with] him," but you never knew when the phone would ring. Months would go by and you wouldn't hear anything. Then the phone would ring and you'd be back on a project. But I was his go-to guy for a couple years. And it was always the same sort of thing: he was doing a spot on a talk show and he wanted to get a trick together. So I would go do it. I would have fun. It would be nerve-wracking. And that would be that until the next time that Orson called.

In my experience, Orson had no interest in talking about his film career. And in being with him in many situations — like at studios — most people knew Orson Welles for his film career and they all wanted to say, "Oh, Orson, *Citizen Kane* was my favorite movie." And Orson was so sick of a lifetime of hearing about that. He'd heard it a thousand times and he didn't need to hear it again. He would absolutely cut people off, saying, "We're not here to talk about movies. We're here to do a magic trick." And, wow, they would get it. I saw him do that, so I kind of got the idea that Orson was not interested in talking about the camera angles in *Kane*. At least to me he wasn't. Now when Peter Bogdanovich was around, maybe things were different.

But what Orson got from me and from the other magic guys was something that he couldn't get from the movie community. And that was a chance to talk about magic theory; about old magicians that had worked in vaudeville and that Orson may have known or seen; or about illusions he had seen or read about. I can't hold up my end of a conversation talking to Orson about directing films, but when it came to magic there was plenty I could bring to the table. And he was very much interested in talking about that. So it was funny to turn the tables and see Orson as the student and us young magic guys as the teachers.

Orson had worked on another program one time with another mutual magic friend of all of ours: a guy named Don Bice. Orson liked Don. One time I was at Orson's and said, "Hey, I saw Don Bice and he said that he always had a great time talking about magic with you, and he mentioned that he'd love to see you again." Orson lit up and said, "Listen, talk to Don and sometime you guys come over here, we'll order a couple pizzas, and talk magic all night." Well, we never did it. But just to think ... that was Orson's idea of a perfect evening, sitting around in his living room, eating pizza, and talking about magic and magicians.

I now think that our failure to follow up on such an evening was a great disappointment not only to us, but most of all to Orson. He was such an awe inspiring person, and in many ways intimidating, that many friends never had the nerve to just call him up and say, "Hey Orson, what are ya doing tonight? Let's grab a pizza and hang out." We all thought that Orson was most likely meeting with some important people or swamped with work but I now believe that he spent many quiet evenings at home with Oja and would have loved to have some friends over. I'm sure that he would have enjoyed it at least as much as we would have.

Caveney, like Dickson and Wayne before him, was involved in the ongoing shooting of The Magic Show.

MC: One day I heard that familiar voice on the line, "Mike, come over." I got in my car and drove to Orson's house. He said, "We're going to be shooting at a little studio in Hollywood and I want to do the Gypsy Thread."[4] Now this is an old trick, well known in magic, and a really terrific trick. It's very simple. You reel off a piece of heavy sewing thread and break it into pieces. You roll them up into a little ball. You hold out one piece that's maybe five or six inches long and you stick this little wadded up ball to the middle of the short piece. Then you take the ends of that short piece and slowly stretch it out and all the broken pieces restore themselves into one long piece again. Very amazing trick.

Welles and Caveney on the set of *The Magic Show* during the shooting of the Gypsy Thread illusion (photograph courtesy of Mike Caveney).

I'm sure Orson had seen it before and decided, "I want to do this trick." But he hadn't done it before and he didn't know what kind of thread to get and he didn't know the exact handling. So my phone rang. Fortunately, I was familiar with the Gypsy Thread. I went to Orson's and we talked about it. Normally this trick is performed sitting at a table and the back edge of the table plays into the secret of the trick. You need that edge of the table to hide a little gimmick at one point. So any magician who was going to perform it on television or in a film, would say, "Okay, put the table here and the camera there and I'll do the trick just like always." But Orson didn't think that way. Orson knew that a television or movie screen has an edge around it where the picture ends. He used the right side of the screen in place of the edge of the table. In other words, he could see, by watching the monitor, when his hand momentarily exited the right side of the picture, and when it was safe to drop something without having it seen. It was just a fraction of a second that his apparently empty hand would disappear from view. The viewers would realize that his hands never came near the table or anything else. The magic happened right out in midair and his hands were completely clean at the finish. It really is an ingenious idea.

He also said, "At the same time, I want the camera to be dollying in, zooming in to get closer and closer." One of the great things about doing this trick on film is that the background of the trick can be your face. And of course Orson had this great face. The restoration of the thread could happen right in front of his face and he wanted the camera to zoom in on this. So the camera was zooming in at the same time his hand was finding the right spot in frame where he could safely drop this thing without being seen.

My assignment was to teach Orson the proper handling and setting up the thread to make sure that the trick was going to work right technically. Then we went to this studio and Jim [Steinmeyer] came along. The first time, we could see Orson drop it. So I set up the thread and we did it again. He had some great patter to go along with it. He did it again and said, "My hand went too far out of sight. It looked fishy. It looked like I was hiding something." I set up another thread and we did it again. This time the thread didn't stretch out smoothly. So we did it again.

For some reason, I kept track of the takes and we shot it 22 times. I don't know if he loved the 22nd time or if he just said, "Everybody's exhausted and hungry and it's late and we've done this enough. Somewhere in here we'll have something we can use." But 22 times over five hours, Orson broke this thread up and recited the patter, the camera zoomed in and the thread was restored.

According to Caveney's date book, the shooting of the Gypsy Thread for The Magic Show *took place on August 27 and lasted from 7:15 P.M. until 2:15 A.M. the following morning.*

MC: It's amazing, but of all the times that I worked with Orson, I never had the sense to bring a camera along and take some pictures. But on this night, my wife Tina (who worked with Orson almost as much as I did), was with me, and she snapped a picture of me standing with Orson between takes. It's the only one I've got of Orson and myself, so of course today, some 23 years later, it's a treasure.

I spoke to a friend of mine this morning and he reminded me of another story. This guy was a movie producer named Bill Self. Back in the '50s and '60s, Bill produced more television shows than I think anybody in the business. Around 1957, he was producing a TV series for Frank Sinatra. One day Sinatra said, "Bill, would you like to meet Orson Welles?" Bill said, "Boy, I would love to meet Orson Welles." Sinatra said, "He's got a film project that he's sort of shopping around. If you want, I'll set up a meeting." Bill said, "That'd be great."

So Orson came in and said, "I'd like to shoot a thirty-minute version of *Don Quixote* in Mexico." Bill said, "Well, it seems amazing, but I would love to see a script and maybe we can do something." Orson said, "Fine," and left. Well, a week went by and Bill hadn't heard anything. So he called Orson's home and the maid answered the phone. Bill said he was calling for Orson Welles. And she said, "He's not here. He's in Mexico shooting a movie." *[Laughs.]* Bill said, "What?" So he went back to Frank and said, "I never got the script because Orson went to Mexico and he's shooting! What are we supposed to do?" Frank said, "Well, I guess we tell him that we're not going to pay for it." So they sent a message to Mexico and said, "I'm sorry, but we can't pay for whatever you're doing down there." That got Orson's attention and he flew back — not to talk to Bill Self, but to talk to Frank Sinatra. He said, "Hey, I talked to your friend and he seemed interested. So I'm shooting it." Orson went back to Mexico and Frank talked to Bill and said, "Look, he's down there shooting and it's not costing that much money." So they decided to pay some bills and get some rushes to see what it looked like. After seeing a few scenes they decided to back away from the whole project, which put Orson in the familiar mess of having a film underway with no money.

That was the great tragedy with Orson. He was so interested in actually doing the project and so uninterested in the financing and the business end. He was an artist and not a business man.

I remember Orson would say — and this was so sad to hear — he said, "Everybody wants to give me an award, but nobody wants to hire me to make a film." And it was absolutely true. They would line up to give him lifetime achievement awards and anything else they could create, but when Orson would say, "Well, thanks, but now let's make a movie," they'd say, "Well ... we don't know ..."

On these talk shows, every star in Hollywood would do them. There would always be other guests — movie stars or whoever — on the shows that we worked. Everybody treated everyone else like old friends. "Hi Bob, how are you?" "Hey Joe, good to see you." And then when Orson would come in, it was completely different: "Hello Mr. Welles," "Yes, Mr. Welles," "Can I get you something, Mr. Welles?" They knew that this wasn't just some celebrity of the week. This was Orson Welles. This was the guy who had achieved everything that everyone in this business hoped to achieve. Whether they wanted to be a movie director — this was a guy that made the greatest movie in history. Whether they wanted to be in radio — hey, this is a guy that made the greatest radio show in history. They were clearly in complete awe of him. I thought that was great. Of course, they all wanted to talk to him about movies and he wasn't the slightest bit interested in that. We were there to perform magic.

I remember we would always see Oja at the house, but she didn't seem to have any interest in magic. She was a really great person for Orson to have around. I always liked her.

Peter Prescott Tonguette: Jim Steinmeyer also told me that Oja wasn't too interested in magic!

MC: Yeah, I mean, Orson truly loved to just sit around and ... we would have a trick that we were working on, but sometimes I would bring a trick over that I was fooling around with. I'd show it to him because Orson just loved watching magic. I'm telling you, he would turn into a 12-year-old kid when you'd show him a trick. Sometimes it would fool him and sometimes it wouldn't, but you could just see it took him back and reminded him of why he got interested in magic and why he loved it.

Orson would read about a new trick or somehow get a hold of a new trick. He'd say, "This is a great trick. I want to do this trick. Now, how can I improve this trick?" And the answer was, "Orson, this trick doesn't need any improving." But no, Orson wanted to make it twice as amazing. I don't know if he was trying to fool the magicians or what. But he would start adding more and more layers until it was very complicated. One of the reasons most great magic tricks are great is because they're simple, because the effect can be described in just a few words.

There were some absolute horror stories. I mean, Orson was just asking for it because these things were getting so complicated. One time, he called to say he wanted to do a new trick that was on the market that involved a little electric clock, one of the first little digital clocks. A magic company had put it out. It was a clock that allowed someone to set the time, and the magician could predict the time. Well, that's a good trick, but not good enough for Orson. So he said, "We're going to change this. Tina is going to be an usher in the theatre. We'll get her an usher's coat at the Merv Griffin

Theatre. And she will be the one that does the dirty work. We'll select a spectator by having names in a fish bowl." And I'm like, "Can't you just point to somebody?" "No, they'll think he's a stooge! And this is how we'll get the names in the fish bowl," etc., etc.

The other problem was that during the years I knew Orson, he was huge. When we would go to his house to work on a trick, he'd be sitting in his big chair in the living room with his little tiny dog in his massive lap. The dog looked like a period. And then Orson would start directing. He would say, "Okay, Mike, you stand there and be me. And, Tina, you're the assistant, so you stand there ..." He would walk us through the routine. During the course of it, I or Tina would say, "Well, wait a minute, what about this, where's this prop going to come from? And when you're done with it, who's going to take it?" All of those details that help make a magic routine flow smoothly. You do it a hundred times and every prop is right where you need it when you need it. And when you are only going to perform a trick once, you try to anticipate every detail. Sometimes we got ninety percent of it right, but it was that last ten percent that looked clumsy.

So Tina and I, under the direction of Orson Welles, would rehearse the routine in Orson's living room. Well, after an hour or two, Tina and I could do it competently. But Orson had never tried it. He would say, "That's it! That's perfect! All right. It's 4 o'clock in the afternoon. I'll meet you at the studio at 7." We would leave and we're thinking, "God, Orson's never even tried this." And the reason why he hadn't was because he couldn't have stood on his feet for two hours. As he was sitting in his chair, directing, he was getting the routine set in his mind. But what we would be talking about between 4 o'clock and 7 is, "What is Tina going to do if Orson forgets to reach back to take this prop? What if Orson reaches back with his left hand instead of his right hand? What are you going to do if he forgets to hand it back to you and sticks it in his pocket? Be ready for anything." So it was always us trying to organize plan B, plan C, and plan D, just so that no matter what happened he could successfully conclude the trick.

There was another time when Orson wanted a stooge. This was for another *Merv Griffin* show. We're going to have a plant in the audience, a guy who's set up. So Tina lined up a friend. We called Orson and said, "It's all set. We have a guy, he's going to be there, his name is Albert. Do you want to meet him?" "No, no, no, I don't want to meet him. Because that way I can say, 'Have we ever met before?' and he can honestly say, 'No, we haven't.'" The key point was that the stooge was supposed to have a girlfriend in Australia. That's all Albert needed to know — he had a girlfriend in Australia. Which was funny, because Albert was gay. But that's beside the point. So everything is set. We're at the studio, they're taping the show, Albert's in the audience, and he's excited that he's going to be on TV with Orson. Orson starts the routine and says, "Now I'm going to pull a name out of the fish bowl ..." And the fish bowl falls over and breaks. There's broken glass everywhere. This is the kind of thing that we'd always worry about. We hadn't thought, "What if he breaks the fish bowl?"

So, to us, this was already a disaster. But nothing fazed Orson. He would roll right along and he would say something amusing about the fish bowl to explain why it happened. He said, "Now the name is Albert. Can Albert stand up?" Well, unbelievably, some complete stranger stands up right where Orson is looking. He asks his name and the guy says, "Albert." We panic. Albert the stooge is also standing but Orson doesn't see him. So now Orson's talking to the wrong guy named Albert. He's not a stooge and has no idea what's going on. Orson says, "Albert, do you have a girlfriend from Australia?" The guy says, "No." It went from bad to worse but in the end, Orson, with his wit and unflappability, managed to arrive at a semi-successful conclusion.

Caveney remembered a very different (and far more successful) television appearance Welles made when he guest-hosted The Tonight Show *one time.*

MC: On one occasion Orson said, "We're going to open *The Tonight Show* with an illusion." This sounded like more fun to me than doing some electronic clock trick. It was going to be a big stage illusion, like Orson used to perform in his USO show during World War II with Marlene Dietrich. So he rented a Sedan Chair and a Tip-Over Trunk. The trick is that a big throne chair is wheeled out on stage with a girl sitting in it. She is placed into a cloth bag which is tied closed and then lifted into a small wooden box that sits on a table. The top of the bag is stuck out through a hole in the top of the box. Then a big cloth is wrapped around the empty throne chair. Orson would fire a gun and pull the bag through this little hole in the top of the box. The bag was now completely empty and the box would be tipped over so everyone could see that it was empty. Then the big cloth around the sedan chair would be pulled away and the girl was discovered back in the chair.

It was a good trick and Orson called me in to help with it. Orson said, "You'll be dressed as a Hindu boy. And the girls will be dressed as Hindu girls." Orson wrote some patter to go with the trick. I'm thinking, "This is going to be great." First of all, it's on *The Tonight Show* and Doc Severinsen's going to be playing the music. We rehearsed until the whole thing could be done at break-neck speed. I wasn't sure what the patter was going to be, but I had high hopes for this spot.

I didn't know that Orson had added something to the opening. He had a metal strongbox that looked like it had been pulled up off the bottom of the ocean. It was frozen into a huge block of ice. I had no idea what he was going to do with it. So at the rehearsal, he pushed it out and said, "200 years ago Cagliostro locked a prediction in this chest and tonight we're going to open it. But not right now. We'll have to do it at another time." And with that, he pushed the table off stage. This was Orson's idea of a joke. He had done the same thing on other shows and the joke was that he never opens it! For all I know, that chest is still frozen in that block of ice.

So I'm dressed as a Hindu boy with no shoes, big blue pants, and a turban. That night I got to hear Orson's patter for the first time. And it was stupendous. You had the presence of Orson, you had the voice, and he told this story which was just a bunch of hooey about some kingdom that had always been ruled by men and now, for the first time, a woman rose to the throne, Leila, Queen of the East. Anybody else telling this story would have been laughed off the stage but when Orson delivered it, it was fantastic.

Then the big throne chair came rolling out and the girl stepped off of it. We put her in the bag and hoisted her up into the box. Like most illusions, the assistants did all the work. Orson just kind of stood there and directed traffic, holding onto this pistol. He finished the story and then shot the gun — but the blank didn't fire. He pulled the trigger again and the blank didn't fire again. So he bellowed out some magic words and we pulled the bag out and the girl was gone. We tipped the box over and it was empty. I pulled the cloth off the chair and there was the girl. Well, the audience went crazy. They just went nuts for this thing. Now I'm standing behind Orson so I really can't see his face at this point. But that night when I got home and watched the show, it was fantastic. The camera zoomed in on Orson and it's my favorite image of him. The applause increased and Orson has a big smile on his face. And the applause increased more and Orson starts to laugh. And then the applause is just deafening and they won't stop clapping. And Orson is just beaming. He is absolutely beaming. In the few years that I knew him, I never saw him happier than that moment.

It was really great. And he had the presence, when the applause finally subsided, he said something to the effect of, "I think it's worth noting that the mysteries of ancient Egypt still hold true, but modern technology is not quite as reliable. I had a feeling that gun wouldn't work!" And it got a huge laugh.

I remember when we were doing these talk shows that Orson wasn't held in very high esteem in the magic world. Because he would do tricks that they had just read about in a magazine and he had complicated them beyond recognition. Those were the days of "Drink no wine before it's time," and his main presence on TV was doing wine commercials and then an occasional magic trick on TV. All the magicians — the people that I hung out with — would say, "Oh, Orson did some stupid thing on TV again." I always found myself defending Orson. I always wanted to sit them down and say, "You know something? You have no idea what a great magician Orson was and is and how much he knows about magic. When you put him in front of an

audience — like what I saw on *The Tonight Show* — he puts everyone to shame."
He deserves a lot more credit than he gets in the magic world.

February 13, 2004

Don Bice

Don Bice: I think, at that point, the magic people were just about his only friends. I can't say that for a fact, because I don't know what he was doing when he wasn't around the magic people, but he never mentioned anyone else. *[Laughs.]* And I understand that.

Bice met Welles in "about 1980 or '81, right in there."

DB: I got a call from a magician by the name of John Daniel. And John Daniel and his wife, Kathy, had worked with Orson on *The Jackie Gleason Show* once or twice. Orson had called them because he had been invited to do *The Tonight Show*, and he wanted to do an illusion that he had done with John and Kathy in Miami. While they had had a wonderful time working with Orson, Orson can be a bit demanding in terms of time commitments! *[Laughs.]* So they weren't certain that they wanted to take the time to work with him on this project. John was a very successful train collector and cactus collector and he published newsletters. He and his wife were very involved.

So they gave me a call and said, "Hey Don, would you like to work with Orson Welles on this project? If you will, we'll rent him the equipment and you'll go along with the package." So I said, "Well, of course!" They said, "He's going to be over here Saturday morning at 9 o'clock, so you be here by 8 and we'll talk about it." I said, "Sure." So I ran over there all excited.

But his big concern was, where were they going to seat Orson? *[Laughs.]* We had a little staging there so that we would all be standing in the right place when Orson came in the room so he would be forced to take a particular chair that John felt he couldn't harm! *[Laughs.]* John got along very well with Orson, but like I say he used a lot of time. When they came back from Miami, I remember John saying that they had just had enough of Orson, had been working with him night and day, and they went to bed and took the phone off the hook so Orson couldn't reach them. And suddenly there was a knock at the door early in the morning and there was a messenger with a note that said, "John: Your phone is off the hook. Call me. Orson." *[Laughs.]* And that's the way he worked.

So Orson arrived and I met him for the first time and we talked, and he was doing *The Tonight Show*. He wanted to do those illusions and we set up the rehearsal and everything. He was quite charming and it was really a very pleasant experience to meet him. We started getting the stuff together for *The*

Tonight Show and we needed some assistants. John had a gentleman who had worked with him before, Dennis Parr, who he called, and he would be one of the assistants. I called a friend of mine, Mike Caveney, and asked Mike if he would like to assist Orson and, of course he, like all of us, would have jumped at the chance.

We started rehearsals at the studios at NBC. Johnny Carson was not on the show. This was during the strike. Orson was filling in for Johnny that night and we didn't even have the Doc Severinsen orchestra — at least not Doc Severinsen, it may have been the studio orchestra. But it was a tense situation because even the cameras were being manned by non-union operators, so the studio was continuing to operate but it was a little chaotic.

Bice told me that he thinks Welles rehearsed for two days at NBC for this Tonight Show *appearance.*

DB: It was very interesting. Orson had a unique way of directing magic. He couldn't get up and do the performance. He physically was not capable of long rehearsals. So he would sit there and I was his stand-in. Orson would say, "All right. Show me how you would do it." And I would go through like showing a box empty and rolling it around, the way I would do it. He would look at it and he would say, "Okay, now show me how you would do that with more energy." I would try it that way. He would say, "Well, now, show me how you would do that if you were frightened." And he would give me three or four ways to do it and, golly, I'd never been given instructions that way before. I really had to scratch my head and work at it.

Then after he saw all those ways, he would say, "Okay, here's how we're gonna do it." Then he would get up and he would walk through it. It was a very, very interesting way because what he did was take all the pieces that he liked and add it with what he had in his mind. It was an education to watch him work that way. I had never seen anyone work that way. Maybe that's common, but it sure wasn't common in the shows that I had participated in.

I was like everyone else. I was in awe. When we arrived at NBC, the word spread through the studio that Orson Welles was here. And everything stopped. They were taping *Hollywood Squares* next door. Everyone from *Hollywood Squares* came over to see Orson. They were all in awe of him. This happened every time we did a taping of anything. Everyone was always that way and I certainly was no different. *[Laughs.]* I was really intimidated by him, not because *he* was intimidating. It's who he was that was intimidating.

So in the beginning I was just very respectful of him, not frightened, but I certainly didn't treat him as I would anyone else that I knew. I did not find him difficult, I didn't find him too demanding. Oja was there rehearsing with us. I adored her. She was just as likable and kind as she could be. She was one of my favorites.

I can tell you when it changed for me, when we became friends. He was doing the second special, I think, for David Copperfield. He was a guest. We had rehearsed all afternoon and we were shooting in the evening hour. There was a break of several hours between the afternoon and the night shooting. Orson said he wanted to take a nap. He asked for a call an hour before the taping so that he could get back in make-up and wake up and get dressed and so forth. And they said, "Fine." Well, they knocked on his door at fifteen minutes to taping session. And here he was asleep and no make-up and not prepared to go out and work. Well, he went through the ceiling. He absolutely screamed and hollered at how unprofessional this was, that he had made a very reasonable request and that he expected when he was dealing with professionals for them to behave as professionals and to get his call.

Well, everyone panicked and the director came in and said, "Mr. Welles, we'll delay the taping. We'll give you plenty of time, take all the time you need." And Orson said, "Absolutely not! I mean, these people have been standing in line waiting to see a show and now we're going to say, 'You have to sit here while Orson Welles gets dressed'? No way. I'll be ready — if I do the show at all." Well, that was all it took. Everyone went into a panic. They just knew — because of his "reputation" — that he just may not do the show. So the director came to me because I apparently knew him well because I was there working with him — of course, I didn't know him that well — and the director said to me, "Well, do you think he's going to walk out?" And I said, "No." I had no idea, but, hey, why add to the tension? There was nothing to be gained by that. So I said, "No, I don't think so. He's a professional." He had been using that word, so it sounded like a good word to me. I said, "He's a professional and he's going to do the show because that's the important thing here. So just give him a chance to calm down and he'll be fine."

I walked back into his dressing room and Orson is raving and ranting. And I started smiling. And he slammed his hand on the desk and said, "Young man, do you find me amusing?" I broke into laughter. I said, "Orson, frankly, I think you're *hysterical.*" And he started laughing. We stood there and laughed and everything was fine. He said, "Would you like to have dinner after we finish tonight?" I said, "I think it'd be great." That changed the whole atmosphere. From then on, it was different.

We were very friendly after that. After that time, I don't know that I ever worked for him again. We stayed in touch and I was there for various projects and things, but I was never a "magical consultant" for him after those — I think it was maybe three — projects. I had a business doing industrial shows and that's where I spent most of my time. I wasn't a working magician.

But after that point our relationship changed entirely. It was like I saw through the act and he knew that I had seen behind the curtain and it was just fine. It was just totally different and I didn't have to walk on eggs. And there was no reason to because he wasn't a tyrant, that was it.

Peter Prescott Tonguette: Do you think that the ranting and raving really was an act, as you say?

DB: Oh, I believe it. There's no way to prove it, but it was protective. I think it was protective, one, because I think he had a lot of characteristics of being a loner. Whether he was or not, I can't say, but he had some appearances of that. Second of all, everyone wanted to talk about the past. Everyone wanted to talk about his old movies. I remember when we arrived at the studio to do the David Copperfield special, the director and some other executives came in and Orson was seated there in the front. They said, "Oh, Mr. Welles, it's so nice to have you here. I'm such a fan of yours, I've seen all your films, I admire your work." He was trying to make Orson comfortable. What he didn't know was that it was having the opposite effect. Orson screamed at him, "We didn't come here to talk about my goddamned movies, we came here to make a show!"

Well, it did two things. The man said, "Yes, sir, yes, sir." He backed off, then he kept his distance, he was afraid of Orson, and Orson didn't have to talk about old movies.

> *Bice didn't work on any segments of* The Magic Show, *though he did observe the filming of several of them. Seeing Welles shooting a portion of the Abu Kahn slapstick sequence at the Variety Arts Theatre in Los Angeles is, for Bice, "the saddest memory that I have of him."*

DB: So I went down there because one of the guys that worked with me in my business was assisting Orson. That man was David Egan. I went down to see how progress was going and it was, for me, just a tragic scene. Here was this darkened theatre, no one there but one cameraman and one sound man, and Orson all dressed up with the turban and everything, sitting in a wheelchair. When I arrived, he said, "Well, look who's here. What are you doing here — slumming?" *[Laughs.]* It just looked like a dark B-movie. Orson's sitting there eating Chinese food and when he got ready to get up on the stage, they had to roll the wheelchair and then they helped him and he would limp up onto the stage and get into position. Everyone would get into their places. Orson would say, "I can't stand anymore, I can't stand anymore. The chair, quick," and they would run with the chair and push behind him and he would sit down. He would try and catch his breath and wait. Then he would stand, take the chair, and shoot just a little more.

And here was one of the greatest talents ever at the end of his life, sitting in this empty theatre with a skeleton crew and shooting this film, getting in and out of his wheelchair. It was just the saddest sight for me.

Even if you didn't know him and care for him, it was just a heartbreaking thing to see a talent like that at the end of his career, suffering so much to perform. When I was there, he was doing the Lazy Magician trick, and he said to me, "Do you think it would be all right if I did part of this trick just sitting in the chair?" And I said, "Well, I think it'd be fine because originally the Lazy Magician was done by Dante and, if I'm not mistaken, he sat in a chair to do it and the girls moved the rope back and forth." I knew that he knew that because he was so knowledgeable and if I knew it, he knew it. But it just seemed like he was looking for someone to confirm it was okay. It may have been for the benefit of the other people on the stage, I don't know.

You judge people by the side of them that you see. I only saw him tyrannical when he was protecting himself. We had lunch one day at Ma Maison. I had never been to Ma Maison and he had given me the address. I tend to write things on scraps of paper and I couldn't find it. So I thought, "Well, I'll call and get the address," and of course their phone number was unlisted. [Laughs.] And I couldn't get over! It was a restaurant and the phone number was unlisted. So I finally found the place and had lunch with Orson, and that day Tony Curtis joined us. It was so neat for me because here was Orson, who I had admired and shared the magic with, and of course Tony Curtis, remember, was from *Houdini* [1953], the movie, so to me I was in the center of the magic world! [Laughs.]

Orson always got a note part way through the meal. His driver would come in and hand Orson a piece of paper. Orson would say, "Thank you," and he would open the note and read it or put it in his pocket. It was his way of getting out of a conversation if he was not enjoying it. There was nothing written on the piece of paper. If Orson was comfortable, having a good time, he just put the piece of paper in his pocket. If he wanted to leave, no matter when it was in the meal, he could say, "Oh my goodness, something has come up. I'm sorry, I'm terribly sorry, I have to leave." And that was his escape. Again, another way to separate himself if he needed to.

Bice's meal-time conversations with Welles were wide-ranging.

DB: We discussed acting. I remember Abb Dickson, who he was very fond of, and tried to help his career when Abb was out here. Orson saw a lot of talent in Abner and he really did encourage him and try and get him into the acting business. I know we talked about acting a lot. One of the things I asked Orson is if he really thought that acting could be taught. He assured me very definitely that anyone could learn to act, in his opinion. Now there were people more gifted than others who could become more skilled than others, but acting was a skill that anyone who wanted to learn could learn. And that kind of surprised me. That was not the response I expected from him.

I also remember we discussed the fact that I had seen him in a film, *Compulsion* [1959], as a very young man, and that I was so impressed with his performance as Clarence Darrow, the attorney, and his plea to spare the boy's life. I said, "That really, really impressed me. In fact, I went out and started reading books on becoming a lawyer and I read the speeches of this attorney. I decided at that point in life that I really wanted to be an attorney." And he died laughing and said, "My God, I would have hated to have that on my conscience!" *[Laughs.]*

Bice remembered Welles's poodle, Kiki.

DB: You'd sit there and someone would always approach the table to tell him how much they appreciated him and what a fan they were and he would grab the dog, put his hands on the dog, and scream, "Mad dog! Back! Back! Stand back! Stand back!" And, of course, with that voice people would just automatically recoil from the table and they would talk from a distance, so they couldn't say too much. *[Laughs.]*

A number of Welles's magician friends got together after he died.

DB: We had our own little private service for Orson. Jim [Steinmeyer] said, "Let's just get together and trade Orson stories and talk and have his favorite dessert." We got vanilla ice cream, fresh raspberries over it, and Bacardi light rum poured over it. *[Laughs.]* That was Orson's favorite desert, according to Jim.

My favorite film piece of his will really surprise you. My favorite film piece is in *Someone to Love* (1987). What you think of the movie isn't really important, but the last sequence when Orson is in the back of the audience talking — some critics have said those were his words and his final farewell, others have said that's just a myth, it was all scripted for him. Makes no difference — that was Orson. That was pure Orson. That was the Orson I knew: knowledgeable, deep, his laughter; he laughs in that last sequence and I just get chills. That was Orson's laugh. That's my favorite piece of film. I can watch that little bit of video and I feel like I've visited Orson.

July 17, 2004

Allen Bracken

Bracken was "a young actor and a magician" working with Abb Dickson in Atlanta in the early '80s.

Allen Bracken: I had occasion to go out to Los Angeles and stay with some friends of mine out there, Don Keller and Ron Surma, who were local magicians affiliated with The Magic Castle and who I knew through Abb. While I was in Los Angeles, I believe it was in 1981, I got a phone call from Abb asking me if I would like to meet Orson and maybe work with him. And, of course, I immediately said yes. I obviously heard of and studied his work through my college stuff. So he called me up. We were going to go eat at Ma Maison restaurant, which was a place that Orson ate on a if I'm not mistaken, almost every evening meal.

It was 6 o'clock in the evening. It was in the summer, as I recall. We went to his house up in the Hollywood Hills, which wasn't too far from where I was staying at the time at The Magic Hotel. We were met by [Alessandro] Tasca, who was kind of his valet and man-about-town guy, and then Oja, who was his companion at the time. They met us at the door and invited us in. We sat in the library. Twenty minutes went by, no Orson. Thirty minutes went by, no Orson. An hour went by, still no Orson. And we just kind of sat patiently in the library waiting for him to show up. *[Laughs.]*

Then after I would guess it was probably around an hour-and-a-half or so, this man walked into the room. And he was short and he was fat and he could barely walk and he had a cane and his hair was disheveled. I couldn't believe that this was Orson Welles. He was wearing a mumu, but it had to be custom made because it was so big and so wide. I was a little bit kind of disappointed. I mean, I was actually shocked, which I think is probably a good word. He introduced himself. We said, "Hi." He said, "I just need to go clean up and then we'll go eat." And, as I said, by now it's probably 7:30 or 8:00. And he walked away.

So Abb and I chit-chatted a little bit. And then another hour went by and another hour-and-a-half went by. So now it's closer to like 9:30, I'm guessing. And he walked back into the room and he had on a tuxedo. His hair was combed and his beard was trimmed. He had that twinkle in his eye that you can see when you look at Orson and you know that he knows — it was just spectacular. It was the most unbelievable transformation from this kind of old, fat looking guy to Orson Welles, to the persona. It was incredible. Even today, thinking back on it, I have chills.

We all piled into the car and we drove down to Ma Maison. We sat down at dinner and he ordered, of course, wine, which he often did — always did, I should say. We ordered food and we had some unbelievable bottled wine that he loved — and, actually, as I recall, probably more than one. In our hour-and-a-half or two hours of sitting at dinner and him telling stories and stories and stories and answering my questions as best as he would or could, while we were there George Lucas came by and said, "Hello." Oh gosh, I wish I could remember. I think Sylvester Stallone happened to be in there and came by and said, "Hello." And these people came to the table with this reverence almost of royalty. A note would be passed and Orson would read the note, he would nod his head, and then George Lucas walked up.

And it was just incredible. I was 21 or 22 years old, I guess, and I was just awe-struck by the whole thing. And then I don't know what there was, but it was a signal that he had with Tasca that would be — and I don't even know what it was — but suddenly he would appear and everybody got up and left. *[Laughs.]* No bill ever changed hands and I don't know what the arrangement was. There were rumors that he never paid for food at Ma Maison because just his presence there was enough that it got customers in. I don't know that to be true or not, but that was the rumor. I never saw a bill, he never signed anything. We just kind of all got up and left and it was just incredible.

Of course, I immediately phoned home and told my family that I had dinner with Orson Welles and what a great experience it was. At that dinner we started talking about the movie that he was in the process of doing, this Abu Kahn magic film that he had worked on previously for even a couple years before I became involved in it. And then he worked on it for years while I was involved in it and then for a few years *after* I had no longer been involved in it! *[Laughs.]*

> *"The movie that he was in the process of doing"* was, of course, The Magic
> Show. *I asked Bracken how Welles described the project to him.*

AB: Well, you know what, he wanted it to be ... and Orson, as long as I knew him, for the few years that I knew him, he wanted to be remembered as a magician. He was very, very much interested in the magical arts and in performing. And one of the lines that he told me, and we often laughed about, was he felt directly responsible for killing vaudeville. He said, "Every time I worked a vaudeville theatre, after I left it closed." He used to do his magic acts and vaudeville and he did them all across the United States and then in Europe. He really loved magic and he loved magicians.

So this was what he was describing to us. He wanted it to be his crowning achievement. Again, Orson Welles wanted everything, I think, to be his crowning achievement. Every film that he was working on was going to be the masterpiece. But the way he described this to us, he wanted this to be the crème de la crème of magic movies.

He was describing scenes over dinner, at which point he invited me to participate. As an actor, I thought, "Now, of course, my career is launched because I was going to be working with Orson Welles." I was really excited.

The other thing about Orson that was just almost frightening was the phone would ring and it would be Orson. *[Laughs.]* "We'll be at La Brea Studios at 10 o'clock. Be there." And he'd just hang up. "Allen, this is Orson. Meet me at La Brea Studios at 10:15." And hang up. I'd go, "Gosh, it's like a quarter after 9!" And then five minutes later, "Allen, we can't get La Brea Studios today. We'll be there tomorrow at 7. Can you make it?" "Yeah." Click. That was it. The phone would ring and you'd start going, "Oh, Christ, it's Orson. Are we on, are we off, what's going to happen?"

And that's the way he worked. We would shoot for a day and then I wouldn't hear from him for a week or two weeks or a month. And then we would shoot for two or three days and then you wouldn't hear from him for a while.

Bracken told me about the friendship between Welles and Abb Dickson.

AB: Abb Dickson was one who, for some reason, Orson just really took a shine to, and used him for counsel and for all kinds of other things. And when anything would happen with Orson, he'd call Abb and tell him. He was always excited to tell Abb about the good things that happened. I remember being in Atlanta and the phone rang and Abb picked up the phone. And he starts, "Oh, hi, how are you?" And it was just a kind of casual conversation. Orson had called out of the blue to tell Abb about some little event that had happened in his life that week as like a confidante.

In The Magic Show, *one of the roles Bracken played was a deputy police officer to Dickson's police chief in the Abu Kahn slapstick sequence. Bracken described his first day of shooting on the film.*

AB: So this particular scene that we were filming was The Disembodied Princess. It's a box where you put a body in and it's got four doors around the mid-section and so you can see the legs and you can see the head. You slice swords through and then you open the doors and the middle is gone. And that's why they call it The Disembodied Princess.

So we're doing this and we have it rigged where all the doors are going to open — by magic — and, of course, the body's not going to be there and then now the body's going to be somewhere else. We finally shot this scene of the doors opening, which was a major trauma. And the other thing that Orson did that I found was that he rehearsed and rehearsed and rehearsed and rehearsed and he would rehearse forever. Then he would shoot it once, maybe, or twice and then move on. But, in my experience, he would never shoot anything until he rehearsed it to death.

And so we had rehearsed all morning. We finally got that shot. Now it was going to be my first shot in the movie and he said, "Okay, Allen, I want you to ..." We're on a pitch black set with lights glaring down on the soundstage, Orson is off in the shadows behind the cameras, and he says, "I want you to cross from up camera left to down camera right, from off camera right across in front of the Disembodied to off camera left." And I'm in a policeman's outfit — a bobby's outfit, actually, an English bobby with the hat — and a flashlight. He says, "Okay, let's try that. Action." So I crossed down and I crossed back and he goes, "Okay, fine. Let's try that again." And he adjusted some lights and had some cameras move around and he yakked for a little while and we did it again. He goes, "Fine. Back up to 1, back up to 1." And this went on, I would guess, for an hour.

And finally, I had no idea what he wanted from me. *[Laughs.]* I'm sitting there and I'm thinking to myself, "You know, is it me?" There's a whole camera crew, there's all these people, and it's like my fifteenth or sixteenth time. I mean, how hard is it to cross from one side to the other? And I'm standing in the middle with these lights and I'm the only thing on stage and I said, "Mr. Welles?" "Yes?" "What's my motivation?" *[Laughs.]* Here I am, 21 years old, and I was asking Orson Welles what my motivation was! And from behind the camera he goes, "*Motivation?* Oh my God, I've been directing for 35 years and no one has ever asked me what their motivation was!" And he just really kind of teed off on me. I was like trembling. And, as I said, I'm on stage by myself and he's just yelling from beyond the camera in pitch black — I don't even know really where he is — about, "You know, I did this and the amazing Albertsons and I did all this stuff and the actors that I've worked with," and he goes on and on and on for 15, 20 minutes — well, maybe not that long. It seemed like that long. I'm sure it was five minutes. And he said, "You know what I think, I think you're motivated by the fact that they're all these spirits around and so you're probably a little frightened, but you're a cop so you're still determined." And I went, "Okay! That's really all I wanted to know," after him yelling.

So at the end of the day, I was like, "Well, I'm fired. I'm sure I'm fired." And so as I went home, he told Abb Dickson, "The motivation kid — what's his name, Allen? Make sure he's back here tomorrow." So I was hired. And from that point on, we worked together off and on for about the next three or four years, whenever he would get an infusion of cash or whatever it took for him to shoot the next scene.

We kind of finished our stuff up around '84-ish, I'm guessing. And it was always, "We're going to get back to it, we're going to get back to it," but then he went to Europe and he was having some other problems and then he died.

I don't want to make it sound like we were best friends or anything, but we did have conversations and we did have dinner together. I was at his house on several occasions where he would just chit-chat. So I did get a chance to know him at a certain level, not nearly as well as Don Wayne or those guys, but I was lucky enough to kind of get in there at a time where he would chit-chat with me.

As a matter of fact, one of the things that Orson did do for me was he kind of validated my acting career with my father, who had wondered for years when I was going to really kind of get a good, real job, because I'd been acting since I was literally in elementary school. But my dad always thought, "Well, he's going to grow out of this. He'll settle down and he'll get a real job." When I told him that I was working with Orson Welles, from that point on my dad never questioned me as an actor. Even though the movie was never finished, as far as I know, and it was never seen in this country — apparently, I heard that there were some showings of snippets of it along the way — once I worked with Orson Welles, my dad was like, "Oh, my son's an actor," because he knew who Orson was.

Peter Prescott Tonguette: When you appeared in *The Magic Show*, was it always in the role of the police deputy?

AB: No, it was always something different. I mean, that was the other thing. Again, it was back to, "Don't you think people are going to recognize me?" *[Laughs.]* It was in the background, obviously. I was kind of a background character. I was never like a main character. But at one point I was a Moorish boy in a Moorish hat and a vest and balloony, Arab type pants. I did the policeman thing. I did a stagehand deal where I came out dressed as a stagehand on stage.

So there again, I was like a utility player through this whole thing in different costumes and different segments, never really one thing.

Bracken said of the Magic Show *footage, "I didn't know how a lot of it was going to fit together."*

AB: Of course, one of the things that I always understood even from my film training and stuff was that Orson Welles's genius was in the editing room. And from what I knew, it would have had to be because of the way he shot stuff. He shot stuff so disjointed.

We would sit down, I remember at the Variety Arts, and he would tell stories and we would laugh because a lot of times he would tell similar stories from when he was in Europe and from vaudeville. He always loved to talk about magic. He didn't really want to ever talk too much about the entertainment or the film stuff. Sometimes you could goad him into it or he would get excited about something and he would start on a story. But his stories oftentimes had different endings, based on who he was talking to and what brought the story up in the first place, so he could relate it to the conversation.

He said there were never any authorized biographies of him. But he was going to write his biography and he had gotten an advance from the French, from some publishing house in France, of a million dollars to write his biography. He told us it was going to be in three books; it was going to take three different books to write his biography. And we joked behind his back that it was going to be like the stories and then the alternate endings were going to be the other books. *[Laughs.]*

Nobody ever really knew what was the truth, but that was the beauty of Orson as a storyteller too. I don't know if you can verify — so much of that stuff is unverifiable, but it's so entertaining that it doesn't really need to be.

We did hit it off. Obviously, I had really a great deal of respect for him going into it. Of course, my "motivation" afternoon I think kind of set the tone for our relationship. He always kind of joked with me about stuff like that and he knew I was an actor. Most of the guys that he worked with were magicians first and then they had their other kind of trades that they did and helped him with afterwards. I was a magician only because, as a magic assistant, I had done some small magic, but I was more an actor first and then a magician second. And so he knew about that.

PPT: Since he thought of you as you thought of yourself, which was first and foremost as an actor, did he ever discuss you appearing in films of his other than *The Magic Show?*

AB: You know what, he never did. We had discussed things that he was doing, but when he was working on a project, from what I knew of him, he was really kind of one-minded. At that time, he had kind of come through — and I'm not sure, I don't want to be wrong with the timing — but I'm pretty sure that he had already come through the "No wine before its time" thing, and he was embarrassed by that because a lot of comedians were making fun of him and it turned into kind of a pop culture joke. And I think that bothered him. He never wanted to talk about stuff like that. So he was kind of in a transition right then and there and also he was really excited, as I remember him, talking about writing this book and how this was going to be really important. And one of the reasons that I think he kind of set aside the movie and didn't continue on with it was because he really was interested in writing his book.

I was doing an audition for a major motion picture. I can't remember, but it was probably around '86 or '85. Orson may or may not have been alive or dead at the time. A guy said, "Hey, tell me an interesting story." So I said, "Oh, I can tell you my Orson story about the balloons." We're sitting there in the Variety Arts center and we'd been there all day. He'd already fired an entire camera crew, which is another story, and replaced them. It's probably 10 or 11 o'clock at night. And we've got these helium filled balloons and the deal is Orson lays the girl down, hands the balloons to her, and she floats up, as if the balloons were lifting her up. So we'd rehearsed and we'd gone on and off and people were running around like crazy. Orson is sitting in his wheelchair on stage and he's like, "Bring me the balloons. Can someone please bring me the balloons?" And people are kind of scurrying about, doing their thing. And it's like, "Excuse me, can I get the ... I need the balloons over here." And nobody's paying attention to him. And at the top of his lungs he says, "*Bring me the goddamned balloons!*" And everybody stopped! It's like, "Oh, okay. Let's get the balloons because right now the balloons are the most important thing!" So we gave him the balloons and he's like, "Thank you very much. Please continue on." He apparently wanted to do something with the balloons.

So I told this story in this audition and the guy kind of chuckled and everything. He goes, "Okay, thank you very much." As I was leaving, he goes, "Hey, you know what? Don't tell the Orson story in auditions." "Why not?" "'Cause you're kind of trying to impress people that you worked with Orson." "Well, yeah." "Yeah, everybody's worked with Orson." *[Laughs.]* You know what, it's funny because it seems like everybody has worked with Orson. I don't know why.

PPT: What was the story about Welles firing the camera crew?

AB: We were working and I don't remember exactly what we happened to be shooting. It may have been the levitation that day. And we got late and Tasca or someone came up and whispered into Orson's ear that it was time to break, that the crew needed a break for dinner. And he had not been happy that day. As a matter of fact, it was told to me — and I don't want to attribute it to anybody, but I think it may have been even Jim Steinmeyer — that if you want Orson to respect you, you treat him like a five year old child. When he yells at you, you yell right back at him. And then oftentimes I would see that. I couldn't do it because I was a kid, but I saw these guys who really were his confidants who really he had a great deal of respect for, when he would have these big explosions and yell at the top of his lungs and demand things and really throw a temper tantrum like a five year old, someone would come over and scold him and then he would be okay again.

But he had not been happy that day and he was irritated about the way things were going, so when there was a dinner break — because I'm guessing it was 6 or 7 o'clock at night — we went upstairs to the restaurant on top of the Variety Arts center. We sat down, ate, and it was a great meal because again you're sitting with Orson and he's telling you all these stories. We sat there for an hour or so and we came back downstairs and we noticed the camera guys were kind of scurrying around and the sound guys were setting stuff up and the grips. And I didn't recognize any of them. I was kind of surprised, I was a little shocked even. The camera guy's sitting there and I was like, "Hey, how's it going?" "Good, how are you doing?" "You just gettin' here?" "Yeah."

He had fired the entire crew before he went to dinner and had them replaced inside an hour for him to come down for dinner. Now we're not talking about a 200, 300 person crew. It was only probably 6 or 8 guys, 10 guys and girls total, but everybody was fired. He was just mad and irritated with them and so he said, "I want everybody out and call whoever and get a whole new crew in," and that's what he did. I was just amazed that he could do that. And again, I never saw money change hands; he paid me, I'd get checks from him, but I don't know how he was able to do that even financially.

PPT: Why do you think that Welles, as Abb Dickson put it to me, "preferred the company of magicians" later in his life?

AB: There again, I don't know except for the fact that it may have tied him to his youth, because I know that's what he was doing and that's really how he kind of came up and really made his name, in magic and in the vaudeville set. I mean, he was disappointed often in his movie[s] and his relationships with movie people and the movie industry. I'm an Orson Welles lover so that may taint what I say, but even beyond *Citizen Kane,* which I thought obviously was brilliant and may be the best piece of film *ever,* but his other stuff showed a real sense of brilliance. But he was disappointed a lot and he didn't get his way, but he often got his way — I think maybe he always got his way — in his magic dealings, working with magicians. There was a kindred spirit there.

July 18, 2004

Tim Suhrstedt

However rare, there were inevitably occasions when Gary Graver was unavailable to work with Welles. Suhrstedt was a cameraman who subbed for Graver in one such instance, working as cinematographer on The Magic Show *for two days in October 1982.*

Tim Suhrstedt: I'm 90 percent sure — well, I never spoke to him directly — but Gary gave him my name. At that time in Los Angeles, there was a relatively small sort of pool of non-union independent crew people. And I had sort of followed some years behind Gary through that low-budget world, related to Roger Corman and things. When the gentleman who was working as Orson's producer called me, he said that Gary had given him my name as a possible substitute. Gary was working out of town; he had some other work.

Peter Prescott Tonguette: Do you remember which sequences you shot for *The Magic Show*?

TS: Well, that was one of the things that was so bizarre about it. There was never anything on paper. We were just kind of doing what he wanted us to do. My only memory of it was all of the shooting happened at a place in L.A. called the Variety Arts Theatre, which was sort of a theatre that kind of specialized in ... it was an old theatre and they had stuff like, it's hard to describe, sort of revival stuff or tributes to vaudeville. And it was a fairly common film location because they were happy to rent this out to people who needed a stage, who needed a proscenium stage.

I just remember that we were down there and all the shooting took place on the stage, literally on the stage in the theatre. There was someone else that we were shooting with Orson, but I cannot remember, for the life of me, who it was or what he did. All I remember was Orson up on stage in kind of a robe at a certain point. And there was nothing on paper; there was nothing resembling script pages. It was completely out of his head. I knew we were shooting for something called *Orson Welles's Magic Show*, but I had no idea what we were doing.

This was strictly Orson on stage. I'm not certain that there was someone else up there, but there must have been, because one of the things that I remember is that it was literally very difficult for him to stand for any length of time, he was so overweight. So he couldn't have been doing much, because I remember when he actually stood up to do his part, we were all kind of worried. Over the two days, I know we were shooting something other than Orson. But I also remember him standing up there in kind of a robe and turban-like hat.

I remember his producer, who was this lovely, older Italian man named Alessandro Tasca. He was just a charmer. I really enjoyed him.

PPT: How did you and Welles work together?

TS: Oh, it was pretty bizarre, because he was basically just kind of setting these shots up and I was just kind of trying to do what he wanted, but without the benefit of having any kind of overview or any sort of context. So I was just pretty much setting up the shots the way he wanted. We were using his old Éclair CM3 cameras. We weren't recording sound. We were just kind of doing what he wanted to do.

To me, of course, to get a phone call when I was that young, had only shot a couple movies, saying, "You want to do a couple days with Orson Welles?" — at first, I thought it was almost a prank. And then I went to his house for kind of an interview. Then I was kind of on stand-by, where Alessandro would call and say, "He's not feeling well, he's not feeling well," and then, "Okay, we're going to go tomorrow." And then we did two days.

PPT: What did you and he discuss when you met him?

TS: Well, oddly enough, he wanted to know if I was familiar with the camera and could load the camera. I sort of did it, but I said, "Well, I'll actually have an assistant there to do that. I can do it, but it's not really what I'll be doing." Going to his house, you probably couldn't have scripted it to be more appropriate to his image and legend. Just the whole interview process and the way this house was and the way he was ... *[Laughs.]* The house was kind of dark and extremely cluttered.

[Oja Kodar] was there[...] She had brought him this gigantic plate of stuffed peppers. So I'm sitting opposite Orson Welles, who is in this terry cloth robe. And, you know, just gigantic.

Someone told me that in the years after I spent these two days with him, he actually dropped some weight. He certainly didn't get slim, but I think this was about as heavy as he ever was. When he was down at the Variety Arts Theatre, he was in kind of a double-sized wheelchair. Literally, when he stood for five or ten minutes, he would perspire and his eyes would bug out. Actually, I joked with my crew, but it was true, that my greatest fear was that I would be a small footnote in cinema history: that I would be the cameraman working with Orson Welles when he keeled over, because he looked to me that at any time he could just keel over. He was so grotesquely overweight. That if the act of standing caused his eyes to bug out and cause him to sweat, I figured that it's only a matter of time before he has a massive heart attack or stroke, and I'll be the cameraman standing next to him and that will be my place in film history. That concerned me, actually.

And in fact, several months later I was called back by Alessandro to do some more shooting for one day, and that's why I didn't do it.

PPT: Really?

TS: Because I felt that I was literally too worried about being the guy there when he died. The project to me seemed so ... I had no handle on where he was in it, how much he'd completed, how close he was to completing it. But it seemed, to be kind, to be very disorganized. It really seemed like we were working on his own little home movie. And so I felt, "Look, for one more day, it's not going to complete the film, I don't even know what the film is. I don't want to be there when he dies." I was that worried that he was going to keel over.

I mean, if there had been a script and I could say, "Good, this is one more scene he needs," or if I had some sense of what I was doing, I would have probably gone back. But I felt that it was completely random shooting that was just in his head. And even Alessandro alluded to me, very kindly — he was very affectionate with him, I think he had told me that he met Orson in the early '50s on his Shakespeare films. And he really liked him, and Allesandro kind of was sort of rolling his eyes, saying, "Well, this is just Orson's thing."

> *Given Welles's working methods, the fact that Suhrstedt was kept in the dark as to the context of what he was shooting is not surprising. As Abb Dickson told me, "Orson, for all of his good points, sometimes was not the best 'communicator' of exactly* why *he was doing something. Sometimes, he just 'shot.' And once it was done, he said thanks and that was it. ... he never let us know further what was going to be done with it. The film was just printed and delivered to Orson. Period."[5]*

PPT: You were talking about the experience of going to his house.

TS: Oh, God. Well, the house was very dark. I came in and, again, there's a part of me that's almost thinking, "This is a prank." Someone's called me and said, "Come to Orson Welles's house." But I walked in and he was sitting in a big easy chair in a terry cloth robe with his feet propped up. And it was not a pretty sight. His robe's kind of falling open. And she brought him a gigantic plate of stuffed peppers which he consumed as he was talking to me. It's just bizarre. You couldn't describe a sort of weirder meeting. So I'm taking in his physical condition and I'm watching him just gorge himself on these stuffed peppers. And he's asking me ... he's very respectful and he asked if I knew the camera. I said, "Well, yeah, I can load the camera ..." And he actually had me load the film while I was there to make sure I could do it. Though, as I told him, I would actually have an assistant who would be doing this.

And then Alessandro called me back and said, "We're ready to go." And that's when we got into this kind of holding pattern for a week because he wasn't feeling well.

The thing was, I don't have that much of a recollection of what we shot. I do know it was all on a stage and it was all magic oriented.

I remember the most fun part of it was, of course, sitting there with him in between shooting, or when he would be sitting in his wheelchair and we were in the theatre. I just started asking him about Gregg Toland and ... his storytelling was just ... well, you know. That was just really a treat to find yourself sitting there with him being the raconteur.

PPT: Did you find him to be disposed to talking?

TS: Oh, God, yes. Really, really sharp and really just that ultimate raconteur. That was just a treat, to hear all that. He told me — I don't know if this is true, but I tell it because he told me directly — that when they were shooting *Citizen Kane*, he paid Nat King Cole fifteen dollars a day to play piano on the set while they were lighting. Now that's directly from him. It's a great story. And that fits in with the time frame, because in the early '40s Nat King Cole was pretty unknown, playing in bars with his trio. And he said that they had heard him and he gave him fifteen bucks a day.

Just to be sitting with Orson Welles and having him tell me that Nat King Cole played during their lighting set-ups was just ... all the sort of Americana-meets-film-history you could hope for.

The whole experience for me was just spending two days with him. The filmmaking part was sort of not much. But the other funny story that I tell about that — and this is true — is he kept saying to me, "Do you have a still camera? Can you bring a still camera?" I said, "Okay, I always have a still camera with me." He said, "Well, you know, they want me on the cover of *Paris Vogue* for December." And I thought, "Yeah, sure they do." *[Laughs.]* And I shot off a roll of stills with him standing up on the stage at the Variety Arts Theatre, in his robe — a kind of bluish robe — kind of posing like the grand magician. I handed him the roll of film.

I remember I was walking through a mall two months later, in December, and walked by a newsstand, and there was my photograph of Orson there on the cover of *Paris Vogue*. So I thought, "Okay. Funny that I doubted him and find that I have the cover of *Paris Vogue!*" Not that that's my line of work, but I had no credit!

Suhrstedt's photo of Welles—wearing the aforementioned "bluish robe" and motioning to a girl behind him who is in midair—graces the cover of Paris Vogue, *December 1982/January 1983. The issue was guest-edited by Welles.*

PPT: You didn't get any credit for it?

TS: Well, no, because I thought, "Yeah, sure, right, here's your roll of film." So the joke was on me. I probably could have at least gotten credit. The double take I did when walking by a newsstand and I saw the photo was really, really funny. So the laugh was on me on that one.

Like Eric Sherman, crew-person on The Other Side of the Wind, *Suhrstedt was impressed by Welles's knowledge of the camera. Sherman's comment to me that "[Welles] had absolute certainty on what was being seen when and where" is echoed in Suhrstedt's recollections below.*

TS: The other thing that I remember is that he would call for a focal length lens and he'd be sitting in his wheelchair on the floor of the theatre. And I'd be on the stage setting up a shot. This is why I know we were shooting someone else. But I can't remember who it was. Because I remember clearly standing at the camera shooting someone, as Orson was directing me from the floor in his wheelchair. He really knew. If he said to me, "Put up a 50mm," he knew exactly what I was seeing. He had a very good sense of ... of course, we didn't have video assist and he wasn't looking through the camera. But he had a very, very good idea of where the frame was. He had a good knowledge of what I was doing, clearly.

I'm surprised that I don't remember what we shot. All my memories of that day are being up on stage—I'm not even sure we ever ventured off the stage. We didn't get a lot done. We didn't work a lot of hours. And I clearly remember shooting Orson in this sort of bluish robe, doing a trick and sort of intro-ing things. Of course, it was weird because there was no sound and he was just kind of talking everyone through it. I clearly remember having my eye to the eyepiece and shooting someone with him directing, although I don't remember what I was shooting.

It was a very strange, sort of odd memory. And, interestingly enough, it had very little to do about filmmaking. It was more about the stories and going to his house. I never saw the footage. They took the footage, they weren't sure when they were going to process it, and I remember I never even got a chance to see it. They weren't even sure what lab they were going to send it to.

It was so sweet because Alessandro was a really lovely, very cultured, very European man. And I really liked him too. I ended up spending a lot of time talking to him just because he was so sweet, and so sort of old-worldly, classy. When he called me back, he had this lovely kind of cultured accent. I remember he said, "Orson really liked you and would like for you to do another day." I actually felt bad because I sort of made up an excuse. But I'm telling you — I didn't want to tell him because they had such a sweet relationship — I literally didn't want to be there when he died. And I felt that it was imminent. I felt that it could clearly happen at any moment. As I said, if I knew where I was in the project or what I was doing or that it was really sort of cogent, the whole plan for the project, I would have done it.

PPT: Did Tasca have a lot of stories about Welles?

TS: Oh, I remember he talked about meeting him. He was very kind, but the subtext of what he was saying was, "Oh my God, this will never get done. But he's my friend."

Alessandro lived very close to him in a condo right off Hollywood Boulevard. I remember he and his daughter came by the set. I just really liked him. I was really kind of charmed by him and sort of taken by his sort of old-world gentlemanliness and how sweet he was with Orson and how very caring he was about it. I don't remember the credits, but I remember being fascinated by all the things he had done, both film in Europe, theatre, opera. He was a real class act. I don't know if he told me or Orson told me, but he was some sort of nobility, a duke or whatever you are in Italy.

It was a pretty interesting two days.

April 23, 2004

Jim Steinmeyer

Steinmeyer arrived in Los Angeles in 1981 to work with famed magician Doug Henning.

Jim Steinmeyer: Many of my friends here in Los Angeles were magicians, and some had worked with Welles as consultants, or helpers and assistants for his magic projects. At that time, he used to appear on *The Merv Griffin Show,* and he would perform some piece of magic. So he always had associates who helped him with those projects. My friend Mike Caveney, a professional magician, and another friend, magician Don Keller, used to help Orson regularly on those shows. Don Wayne, another magic inventor, also used to help him at that time.

And so I knew them and they used to talk about working with Orson. And Don Keller gave him a book I had just written on magic, a historical book about stage magic published in Chicago before I came to Los Angeles. Don said, "Oh, I gave Orson Welles your book and he really loves it." Well, of course, you don't know what that means, so I just said, "Oh, that's great." "He's gonna call you." So I answered, "Yeah, mm-hmm." *[Laughter.]* Orson Welles is going to call me, right.

And at that time, I was staying in some little apartment — because I was out here for just six months of work with Doug Henning — so I was at a little apartment just over the hill from Hollywood. And one night — wouldn't you know? — I come back and there's a message on my phone machine from Orson Welles! That voice! And you think to yourself, this is completely unbelievable. So I went to meet him.

Steinmeyer's first meeting with Welles occurred the evening he was shooting the Gypsy Thread for The Magic Show.

JS: So I ended up being in the studio the night that they filmed that trick. And it was a really, really tiny studio and part of the presentation is that he was smoking a cigar and blowing smoke through it all. And it was a studio about 15 × 15 feet and they were doing a little camera move in it too, so they had track down on the floor. It was almost impossible to stand or sit anywhere out of the way. Because of the camera move and everything, I ended up crouched on the ground, very close to him, and low so I wasn't in his eye line. The trick took hours and hours to shoot, because it was all one long take and it was tough to get the camera move to time perfectly with the trick. So I got to watch performance after performance. Just fantastic. And his presentation was wonderful and his voice was unbelievable. Of course, we all stunk like cigar smoke at the end when we finally left.

And he said, "Oh, I'll call you and we'll have dinner sometime." And he did. And I went down to his house and drove him to Ma Maison. I was driving a little rented Mustang at the time — and he was not self-conscious of that at all. He got in the Mustang and he wanted to go to Ma Maison.

While I was in L.A., we had dinner maybe once a week, certainly once every two weeks. And I would certainly talk to him once or twice a week. Now that I look back on that time, I really didn't really work with him that much. He only asked me to help with about two or three of those Merv Griffin shoots. I was pressed into service to put those tricks together for him. He talked to me about other projects as well, and some of these were illusions that he wanted constructed for his magic special. We built a few effects, in a very leisurely way, that he wanted to shoot.

Mike Caveney and Don Keller were still helping with the television shows, so I didn't really become one of those guys that worked with him. Occasionally, like I said, he asked me to help with an appearance, but mostly my time with him was conversation about magic and other things, like politics or the latest news. I remember several evenings there, thinking to myself, "This is ridiculous that I'm here, talking to Orson Welles. There are so many people who want to be here, asking him about his films." *[Laughter.]*

But, you know, I also was aware that the reason I was there was because I wasn't asking him all those questions about his films. He really wanted to talk about other things; he wanted to talk about magic and historical magic, and the projects we were planning for Doug Henning's television show or his upcoming Broadway show — he was really, really knowledgeable about magic. I probably don't need to say that. But as far as magicians go, he had amazing insights: the people he knew, the performers he'd seen, and his ideas about presenting magic. He talked to me about a magician named Thurston, who he had seen as a boy, about what he was like. And David Bamberg ... he trained with David Bamberg and he was taught the floating ball routine by his father.

So we talked a lot about magic and we also used to talk about politics and the recent news. And he certainly did talk about his films, because the conversation would drift over to those subjects. Although I was careful not to be the fellow always saying to him, "Tell me about the scene in *Citizen Kane* where you did ..."

Peter Prescott Tonguette: So did you two hit it off immediately?

JS: I would say so. He was an amazing friend. I remember him calling once and saying, "What's going on? What are you working on? How are you doing?" And I said, "I'm fine." "Well, you don't sound fine. We should have dinner."

He loved to go to Ma Maison. He said that the reason he always went there was because they let him bring the dog and he used to go in the back entrance with the dog....

This was his black poodle, Kiki, who was just nasty. *[Laughter.]* It was a sweet little dog, but it was one of those dogs that would bark when you get up to leave. You know, it would go for your ankles when you leave! But Kiki was great with him. He always had Kiki in the crook of his arm and then he would put her down on the chair next to him, where she would sit quietly through dinner. He was always conscious that the management wasn't thrilled that he brought his dog, so he quickly hid her on the chair so the customers didn't see Kiki.

He used to say that it was a very European thing, to bring the dog to dinner, but Americans couldn't abide that. At Ma Maison, they were obsequious to him. But there was a point where going there was a little silly, I used to think, because it was such a production. So sometimes I would bring Chinese food to his house. I found a restaurant in Glendale that had Chinese food that he really liked, and I enjoyed those evenings because it was much more relaxed than Ma Maison.

Then I went to New York to do work on Doug Henning's Broadway show. And while we were planning it, Orson came through New York twice. I believe it was twice. He was always curious about how the show was doing, and I saw him in New York. He stayed on the East Side at the Carlyle.

I'd heard all sorts of stories about how he was difficult to work with, very goofy stories about his impatience or how he asked for something to be done under some impossible situation. But I have to say, I never experienced any of that. I never saw it. I could see that he was the kind of person who attracted those kinds of stories. People liked to tell those stories, or exaggerate because Orson was such a prominent personality in so many ways.

The Cradle Will Rock, discussed below, was a screenplay Welles wrote about his staging of the Marc Blitzstein opera of the same title in the 1930s; the film was never made.

JS: I worked with him on ideas for *The Cradle Will Rock* in Italy. It was going to be done in an Italian film studio. There was quite a bit of planning for *The Cradle Will Rock* when he was writing that script. I wasn't involved through the project, but I was involved in planning the effects and the magic with him. I was fortunate enough to hear all the stories of the real production, because he wanted to portray the magic effects from *Faustus*.

Years before, we'd talked about a historical magician — and Orson said, "Oh, this would make a great script." And we talked about it for a few weeks, off and on. Orson was fascinated with the idea of a turn of the century magician, who faces many different audiences and many different beliefs — that period of time when magic is almost real to the audiences.

This is a project alluded to briefly by Jonathan Rosenbaum in his afterword to the published screenplay of The Cradle Will Rock. *Rosenbaum writes of "a possible film project about magic shows at the turn of the century" which was discussed by Welles and Steinmeyer.*[6]

JS: Orson and I talked about a story. It was based Harry Kellar, who was an American magician who retired in 1908. In the 1870s, Kellar toured the world with his show, a mixture of magic and spiritualism, working for very different cultures with the same show. And Kellar was a no-nonsense American, a tough showman determined to get to the top of the profession.

And I know that the subject really interested Orson. He certainly had never seen Kellar, but he knew about him. The element of the story that he liked was the exotic tour, and the magician's presentations right on the edge of reality and fantasy. I remember that I told Orson about a great story from Walter Gibson. Gibson was a writer who did *The Shadow*, and Orson knew him. Gibson didn't do the scripts; he wrote the books and created the character, under the name of Maxwell Grant. Walter had told me years ago about touring with Blackstone — this would have been in the '40s — and watching the levitation illusion of Blackstone's. He used to go in the basement, under the stage, and watch the machinery work from below. And that's how he used to watch what was happening on the stage — he would watch the machinery rising and falling underneath and he knew how it all connected. And Orson was really fascinated with that image, of elaborate mechanical effects being disconnected from the fantasy on stage, but also connected in some mysterious way. I remember Orson saying, "That's a great scene because it's a great way of showing the connection between the magic and the secret apparatus." In other words, to see some wonderful piece of machinery and then see some fantastic effect on stage. But there's always a mystery because as a viewer, you can't necessarily see how they connect, you know....

PPT: ... how it fits together.

JS: Right, but you realize the complexity of the illusion. That's where the whole thing of watching the footsteps through the holes in the stage came from; the footsteps scene ended up at the beginning of *Cradle Will Rock*. I mean, no one really ever did that. You just wouldn't do that. It's a preposterous way of getting a cue, and Orson knew that. But that was his idea, and I remember him describing the scene to me. He was very happy with it, all the people under the stage watching the little holes above them, watching the lights go out so they can follow the footsteps of the performer on stage. The performer in the spotlight, and the technicians in the shadows: it's a great image.

When he was writing *Cradle Will Rock,* he was talking to me about the script. And he told me a lot about the original *Faustus* on Broadway. He was very proud of it and it was really magical — it was all based in stage illusion. But Orson knew that the problem was that the stage magic in *Faustus* wouldn't translate to the screen, and look impressive enough. So he constructed this great scene, with the technicians following him beneath the stage. Orson is the magician, but he gave himself this great entrance in the film — not on stage, but emerging from a fireproof bag beneath the stage. It's a brilliant, theatrical entrance, both grand and self-deprecating at the same time. Again, it was completely his construction, but I remember that certain elements ended up getting filtered through our story about a magician.

PPT: To your knowledge, was there ever a script for this story about a magician at the turn of the century?

JS: Absolutely not. I have to tell you, I'd be very surprised if Orson ever sat down and wrote an outline of it. It never got that far. We talked about it and kicked around some ideas, but I think the final scenes in *Cradle Will Rock* were as far as it ever got.

In addition to witnessing the filming of the Gypsy Thread, Steinmeyer was at least peripherally involved in several other segments which may have wound up in Welles's final version of The Magic Show.

JS: I remember one routine we worked on. I'll tell you the inspiration. It was that Alexander Graham Bell at the end of his life was working on a machine to talk to the dead. Orson thought that was just fantastic, that kind of mix of technology and pseudo-science. And we talked about a routine that was a spirit cabinet. A spirit cabinet is a really old thing that in fact Kellar would have done. Traditionally, it was a simple wooden cabinet and ghosts would appear inside, a spiritualist's trick. And Orson wanted to do one that was quite technological. He would get an older lady up from the audience and then an image of her would actually appear in this cabinet at a certain point. And I know he filmed it because I was in New York at the time. I was quite surprised because one time I talked to him, he said, "We're going to shoot the spirit cabinet at the Variety Arts Theatre next week." So I know it was shot, but I never saw anything about it ... I later felt Orson wasn't really happy with the final film.

I worked with him on a couple of effects he'd slated for *The Magic Show.* One was an antique piece of apparatus called the "card star." And it was this kind of thing that looked like an antenna with five points on it. He would throw a deck of cards at it and a card would stick to each point of the star. And we had a really nice routine worked out for that, for the card star — a nice version of that old trick. And then we had built a Spirit Painting effect, which was really a beautiful effect that hadn't been done since vaudeville. They were paintings that appeared magically, when the subject was requested by the audience. Our idea came out of a conversation about historical magic. We talked about some improvements and how to change the Spirit Paintings around a little bit so that it had a better presentation. So we had the apparatus made and Orson was really happy with it. And I thought, "Oh, this will be something he'll do on television." Well, he said, "Oh, no, this is too good, this is too good. We're not going to do this on *Merv Griffin.* This is too good for that show."

The Spirit Paintings was a piece that I know he wanted to do at UCLA. I remember Oja gave me a little note that was sitting on his desk when he died that had a list of things that he had written about the show. One of them had my name on it, something about the table for the card star and "Jim's reluctance about using it." I don't remember why I would have been reluctant, or why Orson wrote that note, but perhaps I'd said something about the routine or had a concern about using it in the film.

PPT: Did you know Oja Kodar well?

JS: I wouldn't say I knew Oja Kodar well. Sometimes she was out of the country. She wasn't a magic fan, and she told me that, she joked about that. And I admired her honesty. I really liked her. I thought she was smart and perceptive. She was extremely talented and she cared a lot about Orson.

My observation is that they really loved each other.

Oja had great stories and when they were together you could really see the rapport. Several times — not very often — but several times I went there and he decided to make spaghetti. *[Laughs.]* That was one of the few things he cooked. Very informal; a bowl of spaghetti, a fork and a glass of wine. But I remember a couple times having dinner with Oja and Orson. And she had very funny tales about their films together or working in Europe. She had great stories about working with Jackie Gleason. She really had a better recollection than Orson, because Oja was the lowly assistant who had to deal with it all. And, of course, Orson was treated royally. So she could tell you what it was like working behind the scenes on that show, and how Gleason treated everyone.

Peter Bogdanovich has written of how "disarming" Welles was.[7] I asked Steinmeyer if he agreed.

JS: Oh, I would say so. Again, I've heard many stories about working with him. You know, I've certainly heard that tape of him doing those ridiculous British commercials where he blows up and storms out of the studio. So I suppose he was capable of that kind of behavior. But actually, it was completely the opposite, and it was always charming and incredibly disarming. He was really pleasant — surprisingly pleasant because you might expect a self-centered star. But he wasn't that way at all. He really, really listened to people. He could talk intelligently and engagingly about any subject.

I'll tell you a story that's a really good example of this, of just how disarming he could be. I remember going to dinner with him. It was about a year before he died. And something was bothering him. I don't know if it was when the financing for *Cradle Will Rock* fell apart or all the goofy stuff about the sled selling at auction, when Spielberg bought it. Something was bothering him. And I guess I was supposed to be — you know, he wanted to go to dinner and he wanted a diversion and I guess I was supposed to be it.

We were at Ma Maison and I didn't know what I was supposed to say. I would mention something and he would sort of dismiss it, in a slightly grumpy, in a slightly depressed way. And I remember one of the things I said to him was that I had just read Preston Sturges's first play, *Strictly Dishonorable*, and what a really great play it was. And he kind of said, "Oh, yeah, yeah, I saw that." That was what the whole conversation was like. If I mentioned a subject, he would dismiss it. And I knew that there was something else on his mind.

Then there was this long silence. Just as I'm starting to think, "Well, he didn't see it, and he doesn't want to talk about it," or, maybe "he didn't like Sturges," he looked up and he said, "Tullio Carminati played the Latin lover in that." And he also went on, "Antoinette Perry was in it when I saw it, but she didn't do it for a long time" And he said, "You know, that was also the role that made Cesar Romero a star when Carmanate left." Well, I had just read the cast list and he was completely right. And then he proceeded to slowly recall the entire thing and all the fine points of that story, complimenting all the nice little touches in it — just right after I had thought that he was just trying to cut off the conversation, that he didn't really know anything about *Strictly Dishonorable. [Laughter.]*

He had really seen it all, and he had really been there. See, you couldn't dismiss anything he said, even when he was being dismissive. And it made me wonder how many people had treated his stories as exaggerations, because Orson could talk about anything in an engaging, theatrical way. But damned if he didn't really know all about that play, or thousands of other subjects. Roosevelt, Helen Keller, Joe McCarthy. All unbelievable stories, but all incredible.

On October 9, 1985, Welles appeared on The Merv Griffin Show. *The show opened with Welles performing a quite incredible card trick. Later, he was interviewed by Griffin along with biographer Barbara Leaming. He died the following morning.*

JS: Well, I was there at the last *Griffin* show. I met Barbara Leaming that night and was supposed to go to dinner with them afterwards and begged off. One of the reasons I begged off is because I was shooting a television show at the time and I had to be on a set down in Marina Del Ray early in the morning. So Orson went off to dinner with Barbara Leaming. And I was on the set all day and when I got back to my apartment, 4 o'clock or 5 o'clock, there were all sorts of messages on my phone machine, messages about the fact that he'd died.

He was amazing that night. I helped put together that card trick that he did on that *Griffin* show.

PPT: How would you rate Welles as a magician?

JS: Well, it's a hard thing to answer. First of all, in terms of presenting magic, he was 10 out of 10, because he was so magnetic and he could very easily weave a spellbinding story and make it believable. And he had a really good sense of those presentations. Not only that voice and the manner, but also just kind of as a scriptwriter. I think a really good example of that was that thing he's doing with that thread trick, which he says is part of the legend of the Indian rope trick — all of that is completely untrue. But it's so believable and it's so charming, and he instantly takes what is maybe one of the tiniest tricks in magic and he introduces it by making it sound legendary and fantastic. And he tells you, "This is the real secret." And so as a presenter, he was great.

Technically, you had to be really careful not to underestimate him. He was self-conscious about performing sleight of hand, and his hands were stiff. He couldn't do sleights very well any more. He always liked handling bridge-sized cards, narrow cards, which looked small for him, I thought. I remember once having a conversation with him talking about how he used to do a one-hand top palm really well, which is a move — I'll tell you, for someone not doing magic very often — it isn't an easy move. It's a real knack. And then he picked up the cards and went bang-bang-bang and did a one-hand top palm. I saw and he really did do it. He pointed out to me how his hands now shake a little and because of that sometimes it doesn't fall exactly right. But there's no question he had really practiced years ago.

One recalls Mike Caveney's comment to me: "Orson would read about a new trick or somehow get a hold of a new trick. He'd say, 'This is a great trick. I want to do this trick. Now, how can I improve this trick?'"

JS: I think he has a reputation among magicians of having done some overly complicated tricks on those guest appearances. My observation was that he tended to over-think magic, and when he had doubts about it, he would complicate it in an effort to make it more interesting. And so he would add another layer to the presentation and then he would add another layer to the presentation. And there were a couple of *Tonight Show* appearances with these very complicated presentations. I think that's the criticism of him, sometimes presenting tricks that were too difficult to follow. My observation is that if he spent too much time ... if he spent two full weeks on something, it got too complicated because he would second-guess it. But if I said to him, "I think that's too much," he'd say, "Okay, fine." And I think people seldom said that to him. No one ever said, "I don't think you need to do that, Orson." Because, you know, if Orson Welles was saying, "This is what we're going to do," they went, "Okay, fine."

Maurice Zolotow wrote a piece in *Reader's Digest* just after he died, which is a really great piece about Orson, but he talks about forty years earlier when Orson was trying to learn the trick where he would cut to all four aces. And Zolotow, in this wonderful writer's way, ends up by saying, "Finally, at the end of his life, he learned the secret to that and that's what I saw on *Merv Griffin* that night." Well, that isn't what he saw. *[Laughter.]* But it is kind of a sweet, great way of tying it all up.

I remember having conversations with him, and as he described his solutions in filmmaking, I remember thinking, "This is exactly how a really clever magician thinks." Instead of being intimidated that I was with this fantastic, legendary filmmaker who was an expert in a world I knew nothing about, I realized that he was an expert in a world I knew a lot about. He had a very clever sense of problem solving. Everything was about creating one specific effect and everything was arranged towards that, both in the audience's mind and mechanically. And I think maybe in examples like in *Othello* where he's got doubles everywhere...

Some of that goes too far. Sometimes it's a detriment to always be solving problems, to know that you can work around something. Because you know every trick, and you know what the audience will let you get away with, you can tie yourself up in knots. He wasn't intimidated at kind of changing directions and doing something slightly different. I think he took great pride in his problem solving.

He did approach a lot of problems as a magic show; he looked at creating the maximum effect — the effect in the audience's mind was paramount, and as a magician, you want to leave them with a specific impression. You know, in a magic show, there aren't any base hits. You either hit a home run or nothing happens. So every bit of psychology and every bit of that has to be organized like that.

I remember selfishly thinking when he died — I think I was 27 — that I might have met the most interesting person of my life. He was a remarkable friend.

May 25, 2003

10

The Orson Welles Show

Stanley Sheff

Sheff edited Welles's television talk show pilot, The Orson Welles Show, *in 1978.*

Stanley Sheff: Mr. Welles had recently completed taping of an interview with Burt Reynolds at a local television station. A friend at the station sent Welles to the video post-production facility where I was serving as a director/editor. Being an admirer of Mr. Welles's work, I offered three free days of editing with the option to continue with me if he liked the experience. He did. The three days became a year of collaboration with Mr. Welles on *The Orson Welles Show.*

The Orson Welles Show was a pilot Mr. Welles hoped to sell to a major network. It was a mixture of interviews, comedy and magic. Unfortunately it did not sell. Orson told me, "They said it was too strange for the May sweeps, whatever May sweeps are ..."

Peter Prescott Tonguette: Did you come on board the project after shooting was complete or were you around as segments of the show were still being done?

SS: I began my work after the taping of the Burt Reynolds interview. I stayed on until the show was completed and was present at all other shoots, which included Angie Dickinson, The Muppets, Jim Henson, Frank Oz and Orson's magic routines.

This was Orson Welles's first experience editing with video tape. He was amazed by the technology and loved the speed of making edits, but sometimes became impatient waiting for tapes to rewind!

At first, Orson would give me specific instructions. "Start the edit on this frame, end the edit on that frame." After a week or so, Orson felt comfortable enough with my editing skills that he would allow me to cut sequences on my own. As time went on, we were working as partners on the project's post-production. When Orson was not feeling well, I filled in as director to

Welles and Sheff at work on *The Orson Welles Show*. Sheff is appearing as the gypsy violinist (photograph courtesy of Stanley Sheff).

get a few needed scenes. During the Angie Dickinson magic routine, I played the onscreen role of a gypsy violinist.

PPT: Do you recall which scenes you filled in as director on?

SS: The scenes I directed were audience reactions, some inserts with the magic sequences and a few other bits and pieces here and there.

A typical day would begin around 11:00 A.M. and end sometime after 7:00 P.M., with a one or two hour lunch break. Sometimes we would not want to break for lunch and would send out for food. Other times we would just talk about the show or about the old days. There were always visitors. One day a 90 year old gentleman paid a visit. He turned out to be the former Todd School headmaster, Roger Hill, the man who introduced a very young Orson Welles to his favorite author, Shakespeare. We ended up putting Mr. Hill in the show as a ballistics expert for the Russian roulette sequence.

We worked on the post-production for almost a year, working weekends and holidays when required. One time, we worked over 20 hours non-stop. I would usually give Orson a ride home at the end of the day. This time we were both so tired it took us both a few minutes to realize I was about to drop him off on the wrong street.

PPT: Did you get to know Welles at all during off-hours?

SS: Yes, we had a good friendship.

Orson did not mind talking about his past work. We had many interesting chats about *Citizen Kane, The Magnificent Ambersons, Lady from Shanghai, Touch of Evil* and more. He would tell me about all the wonderful practical jokes he used to play. Once on the set of *Bringing Up Baby* [1938], he threw a stuffed leopard into Katharine Hepburn's dressing room after shouting, "The leopard is loose!" For me, working with him on this project was like having a one year course in cinema with Orson Welles as the teacher.

PPT: Did you work on any other projects with him, or discuss doing so?

SS: Orson used to talk about his *War of the Worlds* radio broadcast as that "Lobsterman from Mars Show." I thought that would make a great title for a movie. So did Orson. I asked him if he would be willing to appear in the film if I ever was able to make it. He agreed. Five years after Orson's death, I directed *Lobster Man from Mars* [1989] with Tony Curtis in the role Orson would have played.

Someone had brought in a picture of Orson Welles taken the day after the *War of the Worlds* radio show. It showed a very young Orson Welles looking terribly upset and concerned about the results of the broadcast that panicked the nation. The caption read, "I had no idea this would happen ..."

Orson took one look at the photo and said to me, "I was lying my head off, I knew exactly what I was doing and what would happen." Orson was always the playful rascal, and this attitude continued even during our work together. Often he would peer out the second floor window of the editing room, then throw his cigar butts at his driver below. As the character George Grisby from *Lady from Shanghai* would say: "A little target practice." Never hit the driver though...

November 20, 2004

11

"Orson's Last Editor"

Jonathon Braun

Jonathon Braun: While I was working on the very first film that I ever cut, there was a gentleman there representing the completion bond company, who I guess took a liking to my work because he recommended me to cut another film for a friend of his. The gentleman's name was Principe Alessandro Tasca di Cuto.

I was very young at the time. I think I was 24 or 25 when I first met Tasca. These were only a couple of little low budget horror type films (which were trendy in those days and actually even have a little cult following today). But I guess Tasca kind of saw something in me and kept talking my praises to people and trying to get me other work, which he did, on yet another low-budget horror film. But I kept bugging him, because I knew that he knew and worked with the great Orson Welles. "I want to work with Orson!" Tasca said, "Oh, you're not ready, you're not ready! You're just a kid!" But he knew that I was also helping out on the production side on these little films and would always call me up to ask me for very peculiar things. "Well, Jon, we're doing this project and we need a circus tent. Where can we get a circus tent?" I go, "What?!" "Well, you see, you think you're ready to work with Mr. Welles and you don't even know where to get a circus tent!" "No, but I can tell you where to get some film stock ..."

I kept getting more and more work in editing. I was working for this production company, doing some commercials, and I had access to a Kem flatbed. Tasca, you know, was in *Chimes at Midnight*. I think he played the Bishop. Welles and Tasca were great friends. They lost track of each other for a while, but Orson had gotten back in touch with him and Tasca was essentially producing a lot of these things for Orson in the '70s and early '80s.

So I think that Tasca knew that I had this flatbed and maybe he could get me to do some work for him — cheap. You know, Tasca was very frugal. Especially because he knew it was Orson's own money. They were shooting *The Dreamers*, which was the first thing that I worked with him on.

The Dreamers was never completed or released, but Welles shot around 25 minutes of material for it in the early 1980s.

In their screenplay for the film Welles and Oja Kodar wove the tale of Isak Dinesen's character, Pellegrina Leoni (played by Kodar in the material Welles shot), an opera singer whose voice is lost in a fire. Welles portrayed her friend, a merchant called Marcus Kleek, who looks after Pellegrina following this tragedy. One central scene takes place in Pellegrina's garden as she bids farewell to her previous life as a singer, and to her friend, Marcus.

The scene was photographed, and for all intents and purposes completed by Welles, prior to his death. He used his Hollywood home as his set for this 19th century period piece. In my estimation, it is one of Welles's greatest works.

JB: I think they were shooting the scene in the garden with Oja and Orson's shadow.[1] Tasca called me up and said, "Do you still have that flatbed?" I said, "Yeah, I'm working on it." He said, "Do you think you could do some work for Mr. Welles on it?" I said, "Oh, yeah, absolutely. I'd jump at the chance!" He said, "Now you wouldn't charge?" I said, "No, I'm not going to charge. It's somebody else's equipment. It's off hours. They don't mind and I don't mind." "Okay, fine, here's your chance to do some work for us. I want you to put some footage together for Mr. Welles. We'll see where it goes from there."

Well, of course I was thrilled. So he gave me the information and I ran over to the lab, which was literally right around the corner, and picked up the footage. In those days, sound and film were separate so you had to sync the stuff together. I got a couple armfuls of boxes and there were some papers with them. I went back to the editing room and synced up all the dailies and put them in order. There were script pages and I saw the notes that Orson had written on them about what he was going to do with the stuff. So I started putting it in order in the way he had described in the notes. It was pretty standard stuff. He'd circled the takes he wanted. I started assembling the scene. It was kind of interesting and I was learning a lot just watching it, saying to myself, "Wow, look at the way he does this or does that."

Peter Prescott Tonguette: Did you put together essentially an editor's first assembly of the material?

JB: I guess so. I wasn't really thinking about it. Just based on the notes and script pages that were with the boxes. Then I was instructed by Tasca to bring it over to Orson. And, remember, I was 25, 26 years old. I'd just barely gotten out of film school. I thought I knew a little something. So I brought the stuff over to the house off of Hollywood Boulevard. I rang the bell and this beautiful woman opened the door, this exotic, gorgeous woman. It was Oja. And with a big smile, she said, "Yes?" I said, "It's Jon Braun. I'm the editor and I've brought Mr. Welles's film." "Oh, hold on just a second." She yelled in the back, "Orson!" "Yes, what is it? What?" "The cutter is here!"

And I hate that term — "cutter"! Welles said, "The cutter?! What's *he* doing here?! Oh, just tell him to leave! I don't have time for him right now. I'm so busy. Why are people always bothering me?" I was really scared, so I just said, "Okay," to Oja. She smiled knowingly. I put the footage down and went back to my editing room. I was working on some apple juice commercials or some-. thing and got back to work on those.

And then I got a call from Tasca about three hours later. He was pissed off. He said, "Jon Braun! What the hell did you do?" What did I do? I tried to think of what I might've done that would make him this angry. I thought maybe Orson was angry because I interrupted what he was doing or some-thing. I said, "Well, I just brought the film over to Mr. Welles ..." "No. What did you do to his film?" "Nothing! I just put it together. Like you told me, 'Just put it together'!" "Put it together?! When I said put it together, I meant to sync the dailies! That's all! I didn't say that you were allowed to edit his material! Nobody has ever edited Orson Welles' material without at least dis-cussing it with him first." I was dumbfounded. I'm like, "Really?" Oops! I hadn't thought about that. He said, "You can expect a call from Mr. Welles."

Of course I was scared. I was shivering. An hour or two went by and I started to forget about it. I went back to work. Then the phone rang and I just picked it up, not even thinking who it might be. I said, "Edit Room." There was this deep booming voice on the other end: "Jon Braun *[long pause]*, this is Orson Welles." The whole fear came back all at once. I was trembling in my boots. Orson Welles was calling me — on MY phone. I said, "But Mr. Welles, I need to explain ... I have never really done ... and I just ..." Orson boomed, "I have never in my entire career ..." "But Mr. Welles, please, you have to understand!" Continuing to boom: " ... in forty years of filmmaking, never has anybody done what you have done —" "But I was just trying to ..." "— and put together this material in a way that I would have done exactly had I done it myself." I went silent, "— — what?" He asked, "How did you know?" I said, "What do you mean? I saw your notes and I saw the footage and it just sort of told me what to do." He said, "But that's exactly the way I would have done it. Nobody's ever done that before." I said, "Uhhh ..." *[Laughs.]* And I'm sure you've heard that Orson had a tendency to change personalities at a moment's notice, so his voice suddenly softened. He said, in this kind of overly plaintive voice, "Oh, Jon, if you could spare me just a moment of your time and please come over. I would love to meet you." I thought, Is this the same guy who was yelling that he didn't "have time for the cutter?" Of course I said, "Yes," and dropped everything and went up to his house. He invited me in and he was magnanimous and gracious.

He didn't understand how I would know what he wanted without him having to explain it to me. I had to explain to him that I don't know either, that's just what happened. You look at the material and the material kind of tells you how to cut it. You can't impose yourself on it. And I also had his notes. He said, "We must work together." I said, "Okay!" And that's how we started working together. He told me his plans for doing this and that and the other thing. He told me he wanted to put a little studio together in his house. We actually designed an editing room in his guest house. He designed a special machine with Prevost[2] and I went over to oversee the construction of it in Milan, Italy. We brought it back, set it up, and pretty much brought all of the disparate pieces of everything he had from all over the world and put it together in this guest house. Part of my job was cataloging everything. When we weren't actually working on something, I was basically sent there to figure out what he's got, where it is, what it is, and just watch everything that I could. I forgot whether he told me if it was okay to do that, but I did it! *[Laughs.]*

And I really learned what Orson was about and what he was doing. We worked together over a course of almost three years. It was the best education. All of the film schools I went to paled in comparison to working with Orson Welles.

Even though he was really dramatic, he also saw the humor in things. Sometimes it was a really sweet humor and sometimes it was kind of a vicious humor. He could be mischievous. He used to pull practical jokes on me. I smoked in those days. He didn't move around a lot, but he would hide my cigarettes! In the edit room, I'd go outside just to go to the bathroom or something, and when I returned my cigarettes would be gone. I said, "Oh, well I was going to take a break ..." He said, "What are you looking for?" "Cigarettes. I was going to have a break." "You don't remember where you put them? Oh, you're getting old! I'm the old one here, I'm the feeble one! What's going on with your mind?" All of the sudden they would show up somewhere else. I'd say, "How'd they get there? I didn't put ..." He'd say, "Jon, you have to be more in charge of yourself if you want to work with me! This is really making me wonder."

PPT: So after you assembled the garden scene in *The Dreamers,* did you both work on it some more or was he so pleased with it that he left it as you assembled it?

JB: Well, boy, wouldn't I like it if that were the case! An editor's life is not one of things being left the way you put them together. We worked together more on it after that.

I don't think there was anything of Orson's that he ever felt was done. *The Magic Show* came closest to almost being done, where he felt like, "I think we finally got it." But then a week later we'd be working on something else. He'd say, "Bring out that magic stuff. I want to see something. I want to look at that." And we'd make a little tweak here and a little tweak there.

One of the things that was really fascinating for me was watching the dailies, especially for *The Dreamers*, and seeing how he directed. Now that's something, I got to tell you, I value the most because people don't really see that. You see what's on the screen, but you don't see what got him to that point. I still remember to this day how he directed Oja. He never said, "Do it like this" or "Say it a little higher" or "Say it a little lower" or "A little left" or "A little right." You hear that a lot from directors. "Give me ten percent more, give me twenty percent less." He never said how he wanted something done. He put people — in this case it was just Oja — in a place emotionally. I remember he said, "Now you're in a field." Of course, she's not in a field, she's just in her garden. "You're out in a field. Take a deep breath. Smell the straw, smell the damp air." And he'd put her in a place and say "Okay." That would give her the resources that she would need to deliver the lines or to be able to play the scene. It was so indirect that it was remarkable to me how much more effective it was. It's something I've kept with me for a long time.

I brought up the sound in the garden scene from The Dreamers, *which Jonathan Rosenbaum commented on when he wrote of the "lonely duet of two melodious accented voices* [Welles's and Kodar's], *accompanied by the whir of crickets and even the faint hum of passing traffic."*[3] *The sound of traffic was a result of the scene having been shot in his garden, but the crickets were added later.*

JB: *[Laughs.]* Orson was interesting. Orson loved technology. Any little thing he'd read about or I'd read about, because I was a young guy at the time and I knew a lot about the latest techniques that were coming out. This time, it was loops where you could have these endless sounds that kept going and going. You could vary the pitch and the sound. He loved that and just played with it. The Prevost itself, the one he designed, could record a soundtrack as well as play back. It was very unusual. Most film editing machines at that time had eight plates or spools: four for picture, and four for sound. This thing was a ten-plate. It had the regular eight plates and it had a separate pair for recording that could be synchronized for 16 and 35. So we did little mixes right there on the machine.

For The Dreamers, *Welles also shot his side of a scene in which his character, Marcus, is speaking to another character off-screen. I suggested to Braun that perhaps Welles would have shot the other side of the scene after he'd cast the role.*

JB: He'd often do that. I don't remember specifically on *The Dreamers*. I was not only a co-worker, but I was also a student. So he would give me assignments, saying, "Before we get to this, you have to watch all of that. That way you'll know what we're doing." Sometimes he'd explain to me what it was that I was watching and sometimes I'd have to figure it out on my own. And I have to be honest with you, there were times when I couldn't quite figure it out and know what exactly he had planned. Sometimes he would tell me and sometimes he would be a little frustrated — "Why aren't you figuring this out on your own?" — and change the subject. He expected me to be a little bit further along than I was.

So I didn't quite get all that. I think you're right because it just seemed to me that that would be the only way to deal with [the black-and-white *Dreamers* footage]. But I often get the idea that Orson didn't know exactly, himself. He knew that he had to do something in order to progress and move forward. He'd have to keep adding pieces. But sometimes I think he figured it out later. I think that may have been one of those situations. Although, being pragmatic as editors are, that's the only thing I can think of to do with it. But he never said that. A lot of times Orson didn't say things. A little enigmatic! But that was done prior to me.

Braun did, however, confirm my impression that the garden scene was a segment which could have been placed into the final film, had it ever been completed.

JB: That was the intention. I know there was talk of whether or not this was just a promo reel. I remember at the time that either Oja or Gary asked why they were devoting so much time to just a promo. And Orson said, "It's not a promo. What makes you think it's just a promo? If that's what it takes for us to get more money, fine. But this could be stuff that we could end up using."

If it was good, Orson would use it. In my career, one of the things I learned from Orson was how to get the most out of something and not discard it too quickly. If there's some value to something, work it as best you can. People will accept it if it makes sense, even if it doesn't look perfect or isn't slick and polished like a gem. If it has emotional value and impact, people will accept it. In that respect, I think Orson would try to keep as much as he could. Unless somebody gave him enough money to start from scratch, if he felt these things were better he would have kept them.

PPT: Now you indicated that you revisited *The Dreamers* ...

JB: Actually, toward the end, not really. Once we started getting really involved in *The Magic Show* and then *The Cradle Will Rock*, certainly once *Cradle* started to become real, we pretty much focused on that. We talked about that, how to prepare for that. For fun, we'd go back to some of these other segments. He used to do these sketchbook things. He did some segments on English stately manors and a one-man-band guy. There was one called "Four Clubmen." Some of them made sense, some of them didn't!

These were segments which years earlier Frederick Muller had a pass at editing.
By this point, the sound was missing from the "Four Clubmen" sequence.

JB: That didn't stop Orson from wanting to re-cut it! *[Laughs.]* He also called me a Swiss editor. He said, "You're just so precise and mechanical. You always want to have the sound in sync!" I said, "Well, how about just have the sound to listen to?" On the "Clubmen" sequence, there was this big search to find the audio. We called all over the world, from one cutting room in France to another in Rome. On *Don Quixote*, he'd say, "Well, we have to change this scene and we're going to record this new dialogue." I'd go, "But Akim Tamiroff is dead, Orson. How are you going to get him to re-voice it if he's dead?" He said, "Oh, you're so Swiss! Whose voice do you think is in there right now?" I said, "Orson, is that your voice?" He said, "Jon, I do all these voices."

Braun talked about his working relationship with Welles.

JB: He obviously couldn't afford — and I didn't want to ask him — to keep me on staff. And I was earning my livelihood at the time doing freelance work. So I had to take other jobs, but I always gave Orson priority. When he had something he wanted me to do, he would give me enough notice where I could work it into my schedule either by taking a few days or a few weeks off or sometimes months off. Until toward the end, during *Cradle*, I devoted almost all of my time to him and that project because we thought it was so imminent and so close.

So I was sort of more on call than on staff. He was certainly my priority and when he beckoned I came running. I was there when he needed me, unless there was some other project. And he was very understanding about that. He would leave me these messages on my answering machine sometimes, like, "Oh, please, Jon, if you could just find the time for this poor old man ..." Oh my God, what, are you kidding me? *[Laughs.]* But I think he knew I'd be there whenever he needed me. In that sense, he kind of played with me.

He spoiled me. It's hard, because I have a hard time discussing this with directors now. He knew what he wanted. But he left me alone a lot in the editing room. Whenever I was working for him, the first thing I'd do is come up to the house and tell him I was here and discuss what we were going to do or what he wanted. Then I would say, "I'll talk to you later this afternoon. I'll check in with you and tell you where I'm at." If I had something that I must show him, then he would come down. If it was something I didn't have to show him, he would come down another time. So he left me alone a lot to work on things, which spoiled me. I would say, "Well, Orson, don't you just want to sit here with me?" He'd say, "I already know the way I want to do it. But I need your point of view, your perspective. If I don't like what you do, I can always do it the way I knew I wanted to do it in the first place. I want to see what you're going to bring to it." That's not to say that there weren't long times when he'd sit next to me and be very specific: "Cut here," "Cut there." But I really liked the former method. It made me work harder. I had to think more.

Echoing editors Frederick Muller and Marie-Sophie Dubus before him, Braun never saw Welles personally cut his work.

JB: You mean, physically cut and splice the material? No. But there were times, like I said, where he would sit next to me, or a little behind me because he was too big to actually sit next to me, and he would be very specific. "Cut there and cut there."

As I say, I was fairly young and a little bit naïve back then, maybe even a little full of myself. You know, the hubris of youth. One time Orson said, "Okay, cut there. Stop! Cut there." I said, "No, no, that's not going to work." *[Laughs.]* And there was a long pause behind me and I realized that I just told Orson Welles, perhaps the greatest film director ever, that a cut was not going to work! I turned around and very humbly said, "Well, you know, Orson, it's just my opinion! I think we should really wait for ..." He said, "Really, Jon? You really don't think that's going to work?" I said, "Well, no, I ..." "And you think that your grand experience in filmmaking — now, Jon, how long have you been doing this?" "Oh, I don't know, maybe five years." "Well, I've been doing this for almost forty years and I don't know if it's going to work. How do you know if it's going to work? Don't you think you should just try it? Maybe just humor me and try it?" "All right, Orson, I'll try it." I cut it and of course it did something magical, as it always did. So, in my most humble way, I turned around and said, "Ok, I guess you were right." He said, "I knew I was right!" I said, "Well, Orson, you don't have to be so mean and rub it in my face. I'm swallowing my pride here and agreeing that you were right." He said, "But I'm not being immodest. It's not that I knew I was right the cut would *work*. I didn't know whether the cut would work, who knew? I just knew that we should *try* it." I said, "Oh my God, that's absolutely right." And that's again one of those lessons that stuck with me. You gotta try it. You just never know.

When we were working together like that, I just sat back while my hands did the physical part, but I was just sort of watching what was going on to see what would happen, how the material would come together. Once again the student just observing the master. Most of the time what came out was something pretty amazing. Not always what I expected, not always something that we would keep, and not always something that worked great. Sometimes it was sort of like an interesting idea and then later I would fix it up.

An editing room is a remarkably jumbled and confusing place. In those days especially, you had film everywhere, little 2-inch pieces of film all over the place. You didn't know where everything was. Imagine taking a big block of ice, hitting it with a hammer, all the pieces went all over and you didn't put it back together! That's sort of what it felt like. Orson thought very quickly and I had to keep up with some of the things that we were trying. I was trying to keep everything in sync; he just wanted to cut the picture and get the thought across. He would leave and I would fix it up, as it were: put the sound back in sync, fix something up if it was a little off or didn't cut, adapt something that was really glaring. I'd tell him all the places where I would do that so that it wasn't a surprise. And then we'd watch it again and watch it again.

Physically, I never saw him actually use the splicer. But maybe he kind of used me as the splicer from time to time. But he also allowed me input. I was flattered that he would allow me to collaborate with him. Obviously, it was 99 percent Orson and 1 percent me! It was a very humbling experience, I have to tell you.

It's an education that I could never have gotten anywhere else. Not just about film, but also about life. There were times when he was too tired to walk down to the editing room. He didn't want to make the journey. He would have to stop twice along the way to catch his breath. He wasn't in the best of health, you know. It was hard for him just to walk. Quite often I would come up at the end of the day and say, "Orson, you didn't come down." He would say, "Oh, I was too tired ... so what do you think about the situation in the Middle East?" He knew I lived in Israel for a few years. He'd start asking questions. We would sit there for hours and talk about non-film related things. We'd talk about life or politics. Sometimes we'd just sit there and watch stupid TV. He loved to watch the news and *WKRP*. It was kind of sad in a way, but it was great to see him laugh because that show would make him laugh. I think he just liked having company and somebody to talk to. We talked about things and sometimes it got kind of personal. He recognized some of the things that I was going through at the time and would give me advice about life.

You're too young to remember, but in those days there was something advertised on TV called Sylva Mind Control, which was about "how to harness the power within you." Nowadays it would be one of those infomercials, one of those self-help type things where you would use positive thinking to help you be positive about life. He said, "You're going to one of those seminars? That's ridiculous! That's all phony. I can read people's minds! Want me to read your mind?" He started telling me how to do mind-reading tricks! *[Laughs.]* I said, "Orson, that's not what it is. It's about how to take charge of your life, take stock of yourself, not about how to ..." He'd go, "Oh, that's just nonsense! Don't waste your time!" He told me about how he went through a process to be self-confident. Like all great people, there was a side to Orson that was really very sweet and insecure. He thought people didn't really understand him and didn't really know who he was, but in order to succeed in Hollywood and in life you have to exude a certain confidence and be able to convey that to people.

Braun also worked on The Other Side of the Wind.

JB: As I said, part of my responsibility was cataloging things because Orson didn't know or wasn't sure where everything was. You had to try to track things down and find things wherever we could. He had storage rooms all over Hollywood. Even in Europe, they sent some stuff back. So one of the things that was very important was *The Other Side of the Wind*. Some scenes were shot in 16, some in 35. The negative was locked up tight in Iran at the time. We weren't even sure we'd ever get it back.

Again, I had the chance to watch a lot of the edited material. Occasionally, Orson would come down and would want to view some of the material. We would view a scene here, a scene there, and we'd view some of the dailies. And he'd say, "Jon, what would you do with this?" I was like, "Well, in my opinion, based on the last script that you had"—because he had a bunch of different versions—"I think there's a way to incorporate this scene into that scene, blah, blah, blah." And we'd talk about ideas. In the beginning, we'd never really edited any of it. I thought this was just something he was planning for down the line. So I was pretty comfortable just jawing about it. Then one day he came down and said, "I really want to work on *The Other Side of the Wind*." So we put everything else on hold and we started cutting it.

We worked a lot on the party scene. Talk about non-linear! Orson was the inventor of non-linear. He loved being on the forefront and cutting edge of technique and technology. It boggled my mind, but he was able to keep track of it all. I would contribute what I could. I think Orson used me to bounce ideas off of. "Does that make sense, Jon?" He used to say that a lot. I'd say, "Well, yeah, I guess so." "Why?" "Well, because of this and this." "That's right!" *[Laughs.]* He'd then say, "Okay, let's do that then, if you're that convinced!" I'd say okay and all of the sudden I was invested.

He had a lot of material. The negative was stuck in Iran, so we never had the negative. And there were scenes that he had put together and shown to the AFI about ten years earlier, which were segments which were as complete as he could make them at the time. But I watched as much of that stuff as I could. I don't know if I watched all of it. There's definitely something there, but I'm not sure that it's *there*. Based on the scripts that I read, I'm pretty sure that he wasn't done and it would take quite a bit to complete that film. He had a lot of stuff that he carried around in his head that he would sort of allude to. Again, he'd keep me on my toes. A lot of times, he'd say, "Well, I think the scene where blah blah blah ..." I'd go, "Oh ... yeah. What scene?" *[Laughs.]* He'd say, "Why don't you know about that scene?!" "Well, I read the script." And I'd get all freaked out, like I missed something, and I'd go back to the script and it's not there! It was in his head.

So he told me about a lot of these scenes. And they made sense. They were kind of the glue that held everything together, that joined everything, and I wish he'd gotten them down on paper somewhere.

In that one, a lot of it had already been done before I got there. A lot of what I had to do was adapt myself to the way he was doing things. He had pretty much started that technique and style before I came on. On that project, my thing was to just kind of continue it. So it was more about trying to polish and finesse things than it was to start anything from scratch.

I'm pretty sure this was on *Wind*, but I spent a week once reassembling one scene. He said, "I just don't like the way this is going. This other editor was an idiot, Jon, an idiot! That's why you're here!" *[Laughs.]* I said, "Thank you. I see what's coming." And I had to put the scene back into its raw form, which was very time-consuming with all those fast cuts. We put it back together. We weren't cutting from scratch, because he already had something in mind, but we pretty much started over. Was that the train scene? I can't remember. It wasn't the party scene, which was more like pruning a bush. The bush had already been formed and now the key is to prune it and trim it and pretty it up here and there. We added new characters here and there, by which I mean we brought in the character more here and there.

Braun also re-cut portions of Don Quixote.

JB: The film had pretty much been cut already. I know we had to do a little bit of a restoration process on it. Because opening up these splices, decades-old cellophane tape splices, the film would fall apart. So we had to have it restored before we could start physically working on it. I remember that there were some scenes where he was just not satisfied. He was very proud of the majority of it, but there were some scenes where he said, "I just didn't quite get it," and he wanted to change some of the dialogue and have them say different things.

We started to with some scenes. I'm thinking of a scene with Akim Tamiroff and they're on the top of a hill. That was one where we tried to re-approach it. It's re-cutting, putting in new dialogue. Orson did a rough track for it. As I'm thinking about this, I realize that I use these techniques all the time nowadays, how to put words in people's mouths that they didn't really say at the time, that weren't in the script originally. So we took new approaches to some scenes, but it was mostly re-cutting because it had pretty much all been cut by the time I got there.

Braun said that the version of Quixote *he worked on "was close" to the point where Welles could have released it as it was.*

JB: We would have had to clean up some stuff. Again, learning from Orson about what's acceptable and what's not acceptable, where do you have to polish and where can you let it stay rough and the emotion will still come across. There were passages that just felt draggy and it wasn't propelling along the way it should, and once we smoothed that over ... I actually tried to encourage him because I honestly wanted something to be finished that I was working with him on. And this one felt like one of the closest things. I tried to encourage him, saying, "Orson, let's work on *Don Quixote*." But his mood dictated what he wanted to work on, not my encouragement.

Of editing segments for The Magic Show, *Braun said, "I remember working on them all pretty much separately." This suggests that most of the individual scenes were edited, but as Braun put it to me, they were "not put together as one intentional piece of art."*

JB: The Abu Kahn one, where he gets hit on the head, that's the one that we worked on the most and I felt that it was almost done. It was an interesting idea that all of a sudden a magic show goes awry and actually uses real magic as opposed to tricks.

I mentioned to Braun that The Magic Show *and* The Dreamers *were my two favorites of Welles's unfinished projects.*

JB: It was kind of hard to understand everything that [Isak Dinesen] was trying to do. I think that was probably the reason why Orson combined the two stories, to try to make it a little more accessible to people. My head kind of hurt when I read *The Dreamers*! I had to actually think! *[Laughs.]* Whereas with *The Magic Show*, you just sat back and you just sort of let it happen to you. I think that's also Orson.

There are times in his movies when he encourages you to be a part of the process. You have to think. You would never enjoy *The Trial* if you just sat back and let it happen to you, as audiences do now. I happen to like *The Lord of the Rings* [2001], but nonetheless it's that sort of thing where you sit back and let it happen to you. But *The Trial* or *The Dreamers* are movies where if you're not participating along the way — trying to figure it out or put yourself in that position or try to understand what this guy's thinking or doing or what he really means by saying that, constantly asking yourself questions and being involved — the film would make no sense. It's a real participatory kind of experience. But what I liked about *The Magic Show* was that it was something where you sat back and you could be a kid again.

Braun also worked with Welles on The Orson Welles Show, *which was initially edited by Stanley Sheff.*

PPT: Was he still trying to sell it?

JB: You know, I don't think they really thought I needed to know much about the business side. I always felt that if we were working on something, that meant that he was trying to do something with it. Except for *Wind* and *The Dreamers*. Both of those were more because he just wanted to work on them. A lot of times it would be that he just pulled it out because it had been a while since he got to that particular canvas. He just wanted to apply a few more strokes of paint on it.

If I remember correctly, he was trying to use *The Orson Welles Show* to get another, newer show going, a more contemporary show. But I do remember trying to get Orson to move into the electronic editing world, cutting on video, and it may well have been on this project.

PPT: Were you successful?

JB: No. *[Laughs.]* These were in the days when video editing was just getting going. I said, "Well, why don't we bring a video editing system into the cutting room?" Orson said, "Well, if you can arrange that, Jon." So we brought one in. It was a linear ¾" cassette system, called an ECS 90, or something. It had two decks, one for playback and one to record and a box in between with a joystick on it to control them.

In those days, you could set the machines to be as accurate as you wanted. If you wanted to be really accurate, to edit right on a particular frame, the machines would really have to line up just right to "take" the edit, and it might take a few attempts. Three or four, sometimes. I mean on *each* edit. That could really slow the process down, believe me. Of course, I didn't know that you could set them to be a little looser, which meant that even if you wanted it on a particular frame, if it's within a few frames of that point, that's okay, the machines would slip a little but the edit would "take" right away and the editing process would be a lot faster. Not as accurate, but a whole lot faster. But I didn't know that. So I brought it down and said, "Here's the set-up. What do you think?" He said, "Let's see this thing work."

Like I said, he didn't sit next to me, but kind of behind me. And he had a cane to help him walk. I'd be editing some stuff and he'd watch me putting these little pieces together. I'd say, "See how easy this is, Orson? There's no razor blades, no physical splicing involved, you just press a few buttons and the machines do all the work!" And then of course the machine started acting up a little. It'd try to sync up and make an edit at a certain point and miss it. Remember, I had the machines set to be exactly frame-accurate, no slippage allowed. It'd then recycle, which would take another ten seconds, and try again. Eventually, it got so frustrating that he started saying, "Jon, you said this was going to work! You said this is the latest technology, fast, fast, fast! What's going on here? Jon, you're always trying to get me to do things differently!" And he started hitting me with his cane! *[Laughs.]* I mean he actually started smacking me and it was stinging a little bit! He was laughing along the way, but some of those little swipes hurt! I'm like, "Ow, Orson I'm trying! Ow!" But he had a good sense of humor about it and we tried for a while more, but again I think he felt it was too "Swiss." To him, it didn't need to be so damn precise. Just get it in shape, get it close, and then you can screw around with it later. We went back to film after a few weeks of that.

We did like new technology. He always wanted to know about the latest thing. I think he was enthralled with the concept of it. If he could see the way we do it now, all on computers, 8 to 16 audio tracks, maybe 8 video tracks, all at one time, real-time dissolves, real-time blow-ups, zooms, blue-screen keys, all of it, I'm sure he would think it was truly remarkable. He could do so much. Talk about "the biggest electric train set." Imagine what he would have been able to do.

PPT: Would you have edited *The Cradle Will Rock* had it happened?

JB: Yes, I think so. I mean, that's what I was there for. As a matter of fact, Tasca joked about how I'd have to pay for my own ticket to go over there. And I don't know how much he was joking, but I said, "Well, I'm doing it!" *[Laughs.]* The producer, Michael Fitzgerald, was so close to putting it together, so close.

Again, I was close to Tasca as well as to Orson, so I saw it from Orson's perspective as well as from Tasca's. Tasca had done all the production work on it and he had everything ready to go: the crews were lined up in Italy, locations were initially going to be in New York and when they found they couldn't do it, they were building huge sets at Cinecita, the largest film studio in Italy. Tasca's grand-daughter was helping him do some of the breakdowns for the scheduling. Scenes were scheduled. I had begun to learn a little bit about that stuff myself and so I was interested in learning how they took a script, broke it down and scheduled it.

According to Jonathan Rosenbaum's afterword to the published screenplay of Cradle, *casting for the film included Rupert Everett as Welles and Amy Irving as his first wife, Virginia.*[4]

JB: As usual with anything for Orson, nothing felt solid. Things were changing all the time. Amy Irving was in, she wasn't in, to play his wife. I met with Rupert Everett — though, actually, he was pretty much never out. He was always in. But you never knew the next thing that was going to happen.

Braun described the genesis of Cradle.

JB: I think he felt that it was almost his swan song. I think that he felt that it was going to be the way to let people know that Orson's still there, still standing. It's interesting how it came about. Orson was very well admired within the industry, but didn't have a lot of true friends. People were afraid of him, I think people were in awe of him, and I think people were jealous of him, his raw talent. Also, I'm not sure that Orson really let people in. I think that over the years, things had been so disappointing that he just never let people in. But one of the people that he did let in a long time ago and was very close to was John Huston.

One day when I went in to see him, Orson told me, "Read this" and shoved a script into my hands. I said, "What's that?" "It's a script, of course." It was by Ring Lardner, Jr.—I thought, "That sounds familiar. I know that name." So I read the script. It was *The Cradle Will Rock*. Later, he asked, "What do you think of it?" I said, "This is interesting. This is something I never knew about you, Orson. I knew you did the radio stuff, but this is fascinating. A contemporary opera for the WPA? I want to get a recording of the original Blitzstein opera." I was kind of a liberal in those days, and still am, and Orson was fairly liberal too. And this thing was borderline Socialist! Matter of fact, the WPA closed it down on the opening day because they thought it pushed a little *too* far left. The *WPA*, for God's sake!

He said, "Well, were you really moved by it?" I said, "Well, honestly, I wasn't *moved* by it, Orson. I was fascinated by it more than moved." He said, "I felt the same way. So, here, read this one!" Again, he shoved a script in my hands. Only this one was different. Same title, now it has his name on it! I said, "What's going on here, Orson?" *[Laughs.]* And he told me the story. He said, "I want you to read this because I'm thinking of doing it—only if you think it's good." Now that's bullshit, of course, whether he was going to do it depending on whether I thought it was good. But he always did stuff like that.

What happened was that John Huston had done *Under the Volcano* with Michael Fitzgerald. Now they wanted to do this story of *The Cradle Will Rock*, with John Huston directing. I guess John had actually agreed to do it, but he had gotten very sick. He was going to have an operation and was concerned he wasn't going to come out of it. Fitzgerald was concerned, "Hey, I think I've got this thing put together and now this is getting—" Huston had said, "Look, I may not even be the right guy to do this. Why don't you go to the source and get the guy who it's about to do it for you? Why are you going to me to do it? Go to Orson Welles himself. I'll call him!" And he called Orson. Orson said, "Well, maybe I'll just do the script." And Huston said, "What do you mean, just do the script? Direct it! Direct it, Orson!" This is the way Orson told me the story. So Orson said, "Well, I'll only commit to taking a stab at the script and then we'll see."

Not that the first script was bad by any means. It was actually quite good. But Orson added heart to it, as only a) Orson Welles, the artist, could do and b) Orson Welles, the guy who it was about, could do. He brought stuff to it that only the guy who was in it could. It was a remarkable difference between the scripts. You really felt part of what was going on, you really felt what the guy was going through at the time. You empathized with the characters, whereas in the original one you empathized more with the situation. That's how the whole thing got started.

I don't know about you, but I actually started choking up when Orson wrote about when everyone starts to stand and sing from the audience — one person here, one person there. Even when I tell people the story, I start to choke up.

> *When Braun and I spoke of the tragedy of Welles's screenplay of* The Cradle Will Rock *not being produced, and of Welles's attitude about it all, Braun said to me, "How many times can you have your heart broken? That's a side of Orson that I don't think people really knew. He was actually very sensitive, very sweet. He was just nice. Oh, he could be an asshole, too, believe me.* [Laughs] *He yelled at me a few times — but like a loving parent might." Ironically, in the late 1990s a film called* Cradle Will Rock, *about the same subject matter as the Lardner and Welles screenplays, was written and directed by Tim Robbins; it is unfortunate no one has as yet filmed Welles's vision of this so personal project.*

JB: Having had him as one of the mentors of my life, somebody who has really directed my career ... he actually said to me — and I don't know how serious he was — "I'm going to make you a director one day. You just wait and see." And it was like, how could I be in any other business when you have Orson Welles telling you that! I don't know how much I believed him or if he was just saying that to try to encourage me. But the fact is he believed in me, and knowing that somebody believes in you like that gives you a lot of confidence to go out and do things, to try things, to be a certain way, to act a certain way. And then there were times where Orson did things that I did not really like. Not often, but sometimes. He could be very bitter. He could be very upset with people. He could hold a grudge — man, he could hold a grudge! But, you know what, who am I to know what he went through? How do I know how much that grudge deserved to be held? Like I said, I admired him and what he accomplished. He went through a lot to get there.

I sometimes listen down the line from the cast of characters in Orson's life, the Henry Jagloms, Peter Bogdanoviches, Ojas, to the other people around town, and the *Kane*-like reflections of this person, Orson Welles, and how vastly different those perspectives can be and how they can change from moment to moment, person to person. As I said, I don't think that that was wholly unintentional. That was Orson. I think that was what he liked.

PPT: Do you have any favorite memories of Welles?

JB: There's a lot, and it runs the gamut from remarkable brilliance when he would say something and I'd think, "Oh, my God, that's just so brilliant," to times which were really pitiful moments, but very endearing, like moments when Orson was all alone, sitting in his living room, where it would be just him and me together talking and watching TV. You sort of figured that a man like that would never be alone.

But there was one funny moment about *Citizen Kane*. One time I came in and he was on the phone talking to somebody about some project. I guess he was doing a voiceover for some commercial or other to make money which he could put into one of his own projects. I walked in and he was saying, "So what you're saying is that you want it to read, 'To be or not to be.'" I don't remember what the lines were, so I'll just pretend it's from Hamlet. He motioned to me: "Write this down, write this down." Then he continued, "So the line should be, 'To be or not to be.'" I sat down and began to write: "To be or not to be." He said, "Well, I don't agree. I don't think it should be that. I think it should be, 'Not to be or to be.'" So I scratched the previous line out and wrote that one down. He said, "Oh, well we could combine the two lines and make, 'Be, not be.'" And I'd scratch it out. Then he said, "Well, maybe what we could do is ..." and he's talking faster and faster. I kept scratching and writing, scratching and writing. Finally he said, "Okay, I think, yes, we're agreed. Yes, that's good. Okay, fine, goodbye." And he hung up. I said, "Orson, I didn't get the last thing that you guys said. You went so fast that I didn't get it." He said, "You didn't write down what I said? How am I supposed to remember what the line is? I can't remember that line. Oh my God, I sure am glad you weren't there when we were doing *Kane*. It would have been Rose-what — Rose-who?!" *[Laughs.]*

What I take away from my experience with Orson is how to be a person and how to think, how to use my mind. I think that's what he taught me: how to think and how to approach things from a creative perspective. I have on a couple of occasions met Robert Wise. My dad [Zev Braun] is a producer and is a little on the gregarious side. He knows Wise from some project; I don't know where. One day we met him together at a function in Beverly Hills. My dad took us both in and said, "Oh, look, Orson's first editor and Orson's last editor!" And I'm like, "Please don't put me in the same sentence as Robert Wise!" I always felt like I was more of a student of Orson's rather than a full collaborator, like Wise. But we did share a couple of moments where we talked about what kind of a person Orson was. What struck me was how, even after so long a time, he thought so fondly of Orson as a person. Besides the art and the work and the tumult, his face softened when he talked about Orson. He talked glowingly and with great admiration. After all these years and all the successes he's had in his career, he still felt that Orson was the man out front. I think that kind of brings it full circle to really show what kind of a person Orson was, to have that impact on a person's life, with Robert Wise and all he's accomplished, and with me and all the things that I've done in my life — not that I've accomplished anything near what these guys have, but I've had a modicum of success and I credit it to my time with Orson. He stays with me even to this day. Marlene was right: He was some kind of man, all right.

May 21, 2004

12

"He Kept Me Busy"

Gary Graver

Gary Graver: So many people will tell you in interviews, directors even now, that *Citizen Kane* made them want to be a director and make movies. Nobody can get the career that Orson had if you think about it, from the Mercury Theatre, *The War of the Worlds, Citizen Kane*, right to *The Other Side of the Wind*, and all the stuff in between. I'm sorry he didn't get to make more movies, that's all. But Spielberg, Lucas, they can make all the movies they want, all the money they want, but they just are not going to have that kind of a career.

He was always working right until the end. He never was sick, he wasn't expecting to die; he was working. He slowed down a little bit, thank God. *[Laughs.]* He kept me busy.

Welles and Gary Graver (photograph courtesy of Gary Graver).

Chapter Notes

Preface

1. Jonathan Rosenbaum, afterword, in *The Cradle Will Rock: An Original Screenplay* (Santa Barbara: Santa Teresa Press, 1994), p. 116.

2. "The Beatrice Interview," by Ron Hogan, http://www.beatrice.com/interviews/plimpton/.

3. George Plimpton, *Truman Capote: In Which Various Friends, Enemies, Acquaintances, and Detractors Recall His Turbulent Career* (New York: Nan A. Talese/Doubleday, 1997), p. ix.

4. Andre Bazin and Charles Bitsch, "Interview with Orson Welles," *Cahiers du Cinema*, June 1958, collected in *Orson Welles Interviews*, ed. Mark W. Estrin (Jackson: University Press of Mississippi, 2002), p. 40

Chapter 1

1. Norman Lloyd, *Stages of Life in Theatre, Film, and Television* (New York: Limelight Editions, 1993), p. 44.

2. Frank Brady, *Citizen Welles: A Biography of Orson Welles* (New York: Anchor Books, 1989), p. 203.

3. Lloyd recounted to me the events leading up to "the stabbing of Joe Holland" — the actor who was playing Caesar in the Mercury's production of the play. Lloyd said, "This is how I remember the story of the knife. It's true that memory plays tricks, but I think this is pretty much what it was. As the assassins, led by Brutus, moved up to assassinate Caesar, they came from the ramp that led down to the wall of the back of the theatre. They came up from there to Holland, who was on the highest level. As they came up there, they then attacked Caesar. Holland does the 'Et tu, Brute?' line. At this particular dress rehearsal, shortly before we opened, *all* the conspirators had real knives. Holland had an overcoat, and when Orson stabbed him, the blade was to go between the arm and the body of the coat.

"At this particular dress rehearsal, Orson did this, and when he dropped the knife after stabbing him — that is, not really, but in play form — the knife went straight down into the floor. It stuck in there and quivered. There was a light on it, so it had a wonderful shine. Well, this was fantastic. So, Orson decreed, because of the light on it and the effect, that all the other conspirators were to use rubber daggers, and get rid of their real ones. Only he was to have the real one. Now, the play opens and it runs. Every night that he did this piece of business, which went between Joe Holland's arm and the coat, and he'd drop the dagger — and it never stuck in the floor again.

"But he kept trying. And then one day, he missed the place between the arm and the coat, and he actually got the artery of Joe Holland's arm. The amazing thing is Joe Holland said, 'Et tu, Brute?' and collapsed. And do you know that he lay there on the floor, bleeding, bleeding away, all through Coulouris's 'Cry havoc and let slip the dogs of war'? I really can't tell you how long, but it was a length of time. The blood started pouring all over the stage.

"Finally, the lights faded out. When the actors then moved around to get a new position, I was coming on stage. I stumble into Joe Holland! I feel all of this stickiness over me. Joe says, 'Christ, I'm stabbed.' He stumbles off to go to the hospital for two months. He could have easily died, bled to death.

"I never checked again, or even thought about checking, whether Orson kept using a real dagger. But I know that was the end of the dagger with Joe Holland!"

4. Brady, p. 592.

Chapter 2

1. Leslie Megahey, "Interview from The Orson Welles Story," in *Orson Welles Interviews*, ed. Mark W. Estrin (Jackson: University Press of Mississippi, 2002), p. 209.

2. Frank Brady, *Citizen Welles: A Biography of Orson Welles* (New York: Anchor Books, 1989), p. 209.

3. David Kamp, "Magnificent Obsession," *Vanity Fair,* January 2002, p. 130.

4. Kamp, pp. 130–133.

Chapter 3

1. Richard "Dick" Wilson was, in the words of author Chuck Berg (writing in *The Encyclopedia of Orson Welles* [New York: Checkmark Books, 2003]), "one of Welles's closest and most trusted lieutenants" throughout his entire life.

2. Frank Brady, *Citizen Welles: A Biography of Orson Welles* (New York: Anchor Books, 1989), p. 409.

3. Barbara Leaming, *Orson Welles* (New York: Viking Press, 1985), p. 350.

Chapter 4

1. Laura Deni, "The Fascinating Life of Alvin Epstein," http://www.broadwaytovegas.com/May2,2004.html.

2. Barbara Leaming, *Orson Welles* (New York: Viking Press, 1985), p. 405.

3. In act V, scene iii, of *King Lear* (*The Oxford Shakespeare*, ed. W.J. Craig, 1914), Lear says, "Howl, howl, howl, howl! O! You are men of stones," as he enters with the dead Cordelia.

Chapter 5

1. *The Fountain of Youth* was awarded a Peabody in 1958.

2. The second episode (never shot or broadcast) was to be an adaptation of Collier's story "Green Thoughts."

Chapter 6

1. Orson Welles and Peter Bogdanovich, *This Is Orson Welles,* revised edition (New York: Da Capo Press, 1998), p. 254.

2. Richard Marienstras, "Orson Welles: Shakespeare, Welles, and Moles," collected in *Orson Welles Interviews,* ed. Mark W. Estrin (Jackson: University Press of Mississippi, 2002), p. 165.

3. Welles and Bogdanovich, 1998, p. xxxiv.

4. Orson Welles, and Peter Bogdanovich, *This Is Orson Welles,* revised edition (New York: Da Capo Press, 1998), p. xxxii.

5. Welles and Bogdanovich, p. xxxii.

Chapter 7

1. Stefan Droessler, "Oja As a Gift," an interview with Oja Kodar, *The Unknown Orson Welles,* ed. Droessler (Munchen; Belleville/Filmmuseum, 2004), p. 35.

2. Frank Brady, *Citizen Welles: A Biography of Orson Welles* (New York: Anchor Books, 1989), p. 500.

3. Filmed without sound.

4. Welles dyed Hayworth's hair for her role in *The Lady from Shanghai.*

5. Joseph McBride, *Orson Welles,* revised and expanded edition. (New York: Da Capo Press, 1996), pp. 204–205.

6. *The Deep* is also known as *Dead Calm.*

7. In addition to her role in *The Other Side of the Wind,* McCambridge acted in *Touch of Evil* for Welles years before.

8. Ferris is referring here to the birthday party scene in *Wind.*

9. *The Cinema of Orson Welles* was published by The Museum of Modern Art in 1961. It was Bogdanovich's first book.

10. Bogdanovich began his show business career as an actor on the stage.

11. The role of Charles Higgam was re-cast with an actor named Howard Grossman.

12. Yule, p. 64; Welles and Bogdanovich, p. 441.

13. Welles and Bogdanovich, p. xxxii.

14. Bogdanovich ended up having to make the movie in color.

Chapter 8

1. Orson Welles and Peter Bogdanovich, *This Is Orson Welles,* revised edition (New York: Da Capo Press, 1998), p. 224.

2. Raymond Bally to the author.

3. All quotes by Dominique Engerer Boussagol are taken from e-mail correspondence with the author, December 21, 2004.

4. Welles and Bogdanovich, *This Is Orson Welles,* p. 254.

5. Dubus is referring here to some shots in the film where Welles addresses the camera from the editing table.

6. Presumably, this was an alternate title for *Don Quixote.*

Chapter 9

1. The description of this scene is drawn from my own viewing of an extensive amount of material from *The Magic Show* and from Dickson's memory of it, which has aided me considerably in comprehending the narrative.

2. Gary Graver to the author.

3. Graver to the author.

4. Caveney's date book indicates that he rehearsed the Gypsy Thread at Welles's house on August 22, 1981 for 2 hours; August 24 for 4 hours; and August 26 for 3 hours.

5. Abb Dickson to the author.

6. Jonathan Rosenbaum, afterword, in *The Cradle Will Rock: An Original Screenplay* by Orson Welles (Santa Barbara: Santa Teresa Press, 1994), p. 116.

7. Orson Welles and Peter Bogdanovich, *This Is Orson Welles,* revised edition (New York: Da Capo Press, 1998), p. xii. Bogdanovich also used the same word — "disarming" — to describe Welles to me during our conversation for this book.

Chapter 11

1. In this scene, Welles is visible only in shadow.

2. Prevost is an Italian manufacturer of editing equipment.

3. Chuck Berg, and Tom Erskine, *The Encyclopedia of Orson Welles* (New York: Checkmark Books), p. 93,

4. Jonathan Rosenbaum, afterword, in *The Cradle Will Rock,* by Orson Welles (Santa Barbara: Santa Teresa Press, 1994), pp. 116–117.

Selected Bibliography

Berg, Chuck, and Tom Erskine. *The Encyclopedia of Orson Welles.* New York: Checkmark Books, 2003.

Brady, Frank. *Citizen Welles: A Biography of Orson Welles.* New York: Charles Scribner's Sons, 1989.

Callow, Simon. *Orson Welles: The Road to Xanadu.* London: Jonathan Cape, 1995.

Conrad, Peter. *Orson Welles: The Stories of His Life.* London: Faber and Faber, 2003.

Droessler, Stefan, ed. *The Unknown Orson Welles.* Munich: Belleville/Filmmuseum Muenchen, 2004 .

Estrin, Mark W., ed. *Orson Welles Interviews.* Jackson: University Press of Mississippi, 2002.

Leaming, Barbara. *Orson Welles.* New York: Viking Press, 1985.

Leemann, Sergio. *Robert Wise on His Films: From Editing Room to Director's Chair.* Los Angeles: Silman-James Press, 1995.

Lloyd, Norman. *Stages of Life in Theatre, Film and Television.* New York: Limelight Editions, 1993.

McBride, Joseph. *Orson Welles*, revised and expanded edition. New York: Da Capo Press, 1996.

Perkins, V.F. *The Magnificent Ambersons.* London: BFI Publishing, 1999.

Rosenbaum, Jonathan. *Placing Movies.* Berkeley: University of California Press, 1995.

_____. *Movies as Politics.* Berkeley: University of California Press, 1997.

_____. *Movie Wars.* Chicago: A cappella, 2000.

Tonguette, Peter. "The Company of Magicians: Orson Welles, Abb Dickson, Scarlet Plush, and Purple Hokum." *Senses of Cinema*, issue 32, July–Sept. 2004 .

_____. "From the Beginning: Notes on Orson Welles' Most Personal Late Film." *Senses of Cinema,* issue 27, July–Aug. 2003.

Welles, Orson. "A Brief Career as a Musical Prodigy." *Paris Vogue,* Dec. 1982/Jan. 1983, pp. 186–187.

_____. "Citizen Abner" *Genii* magazine. Special Abb Dickson issue. January 1989.

_____. *The Cradle Will Rock: An Original Screenplay.* Santa Barbara: Santa Teresa Press, 1994.

_____. "My Father Wore Black Spats." *Paris Vogue,* Dec. 1982/Jan. 1983, pp. 184–186.

_____. *The Other Side of the Wind: Screenplay.* France: Cahiers du Cinema, Festival internazionale del film Locarno, 2005.

Welles, Orson, and Peter Bogdanovich. *This Is Orson Welles.* revised edition. New York: Da Capo Press, 1998.

Yule, Andrew. *Picture Shows: The Life and Films of Peter Bogdanovich.* New York: Limelight Editions, 1992.

Index